Circumference and Circumstance

Circumference and Circumstance

STAGES IN THE MIND AND ART OF

Emily Dickinson

BY WILLIAM R. SHERWOOD

Columbia University Press

NEW YORK AND LONDON

1968

William R. Sherwood, formerly a member of the English Department at Vassar College, is now Assistant Professor of English at Hunter College of the City University of New York.

The Lucy Maynard Salmon Fund of Vassar College has helped to make possible the publication of this book.

Acknowledgment is made to Little, Brown and Co. for permission to quote from the following: *Single Hound*, copyright 1914, 1942 by Martha Dickinson Bianchi; *Further Poems*, copyright 1929, © 1957 by Mary L. Hampson; *Unpublished Poems*, copyright 1935 by Martha Dickinson Bianchi, copyright renewed 1963 by Mary L. Hampson.

TO MY PARENTS

Preface

In this study of Emily Dickinson's poetry and letters I have tried, accepting and using the chronology established by Thomas H. Johnson, to describe the development of Emily Dickinson's principal ideas and to characterize the mind in which those ideas were held. Where I have felt it to be useful, I have tried to establish some relationship between the shifts in thought and in theme in her poetry and the events in her life, but I have always begun with the poems and the letters themselves and have not tried to force them into a scheme on the basis of biographical data. The assumption that poetry is a form of autobiography is implicit in this book and is argued explicitly in Chapter 3, where I hope I have given assurance that I have not made connections between life and art with a heavy hand or with a simple mind.

What I have hoped to do is to bring some coherence to future studies of Emily Dickinson's work by showing that her poetry, when read as a whole and in the proper order, reveals a development of mind that is both logical and humanly possible. In the process I have of course arrived at many generalizations about Emily Dickinson, generalizations that I think are sound, but I am more concerned with establishing a basis from which future generalizations can be made with more certainty and with more fidelity and pertinence to the body of poetry she actually wrote. I have made explications of relatively few poems, and those that I have chosen to discuss at some length are not always her best or her best-known, and some of the best and most frequently analyzed are scarcely mentioned. Sometimes I have dwelt on a particular poem to show that a point I have made elsewhere does indeed hold and does illuminate the poem in question, sometimes to refute other statements about Emily Dickinson's work as a whole for which the poem in question has been used as the principal evidence. My main intention, however, has been to describe Emily Dickinson's sensibility and to indicate the ways in which it developed.

In the process, I believe I have cast light on certain questions about Emily Dickinson, have discovered some new facts about her, and have applied other information in a new way. The questions her biographers have raised concerning the Reverend Mr. Wadsworth and other candidates for her attention are discussed in Chapter 3, from which the title is taken. "Circumference" is dealt with in Chapters 3 and 4. In Chapter 4 I have included a poem that does not appear in Johnson's edition. The significance of Emily Dickinson's retirement from public life and of her custom of dressing in white is also treated in that chapter, though it is alluded to earlier. In Chapter 5 I have cited specific sources for some of her poems and more general sources of her aesthetic theory, which is discussed at some length in the same chapter. The question, often raised, of whether her poems came down to us by accident or design is answered, conclusively I believe, in Chapter 5. Chapter 2 deals with the poetry she wrote during the first two years in which she apparently felt her poems to be worth saving, and the reason for my considering these poems separately is discussed in that chapter and the one following. Chapter 1 is an attempt to characterize, mostly by means of her letters, the attitudes Emily Dickinson held before writing the poems that she preserved. Some of my reasons for choosing Marianne Moore's poem to introduce this book will be clearer after the discussions of Emily Dickinson's imagery in Chapter 2, but the poem is appropriate for the book as a whole if, as I hope, I have shown the "essential perpendicularity" of this poet who thirsted for so much and forced herself to be so patient.

November, 1967   WILLIAM R. SHERWOOD

Acknowledgments

I would like to express my deep and general indebtedness
to the labor and devotion of Emily Dickinson's principal
editors, Mabel Loomis Todd and Thomas H. Johnson. It
is no exaggeration to say that without their work I could
not have written this book. The criticism and encouragement given me by Fred Dupee and Lewis Leary of Columbia University, where this study was first undertaken as a
doctoral dissertation, and the suggestions, support, and
encouragement offered by Richard B. Sewall of Yale and
my colleague at Vassar, John Aldrich Christie, concerning
the final manuscript for this book were of great assistance.
To my students in American Literature at Vassar College
I owe a special debt for the many ideas and insights they
stimulated me to find and led me to discover. To the late
Perry Miller my indebtedness and gratitude are incalcul-
able.

Permission to quote from the following publications is
gratefully acknowledged: Harvard University Press for
The Letters of Emily Dickinson, edited by Thomas H.
Johnson and Theodora Ward, 1958; *The Poems of Emily
Dickinson,* edited by Thomas H. Johnson and Theodora

Ward, 1955. Little, Brown and Company for *The Complete Poems of Emily Dickinson,* edited by Martha Dickinson Bianchi, 1924. Houghton Mifflin Company for *Emily Dickinson Face to Face,* by Martha Dickinson Bianchi, 1932; *Life & Letters of Emily Dickinson,* edited by Martha Dickinson Bianchi, 1924; *Dear Preceptor: The Life and Times of Thomas Wentworth Higginson,* by Anna Mary Wells, 1963. Yale University Press for *The Years and Hours of Emily Dickinson,* by Jay Leyda, 1960. The Macmillan Company for "An Egyptian Pulled Glass Bottle in the Shape of a Fish," reprinted with permission of The Macmillan Company from *Collected Poems* by Marianne Moore, 1935, renewed 1963 by Marianne Moore and T. S. Eliot. Alfred A. Knopf, Inc., for "Not Ideas About the Thing but the Thing Itself," from *The Collected Poems of Wallace Stevens,* 1957. William Sloane Associates, Inc., for *Emily Dickinson,* by Richard V. Chase, copyright 1951, William Sloane Associates, Inc. The Harvard College Library for letters quoted on pp. 6, 81, 137, 151, 218 by permission of The Harvard College Library. The Mount Holyoke College Library for the letter on p. 239. The University of the South for the excerpt from "Emily Dickinson," by Austin Warren, originally published in the *Sewanee Review,* LXV (Autumn, 1957). *The New England Quarterly* XIII (1940), for the excerpt from "From Edwards to Emerson," by Perry Miller.

W.R.S.

Contents

xiii

Circumference and Circumstance

Here we have thirst
  And patience, from the first,
    And art, as in a wave held up for us to see
    In its essential perpendicularity;

Not brittle but
Intense – the spectrum, that
  Spectacular and nimble animal the fish
  Whose scales turn aside the sun's sword with their
    polish.
      Marianne Moore, "An Egyptian Pulled Glass Bottle
                                in the Shape of a Fish"

Chapter 1

Any biographer or critic who deals with Emily Dickinson soon becomes acutely and depressingly aware of certain problems that arise both from the obscurity and privacy in which she chose to live and work and the fullness with which in letters and poems she expressed herself. We know at once too much and too little about her. The Emily Dickinson revealed in her works is a complex and inconsistent, often contradictory, figure, moving from ecstasy to desperation, from a fervent faith to a deep suspicion and skepticism, from humility and submissiveness to defiance and scorn. She is blasphemous as often as devout, and in her poetry God is accused of petty vindictiveness and cold indifference as often as He is celebrated for benevolence or admired for His majesty. Nature simultaneously reveals to her proof of immortality and reminds her that the mind creates the evidence it seems to see. To us the distance between Emerson's conviction that nature is "one vast picture which God paints on the instant eternity for the contemplation of the soul" [1] and Melville's conclusion that "all deified Nature absolutely paints like the harlot whose allurements cover nothing but the charnelhouse within" [2] seems an unbridgeable gulf, but Emily Dickinson in one light, quick step could cross and recross it. Faced with such perplexing diversity of statement, her earliest editors and her most recent critics alike have attempted to enumerate and categorize the many Emily Dickinsons and to define and describe her major themes.[3] The intent in this book is less to classify than to reconcile and to synthesize, to ascertain if possible the central impulse or impulses that permeate the total work and that hence relate each element of it, in short to identify the "string" – to use the image James had Vereker substitute for the more famous one of the figure in the carpet – on which her pearls are strung.

Such an attempt to characterize the single and consistent Emily Dickinson who expressed such disparate emotions and attitudes and portrayed herself in such a variety of roles is made more difficult by the absence of trustworthy and significant information about her from her contemporaries. Through her own deliberate choice she was in her lifetime considered an oddity rather than a serious artist, and the tributes paid to notoriety are unfortunately more ephemeral than those to fame. Few people wrote about her during her lifetime – a maiden recluse Richard Chase reminds us [4] was an uncommon but not extraordinary phenomenon in New England – and what they had to say was inevitably more pertinent to her as a "character" than as a poet. Nor can the flood of reminiscences and the tales of lovers and forestalled elopements [5] that began to appear after the success of the first edition of her poems be trusted readily. Much of the information we have about Emily Dickinson is either meager or distorted, a fact which only proves what Emily Dickinson and the rest of Amherst knew very well, that the backside of reticence is gossip. Apart from the poetry itself, her letters are the best evidence of her state of mind at any given period. Because they are the only evidence we have of her thinking before 1858, the date of her first important poems, this chapter, devoted to establishing the extent to which the attitudes expressed in

4

her poetry were the outgrowth of those she had held earlier, will rely heavily upon them.

The "surprise" which a recent critic of Emily Dickinson has cited as one of "the distinctive marks of her best poetry" [6] has too often been confused with artlessness by less sophisticated readers with the result that her poems, especially the earlier ones, have been read as if they were the spontaneous products of a naïve and newly emergent sensibility reacting to the beauties of New England nature and the rigors of New England provincial life. When one remembers that in 1858, the first year from which any substantial and significant poetry has survived, Emily Dickinson was not seventeen but twenty-seven, that ten years had passed since her last protracted residence away from her father's house in Amherst and since her last exposure to any sort of formal education, one is less likely to imagine her as a village Miranda. Her "surprise" is, I believe, intentional, the product of achievement not of innocence, and these poems are the statements of a mature artist satisfied that she has at last discovered a way of organizing her responses into a body of poetry she feels to be worth preserving. It is because Emily Dickinson's pride as an artist was greater than her sympathy for future critics and scholars that nothing remains of her early work save a few poems and valentines, and these were saved not by her but by their recipients.[7]

Though she does not seem to have saved poems before 1858, she certainly wrote them. As early as 1853 she had sent poetry to Susan Gilbert [8] and, it would appear, to her friend Henry V. Emmons,[9] and she had announced to her brother, Austin, himself apparently an aspiring poet, "I've been in the habit *myself* of writing some few things, and it rather appears to me that you're getting away my patent." [10] Her sense of the exclusiveness of her vocation and of her need to protect it from infringement, treated lightly here, is given more direct expression in an earlier letter to Susan Gilbert. In 1851 Emily Dickinson had written how both girls "please ourselves with the fancy that we are the only poets, and everyone else is *prose*," [11] and a few months later, when describing for Austin her life at home in Amherst that winter, she writes, "It is pretty much all sobriety, and we do not have much poetry, father having made up his mind that it is pretty much all *real life*. Fathers real life and *mine* sometimes come into collision, but as yet, escape unhurt!" [12] "Prose" has become synonymous with "real" or public life, ironically the "life" which uses patents to protect its inventions and discoveries. The distinction between the public and the private life, between authority, whether it be that of society or that of "Father," and the imagination was one that she had drawn as early as 1851. Already she had begun to feel the opposition of authority to the impulses whose expression would later signify power, prestige, and even life.

The "real life" in Amherst that Emily Dickinson described for Sue, Austin, and others in her many letters of this period [13] was primarily a repetitive, narrow, yet secure routine of domestic chores and entertainments:

I rise, because the sun shines, and sleep has done with me, and I brush my hair, and dress me, and wonder what I am and who has made me so, and then I wash the dishes, and anon, wash them again, and then 'tis afternoon, and Ladies call, and evening, and some members of another sex come in to spend the hour, and then that day is done. And, prithee, what is Life? [14]

Or, as she relates a familiar scene to the absent Austin, it is comprised of quiet, yet somehow tense and stultifying family gatherings in the evening:

We are enjoying this evening what is called a "northeast storm" – a little north of east, in case you are pretty definite. Father thinks "it's amazin raw," and I'm half disposed to think that he's in the right about it, tho' I keep pretty dark, and dont *say* much about it! Vinnie is at the instrument, humming a pensive air concerning a young lady who thought she was "almost there." Vinnie seems much grieved, and I really suppose *I* ought to betake myself to weeping; I'm pretty sure that I *shall* if she dont abate her singing.

. . .

Mother is warming her feet, which she assures me confidentially are "just as cold as ice"[!] I tell her I fear there is danger of icification, or ossification – I dont know certainly which! Father is reading the Bible – I take it for *consolation,* judging from outward things.[15]

She describes a Sunday afternoon once church, or as she called it "meeting," was over and the family had reassembled at home: "Father and mother sit in state in the sitting room perusing such papers only, as they are well assured have nothing carnal in them." [16] As the quotations below indicate, she often avoided attending church, preferring to use that time for her extensive correspondence and welcoming the opportunity for privacy: [17]

They will all go but me, to the usual meetinghouse, to hear the usual sermon; the inclemency of the storm so kindly detaining me; and as I sit here Susie, alone with the winds and you, I have the old *king feeling* even more than before, for I know not even the *cracker man* will invade *this* solitude, this sweet Sabbath of our's.[18]

I will write when they've gone to meeting, lest they stop me, when they get home.[19]

The monotony, and the rebellion against it, are evident, but the security that such a routine afforded Emily Dickinson was equally important. The assertion of private impulse within a framework of fixed and unalterable pattern is already evident, as are the strict husbanding, the "economical" management of resources and the intense yet circumspect manner of expression. The very form of her mature work is one of protest within a convention, in this case that of Common Hymn Meter, and it is not an exaggeration to say that her creative energy was supported, sustained, and organized by the very forces that seemed to restrict it.

It would be a mistake to assume that Emily Dickinson's life in Amherst was one of unending drudgery and routine; there were "sociables," lectures, concerts, sleighrides, fires, northern lights,[20] visitors, even visits, even good sermons,[21] even, at times crime, scandal, and violence.[22] But the normal events of community life, of birth, engagement, marriage, and, above all, death far outweighed these aberrations. The life that Emily Dickinson knew was overwhelmingly one of pattern and process. In the intimacy and exposure of village life the stages of man and the cycles of nature are forced upon one's consciousness, and it would be surprising if Emily Dickinson had not assumed that the clear cycle of the sun's transit and the seasons' progression was the prototype of a larger pattern in human life, the final movement of which remained unseen.

Surprisingly enough, although death, both as the gateway to immortality and as the eternal darkness and imprisonment for those to whom immortality was denied, was to become one of the primary concerns in her poetry, death as a theme does not play a large role in her early letters. Her letter to Abiah Root,[23] apostrophizing the death of Sophia Holland two years earlier seems to be less an expression of sorrow than it is an attempt to convince the recipient of the writer's spirituality, perhaps because it was written shortly after Abiah had joined the church and at a time when Emily Dickinson was trying to come to terms with her own refusal to make this commitment. And, as Chase has pointed out, her letter to Abiah describing the death of Leonard Humphrey does not "use the words of someone personally overwhelmed with grief and loss after the death of a beloved one. They are the words of a sensitive and intelligent young woman trying to master the *idea* of grief and loss (Chase's italics)." [24] Even the letter to Newton's pastor, used by Whicher [25] and Chase [26] as evidence both of her attachment to Newton and of her concern, at this time, with immortality, is a singular document. Nowhere else, except in a postscript in one letter to Austin,[27] is Newton's

8

death mentioned. In short, her letters show no indication that the immediate effect of these deaths, which years later were to provide her with the subject of much of her poetry, was a profound one. Apparently their real importance became clear to Emily Dickinson only in retrospect when she sought for elements of her experience suitable for objectifying the emotions that she needed to convey through poetry. To attribute to Emily Dickinson, on the basis of these poems, a deep romantic attachment to either Benjamin Newton or to Leonard Humphrey is to fail to distinguish between the way she reacted to experience in life and the use to which she put it in art.[28]

Nor, despite what we might assume from the fact that immortality is a central subject in her earliest preserved poetry, did Newton's death have the immediate effect of directing her attention to the problem of man's fate after death. The letter, previously cited, to the Reverend Mr. Hale, Newton's pastor, in which, ten months after Newton's death, she asks if he is indeed in heaven, is her first expression of serious concern about this problem.[29] To be sure, in some of her correspondence of the period 1853–1857, the years between Newton's death and her first substantial body of work, she does deal with the subject of immortality, but the concept expressed is that of the most tedious and saccharine of her poetry, where heaven is a blissful and eternal reunion with those dear to her, a place where, as she wrote her close friends Doctor and Mrs. Holland in late 1854, one could eternally gather golden flowers in pearl baskets.[30] The impulse is regressive and infantile; the concept, by considering immortality as a product of natural rather than moral law subtly denies the religious doctrines she ostensibly celebrates, and the poetry arising from it lacks that probing, explorative quality that characterizes Emily Dickinson's important work.[31]

But Emily Dickinson was at no time a profound religious thinker; rather, as Allen Tate has implied,[32] she used, just as she used the experiences that made her aware of death, the symbols of religion as a means of extending the significance of inner, personal feeling and conflict. If the poles of her "metaphysical" imagery – the human and the divine – are as separate as those of Herbert and Donne, and the force, the spark, that leaps the barrier between them is as electric and as illuminating, yet the direction of the current, to carry out the metaphor, is the reverse of that of the earlier metaphysicals: God is not humanized; He does not through the power of poetry walk the earth once again in the shape of natural man; it is the poet who walks proudly through heaven, or condescends to purchase at His dry-goods store, or leaves Him to cool His heels on her doorstep.

If we realize that behind much of the humility of her poetry lies egotism and that one of the principal functions of the religious elements in it is to express the poet's sense of her own exclusiveness, we will not be surprised by the absence of any expression of profound religious conviction in her early life. Emily Dickinson's conduct at Mount Holyoke was that of the "hold-out," not that of the devout believer. Despite the pressures brought to bear upon her by friends, by groups, by her own conviction that to resist making a public commitment to Christ and to His Congregational Church she would risk both social and spiritual isolation, she refused to make a confession of faith.[33] In refusing she had the model of her father, Edward Dickinson, who, despite the examples of his wife and his daughter Lavinia, did not join the Amherst Congregational Church until the age of forty-seven, in 1850,[34] several years after his daughter Emily had resisted the appeals, the sentimentality, and the warnings of damnation by her classmates and teachers at Mount Holyoke. The spring of 1850 was apparently the time of a powerful religious revival in Amherst; yet Emily Dickinson was still not moved to declare her faith. "Christ is calling everyone here," she wrote her friend Jane Humphrey, "all my companions have answered, even my darling Vinnie believes she loves and trusts Him, and I am standing alone in rebellion, and growing very careless."[35] Perhaps she had inherited her lawyer-father's sense of the sanctity of contract and would not enter an agreement uncertain of her good faith.[36] Perhaps she resented the public nature of such a commitment, the sharing with others less endowed than herself of what she felt should be possessed by her alone, and wished then, as she later stated in her poetry, the exclusive role of wife or queen.

Certainly, whatever her attitude toward God, she had little respect for man's manner of worshipping Him, nor, in the main, for the worshippers themselves. Surely the "Sewing Society" described below was comprised of the same "soft, cherubic creatures" who were to be the subject of one of her most famous satiric poems,[37] and her attitude toward the "good works" accomplished by these "gentlewomen" shows how little the ethical side of Christianity attracted or even interested her:

The halt – the lame – and the blind – the old – the infirm – the bed-ridden – and superannuated – the ugly, and disagreeable – the perfectly hateful to me – all *these* to see – and be seen by – an opportunity rare for cultivating meekness – and patience – and submission – and for turning my back to this very sinful, and wicked world. Somehow or other I incline to other things – and Satan covers them up with flowers, and I reach out to pick them. The path of duty looks very ugly indeed – and the place where *I* want to go more amiable. . . . The Sewing Society has commenced again – and held its first meeting last week – now all the poor will be helped – the cold warmed – the warm cooled – the hungry fed – the thirsty attended to – the ragged clothed – and this suffering – tumbled down world will be helped to it's feet again – which will be quite pleasant to all. I dont attend – notwithstanding my high approbation – which must puzzle the public exceedingly. I am already set down as one of those brands almost consumed – and my hardheartedness gets me many prayers.[38]

Nor was her respect for the church as a corporate body any greater than that for the individual members of the congregation. Meeting was, for her, an experience to be avoided if possible, endured if not,[39] its ritual petty and fatiguing,[40] its ministers bombastic, presumptuous, or dull.[41] She writes Austin "young Mr. Hallock made a prayer which I don't doubt you heard in Cambridge. – It was really very audible." In one amusing account of her reaction to meeting, an account that shows her to be more humorous, more feminine, less bleakly and hypersensitively religious, less, in short, of a trembling, childlike New England nun than some of her admirers might admit, she writes:

While the minister this morning was giving an account of the Roman Catholic system, and announcing several facts which were usually startling, I was trying to make up my mind wh' of the two was prettiest to go and welcome *you* in, my fawn colored dress, or my blue dress. Just as I had decided by all means to wear the blue, down came the minister's fist with a terrible rap on the counter, and Susie, it scared me so, I hav'nt got over it yet, but I'm glad I reached a conclusion! [42]

"Usually startling" – the irony is the function of a profound contempt; it betrays her thirst for an experience, religious or otherwise, that would provide a sense of contact with the genuinely startling. In at least one instance in this early period the church did seem to provide such an experience, one that may have been the source for the poem "I heard a fly buzz": [43]

We had such a splendid sermon from that Prof Park – I never heard anything like it, and dont expect to again, till we stand at the great white throne, and "he reads from the book, the Lamb's book" . . . it was very full, and still – so still, the buzzing of a fly would have boomed like a cannon. And when it was all over, and that wonderful man sat down, people stared at each other, and looked as wan and wild, as if they had seen a spirit, and wondered they had not died.[44]

It is scarcely surprising that this thirst for an apocalyptic experience should make her, before her poetry had come to serve as the mode of relating her wishes and needs to the external world, scorn the gentle, serene religiosity of the schoolgirl-nun for the *frissons* of the romance. She wants to be bewitched, not lulled or purified, as she says in a somewhat mocking letter to her more devout friend, Susan Gilbert:

I have just read three little books, not great, not thrilling – but sweet and true. "The Light in the Valley," "Only," and A "House upon a Rock" – I know you would love them all – yet they dont *bewitch* me any. There are no walks in the wood – no low and earnest voices, no moonlight, nor stolen love, but pure little lives, loving God, and their parents, and obeying the laws of the land; yet read, if you meet them, Susie, for they will do one good.[45]

Obviously the religious atmosphere of Amherst in the 1850s did not provide the kind of experience she was seeking. Her letters of 1850 make the distinction between the tranquility, the gentleness, the kindness of her friends who have answered Christ's call, "on whom *change* has passed" [46] and her own more intense feelings. In a letter to Jane Humphrey, the same one in which she differentiates herself from her friends who have professed Christ – "I am standing alone in rebellion" [47] – she describes in terms of temptation and seduction, the feelings evoked by some unrecorded romantic attachment:

I have dared to do strange things – bold things, and have asked no advice from any – I have heeded beautiful tempters, yet do not think I am wrong. . . . I could make you tremble for me, and be very much afraid, and wonder how things would end . . . an experience bitter, and sweet, but the sweet did so beguile me. . . . Nobody *thinks* of the joy, nobody *guesses* it, to all appearance old things are engrossing, and new ones are not revealed. . . .[48]

The importance of the passage, and of the one above it, lies in the opposition and choice between romantic intensity on the one hand and a vapid sweetness and piety on the other. To the "leveling-out, the slackness, the mediocrity, the softness and bluntness of moral and intellectual experience, the anxious isolation, and the monotony of both private and public life," [49] of Amherst Emily Dickinson opposed her moments of "transport" and exaltation. Yet these precious moments, vital as they were to her and profound as she felt them to be, had, in the context of Amherst Congregationalism, no significance; indeed they were in her mind and in the mind of the community the antithesis of correct religious response. The equation, felt through the metaphor inherent in the words *transport* and *exaltation,* of a heightening of emotion and awareness with an ascendancy of spirit and of status was denied by both minister and believer.

As early as 1854 Emily Dickinson made clear to Susan Gilbert her willingness to rebel against God and isolate herself from Him rather than to forsake the cultivation of that intuition that she has "lived by":

Sue – you can go or stay – There is but one alternative – We differ often lately, and this must be the last.

You need not fear to leave me lest I should be alone, for I often part with things I fancy I have loved, – sometimes to the grave, and sometimes to an oblivion rather bitterer than death – thus my heart bleeds so frequently that I shant mind the hemorrhage, and I only add an agony to several previous ones, and at the end of day remark – a bubble burst!

Such incidents would grieve me when I was but a child, and perhaps I could have wept when little feet hard by mine, stood still in the coffin, but eyes grow dry sometimes, and hearts get crisp and cinder, and had as lief burn.

Sue – I have lived by this. It is the lingering emblem of the Heaven I once dreamed, and though if this is taken, I shall remain alone, and though in that last day, the Jesus Christ you love, remark he does not know me – there is a darker spirit will not disown it's child.

Few have been given me, and if I love them so, that for *idolatry,* they are removed from me – I silently murmur *gone,* and the billow dies away into the boundless blue, and no one knows but me, that one went down today. We have walked very pleasantly – Perhaps this is the point at which our paths diverge – then pass on singing Sue, and up the distant hill I journey on.[50]

The letter's importance certainly lies more in its content than its technique; it shows clearly that the distinction made in earlier letters between the devout who lead "pure little lives, loving God and their parents, and obeying the laws of the land" [51] and the bewitched, between those dedicated to "real life" and "prose" and those dedicated to poetry, has taken on a new and deeper significance. The writer is now a victim of persecution rather than mere misunderstanding, and her mood has shifted from contempt to fortitude. Emily Dickinson, now more conscious of the limited degree to which she can assert herself directly, is learning to convert weakness into aggression and renunciation into a positive assertion of self. The cultivation of suffering and isolation, the roles of martyr for the cause of emotional freedom and rebel against a tyrannic God, the bravado, the reticence, the pride in her meek familiarity with agony and her kinship with death, the arrogance disguised as sympathy for the departed, the resentment disguised as resignation, the aggressor disguised as victim – all these roles and attitudes so familiar to her readers and so characteristic of the poetry she had yet to write are found in embryo here. To Emily Dickinson, even at this early date, pain had begun to appear as the proof of her vocation, and her capacity to endure it as the secret sign, and the only one, of her superiority over her contemporaries. Agony was to be the price of transport, and indeed it was the wealth and currency of the deprived, paid to an exacting and exorbitant God who kept his ledgers scrupulously accurate. As she was to write in 1859:

> For each extatic instant
> We must an anguish pay
> In keen and quivering ratio
> To the extasy.

For each beloved hour
Sharp pittances of years –
Bitter contested farthings –
And Coffers heaped with Tears! [52]

But there is another aspect of Emily Dickinson, one less appealing to those who take her seriously but one which is nonetheless characteristic – that of the poet as child, or better, infant, a placating, innocent, frightened, effusive creature. This is the "Emily," or "Emilie," who appears in her neighbors' reminiscences,[53] her biographers' studies,[54] and her critics' analyses [55] all too frequently. This "little figure," [56] also characterized by the poet herself in such pathetic diminutives as "little pilgrim," [57] "tiny courtier," [58] or even "little Gentian" [59] represents the Emily who could not follow her rebellion through or bear the isolation it entailed, who, at the onset of the terror that seemed to follow every vital assertion, was willing, temporarily, to excuse her guilty actions as childish pranks, to become the "naughty girl" [60] or "little tippler" [61] to soothe and charm into forgiveness her father, on earth as in heaven. We can be grateful to this infantile "Emily," though we may prefer to read Emily Dickinson, for her presence helps us to explain the attitudes she expressed in poetry and the compensation she found in writing it, as well as the compromises she made in life. As a deliberate disguise, a mask, "Emily" is used simultaneously for propitiating and manipulating various aspects of the external world; but the fears which produced this figure are very real ones, and one can speculate that the very tensions and frustrations these fears aroused reinforced the intensity of Emily Dickinson's poetic drive. Those who want to appreciate Emily Dickinson must recognize both the causes and the contribution of "Emily," but, ironically, those whose estimate of Emily Dickinson's poetry is based on their admiration of "Emily" are admiring the manner by which, in her lifetime, the deeper attitudes behind her poetry were concealed.

For Emily Dickinson concealment is first an authentic reaction, then a maneuver; a heartfelt response is converted into an artful strategy, and her sense of vulnerability as a sensitive young girl in a nonliterary family and an aggressively mercantile and political society becomes, through that fine economy of the maximal use of limited resources that characterizes the formal structure of her poetry and the strategy of her life, precisely the means of her protection. That it is a heartfelt response, and that the compensatory process converting deficiency into abundance, suffering into triumph, defeat into victory was developed long before "Success is counted sweetest," [62] one of the earliest and most effective poetic statements of this theme, is shown in the following passages from a letter to Abiah Root, written in 1852:

How very sad it is to have a confiding nature, one's hopes and feelings are quite at the mercy of all who come along; and how very desirable to be a stolid individual, whose hopes and aspirations are safe in one's waistcoat pocket, and *that* a pocket indeed, and one not likely to be picked!
. . . I always try to think in any disappointment that had I been gratified, it had been sadder still . . . consolation upside down as I am pleased to call it.[63]

Chase has ascribed the strained and excessive expressions of ecstasy, grief, and self-pity so recurrent in Emily Dickinson's correspondence with her close female friends Abiah Root, Jane Humphrey, and, above all, Susan Gilbert, later Emily Dickinson's sister-in-law, to a common absorption with a cult of sentimentality,[64] and it is certainly true that such effusiveness was not unique with Emily Dickinson.[65] Still the sense of being at once superior and persecuted, rebellious and contrite, the excessive pledges of love and devotion when she writes, the exaggerated expressions of loss, isolation, punishment, and betrayal when she is not answered – all these emotions and themes recur so often in her poetry that we must conclude that they represent significant feelings on the part of Emily Dickinson, and that the form alone in which these feelings were expressed, was influenced by that cult of sentimentality to which Chase has made reference:

> Will you be kind to me, Susie? I am naughty and cross, this morning, and nobody loves me here; nor would *you* love me, if you should see me frown, and hear how loud the door bangs whenever I go through; and yet it is'nt anger – I dont believe it is, for when nobody sees, I brush away big tears with the corner of my apron, and then go working on. . . .
>
> And I do love to run fast – and hide away from them all; here in dear Susie's bosom, I know is love and rest, and I never would go away, did not the big world call me, and beat me for not working.
>
> . . .
>
> Do I repine, is it all murmuring, or am I sad and lone, and cannot, cannot help it? Sometimes when I do feel so, I think it may be wrong, and that God will punish me by taking you away; for he is very kind to let me write to you, and to give me your sweet letters, but my heart wants *more*.[66]

"God will punish me by taking you away." The phrase reveals that in Emily Dickinson's mind death was the agency through which, as punishment, God deprived her of her friends. In Emily Dickinson's mind, there was little difference between the death of a friend and her prolonged absence from him; indeed, in her poetry the death of another is often a metaphor for his absence, and her own death a metaphor for her feelings of isolation. That death and absence were linked in her mind well before the deaths of either Leonard Humphrey or Benjamin Newton is indicated in the following passage from a letter written to Jane Humphrey in January of 1850 discussing the absence of her sister, Lavinia. "When I knew Vinnie must go," she writes, "I clung to you as the dearer than ever friend – but when the grave opened and swallowed you both, I murmured." [67] To be sure, just as when in 1852 she writes to Susan Gilbert of taking up "my little cross again of sad, *sad* separation" [68] much of this is merely romantic hyperbole. Yet the fear that God will punish his rebellious subject by taking her friends away, the fear that in the Wadsworth episode was amply justified, has already been established.

Perhaps the most shocking aspect of the treatment of death and of immortality in Emily Dickinson's early letters is the lack of compassion or of spiritual depth with which she views these two concepts. Death matters only because it removes her friends: immortality is important because it will reunite her with them. On the one hand she reveals a childish callousness wherein at worst death is a malevolent inconvenience, at best an excuse for literary composition.[69] On the other, she reduces the most profound and awesome drama of sin, judgment, and restitution to an eternal garden-party. Her letters to Mrs. Holland in 1855 "Thank God there is a world, and that the friends we love dwell forever and ever in a house above" [70] and to John Graves in 1856 "It is a jolly thought to think that we can be Eternal – when air and earth are *full* of lives that are gone – and done – and a conceited thing indeed, this promised Resurrection." [71] do not show any intellectual advance over the sanguine optimism of her letters in 1851 to Austin "We will not live here always – but [?] will dwell together beyond the bright blue sky . . ." [72] or to Abiah Root ". . . writing is brief and fleeting – conversation will come again, yet if it *will,* it hastes and must be on its way – earth is short Abiah, but Paradise is *long*. . . ." [73]

A number of the letters of 1856 stress the idea that immortality will reunite absent friends. Her mother's illness and her aunt Lavinia's death may have turned her mind to this subject. But she is still unwilling to face the possibility that immortality might be denied her or, even worse, be a false assumption. There is a great difference between her statement to Samuel Bowles in 1860 "That *Bareheaded life* – under the grass – worries one like a Wasp" (Letter 220) and her repressive, and regressive, response to the same problem in 1856 as expressed in Letter 182 to Mrs. Holland when she discusses her mother's illness, ". . . mother lies upon the lounge, or sits in her easy chair. I don't know what her sickness is, for I am but a simple child, and frightened at myself. I often wish I was a grass, or a toddling daisy, whom all these problems of the dust might not terrify. . . ." Not until 1858, the beginning of her really creative period, does she question the existence of immortality or examine the possibility that she may be denied it. Earlier she was deeply committed to the belief that immortality will compensate for the emotional poverty of her present life, and, as we have seen in her letter to Mrs. Holland, attempted to repress her occasional doubts.[74]

Can one see also in the young Emily Dickinson the first signs of the recluse she was to become? Certainly, whether in the dominant roles of poet, queen, martyr, or rebel, or in the inferior ones of child or prisoner, she often portrayed herself as isolated from both religious and secular approval. Though her letter to Abiah Root in which she refuses an invitation to visit by writing "I thank you Abiah, but I don't go from home unless emergency leads me by the hand, and then I do it obstinately, and draw back if I can" [75] has been used as evidence that she had elected seclusion as early as 1854,[76] the statement is probably a tactful excuse rather than a declaration of principle.[77] For in September of the same year she wrote the Hollands a letter in which she cheerfully anticipates a visit to them in Springfield,[78] and her letters to Susan Gilbert [79] and Mrs. Holland,[80] written during her trip to Washington and Philadelphia in 1855, express excitement rather than homesickness or fear of the world outside of Amherst. A more probable date for the beginning of her excessive attachment to home is 1856, the year of her mother's illness when she and Lavinia took over the management of the household.[81] Perhaps at that time the old association of death with absence was revived, and she reexperienced the feeling that had inspired her to write Jane Humphrey, teaching in far-off Willoughby, Ohio, in 1852: "Why, I cant think what would tempt me to bid my friends Good bye. . . . when some pleasant friend invites me to pass a week with her, I look at my father and mother and Vinnie, and all my friends, and I say no – no, cant leave them, what if they die when I'm gone. . . ." [82]

In any case, by the summer of 1858 her position is clear; her duty is to her father and invalid mother. "I do not go out at all," she writes, "lest father will come and miss me, or miss some little act, which I might forget, should I run away." [83] But this is still a statement of fact, not an announcement of resolution, and lacks the finality which we in retrospect are too likely to attribute to it. Though there is evidence that Emily Dickinson's shyness was becoming increasingly acute by 1859,[84] there is little reason to believe that she took the deliberate step of elevating this tendency into a symbolic act of both wedding and interment until after Wadsworth's departure for California in December of 1861.[85] Thus, though we cannot assume with Chase that by 1859 "the path toward her ultimate seclusion already stretched before her," [86] we can state that the circumstances of her family life and the sense simultaneously of exclusiveness and ostracism generated by her poetic ambitions combined to make her feel at once isolated, defenseless, superior, resentful, and unique. Before Wadsworth's arrival she had already learned to convert her defeats into victories, her deprivation into abundance. The way she had learned to do so was to write poetry.

The world is full of renunciations and apprentice-ships, and this is thine; thou must pass for a fool and a churl for a long season.

Emerson, "The Poet"

Thou that knowest and keepest thy pride and stubbornness and thy distempers, know assuredly thou dost justle God out of the Throne of his glorious Soveraignty and thou dost profess, Not Gods wil but thine own (which is above his) shall rule thee, thy carnal reason and the folly of thy mind, is above the wisdome of the Lord and that shal guide thee; to please thine own stubborn crooked pervers spirit, is a greater good than to please God and enjoy happines, for this more Contents, thee; That when thou considerest but thy Course, dost thou not wonder that the great and Terrible God doth not pash such a poor in-solent worm to pouder, and send thee packing to the pitt every moment.

Thomas Hooker, "A True Sight of Sin"

Chapter 2

The chronology established by Thomas H. Johnson shows clearly that 1858 was the year in which Emily Dickinson first decided to preserve her poetry.[1] The basis for her decision remains unknown. It can be assumed, however, that at some time between 1856 and the summer of 1858 (no letters from 1857 have survived) Emily Dickinson gained the confidence in her talent that allowed her to make the internal commitment that distinguishes the artist from the tyro, though, as her many "occasional" poems testify, she continued to make use of the mask of the genteel amateur poetess, that figure familiar to every New England community, whose work is merely needlework of a higher order. Only in two letters of this period does she allude in language that characteristically combines disguise with revelation to her new vocation, in the first to her uncle, Joseph Sweetser, to its intensity, in the second, to Louise Norcross, to her ambitions:

Much has occurred, dear Uncle, since my writing you – so much – that I stagger as I write, in its sharp remembrance. Summers of bloom – and months of frost, and days of jingling bells. . . .

I would you saw what I can see, and imbibed this music [of birds]. The day went down, long time ago, and still a simple choir bear the canto on.

. . . I hardly know what I have said – my words put all their feathers on – and fluttered here and there.[2]

. . . I have known little of you, since the October morning when our families went out driving, and you and I in the dining-room decided to be distinguished. It's a great thing to be "great," Loo, and you and I might tug for a life, and never accomplish it, but no one can stop our looking on, and you know some cannot sing, but the orchard is full of birds, and we all can listen. What if we learn, ourselves, some day! Who indeed knows? [3]

The "days of jingling bells" may well refer to the days spent constructing poems, for in a later letter to Higginson, Letter 265, dated June 7, 1862, she replies to Higginson's criticism of her rhyme-schemes in the same image. ". . . [I] could not drop the Bells," she writes, "whose jingling cooled my tramp." The "summers of bloom" and "months of frost" are more likely to be statements of metaphor than of fact, signifying the alternation of death and resurrection she observed in the natural cycle, an alternation that gave her intimations if not assurances of immortality. These were images that she frequently employed in her poetry, and so it is likely that in this paragraph she is referring to her absorption in the fashioning of her new creative power. Unfortunately the *terminus a quo* cannot be established; so far, no earlier letter to her uncle has been found.

The equation of the bird with the poet and of its music with poetry made in both these letters can be traced back at least as far as 1854, where it is used in Poem 5, enclosed in a letter to Susan Gilbert. It is, like most of her central imagery, conventional, drawn from a long-established and popular tradition, but pushed to some extent beyond a purely conventional significance. The bird's song rising against the sunset and oncoming night may represent, in its affirmation against the day's death, some knowledge on the part of nature of a life beyond mortality; likewise, perhaps, the poet's intuition of immortality is a genuine source of knowledge. But this is to assume that both poet and bird are divinely inspired, and, as Emily Dickinson discovered early, no amount of perspicacity or ornithology would conclusively verify that assumption.

In the few poems of this period that can, on account of their employment of the imagery of the bird and its music, be interpreted as comments upon the poetic process itself the concern is always epistemological, i.e., with the significance and validity of the evidence of her intuition, or moral, that is in terms of the poet's function as witness to the truth of immortality and consoler of the bereaved. At times the bird represents the artist; [4] at times it is the artist's intuition, that force that has the power to fly beyond the natural world and return, like Noah's dove, with evidence of "land." [5] The overwhelming question for her was, of course, whether this evidence was provided by nature or imagined by mind. The answer given by Emerson was certainly well-known to her,[6] and it was undoubtedly an appealing one, for it gave to poetry a validity both intellectual and moral, and it gave the poet the assurance that, as insignificant and subordinate as the world may take him to be, "he is the sovereign, and stands on the center," [7] that though "isolated among his contemporaries by truth and by his art" [he will] "draw all men sooner or later." [8] It is scarcely surprising that Emily Dickinson in her early poetry is concerned with the possibility that through intuition or perception she can discover conclusive proof of the existence of immortality:

> My nosegays are for Captives –
> Dim – long expectant eyes,
> Fingers denied the plucking,
> Patient till Paradise.
>
> To such, if they sh'd whisper
> Of morning and the moor,

They bear no other errand,
And I, no other prayer.[9]

The mood, however, is optative, not declarative. In the end, the significance of her insight, and hence of the poetry in which it was articulated, depended upon its source, and she was of too empirical a cast of mind to assume that Nature itself necessarily provoked the intensity with which she responded to it. If the intimations she felt from nature were too intense for her to ignore, immortality was too magnificent an hypothesis to be proved by them alone.

In a number of poems written in this period she refers to a mysterious force that is apparently transmitted through nature:

The Murmur of a Bee
A Witchcraft – yieldeth me –
If any ask me why –
'Twere easier to die –
Than tell – [10]

Musicians wrestle everywhere –
All day – among the crowded air
I hear the silver strife – [11]

I taste a liquor never brewed
From Tankards scooped in Pearl – [12]

A something in a summer's Day
As slow her flambeaux burn away
Which solemnizes me.[13]

As she contemplated the seasonal cycle, the movement from funereal pomp to frost to spring's reawakening to summer's fulfillment, Emerson's question "But is there no intent of an analogy between man's life and the seasons?" [14] must have occurred to her, and the corroborative "evidence" of the solar cycle from sunset to night to dawn to noon, of the flowers blooming again, of the butterfly emerging, of the birds that had returned – to cite the images she used in many of her poems – must have led her tentatively to assume that certain natural phenomena might be emblematic of immortality. For support in this assumption Emily Dickinson could have turned to the leading intellectual figure in Amherst, a man whose opinions were certainly regarded at least as highly by the residents of Amherst as those of that radical philosopher, Emerson – Edward Hitchcock, noted geologist and president of Amherst College from 1845 to 1854.[15] While there is no proof that Emily Dickinson actually attended any of President Hitchcock's lectures on the spiritual significance of natural phenomena or that she read them when in 1850 they were collected into a small volume printed in Amherst,[16] she would certainly have been aware of them and would not have been likely to ignore Hitchcock's attempt to answer the very questions that troubled her most at this time.

The surprising thing is that she did not succumb to the temptation of accepting either his answers or Emerson's. But Hitchcock the scientist, the disciplined observer, would probably have attracted her more at this time than Hitchcock the religious philosopher, for in the poetry she wrote during the period of 1858 to 1860 she establishes, tests, and ultimately rejects the hypothesis that nature demonstrates the design God has prepared for man. Unsure from the first whether the poet's observations of the natural order provided insights into the human condition that were more valid than the calculations of astronomers or the cataloging of botanists, she eventually concluded that the gulf between nature and man was too great for nature to offer meaningful analogies. She was forced to the conclusion that her desire to sustain, through the evidence of nature and through the perception that she organized into poetry, the faith she desperately needed would demand an impossible sacrifice, to wit, the suspension of the responsive and inquiring sensibility that her poetic power derived from.

Thus any object in nature could be considered as a revelation or sign of spiritual fact, as an enigma, or simply as a discrete phenomenon to be described rather than interpreted:

> . . . You and I the secret
> Of the Crocus know –
> Let us chant it softly –
> *"There* is no more snow!" [17]
>
> . . .
>
> Flowers – Well – if anybody
> Can the extasy define –
> Half a transport – half a trouble –
> With which flowers humble men:
> Anybody find the fountain
> From which floods so contra flow –
> I will give him all the Daisies
> Which upon the hillside blow.
> Too much pathos in their faces
> For a simple breast like mine –
> Butterflies from St Domingo
> Cruising round the purple line –
> Have a system of aesthetics –
> Far superior to mine.[18]

The mixed feelings provoked by the flowers result from the poet's uncertainty as to their significance, though her response is ecstatic in its intensity. The flower may be evidence of resurrection – the word *transport* is used in a double sense – or only of a renewal in nature that has no implications for human life. It is the meaning the flowers express, regardless of what that meaning may be, that the poet wishes to "define." Nature, to which she had turned with a blithe confidence that it would confirm her hope of immortality and allay her fears that she would suffer in eternity the same isolation that she felt so keenly in Amherst, remained impassive and ambiguous and aroused forebodings as well as ecstasies. The cyclical aspect of nature that seemed at first to be the visible sign of eternity and resurrection could also graphically suggest the passage of time.[19] This uncertainty about *what* Nature intimated concerning human life is evident in her letters as well as her poems. To the Norcross sisters she wrote in 1860 "This world is just a little place, just the red in the sky, before the sun rises," [20] and to Samuel Bowles she affirmed in 1858 that "Confidence in Daybreak modifies Dusk"; [21] but she could also write Mrs. Holland in 1859, reflecting on the autumn landscape:

The gentian is a greedy flower, and overtakes us all. Indeed, this world is short, and I wish, until I tremble, to touch the ones I love before the hills are red – are gray – are white – are "born again"! If we knew how deep the crocus lay, we never should let her go.[22]

And, in perhaps the most revealing letter of all, written about March 1859, she tells Catherine Scott Turner the "qualifications" she must have to be elected to Emily Dickinson's circle of intimate friends. "Are you afraid of the Sun?" she asks. "When you hear the new violet sucking her way among the sods, shall you be *resolute*? All *we* are *strangers* – dear – The world is not acquainted with us, because we are not acquainted with her." [23]

A sense that the laws which govern the world of nature are entirely different from those that govern the lives of men is expressed in several poems of this period.[24] Behind her resistance to Susan Gilbert's suggestion that she eliminate the last stanza of one of her most famous poems, "Safe in their alabaster chambers," [25] is the poet's intention to reinforce the suggestion made in the first stanza that the analogies of resurrection with morning and immortality with noon which those now dead had once perceived in nature had proved to be false, and that the two orders of existence are totally unrelated. In another poem she goes so far as to chide the analogies she had once believed in; the sun, the bird, the butterfly are recognized to be products of human artifice designed to disguise the somber probability of a final and meaningless death, where, to quote one of the

29

variant stanzas of "Safe in their alabaster chambers," "Midnight in Marble – Refutes – the Suns –"

> Make me a picture of the sun –
> So I can hang it in my room –
> And make believe I'm getting warm
> When others call it "Day"!
>
> Draw me a Robin – on a stem –
> So I am hearing him, I'll dream,
> And when the Orchards stop their tune –
> Put my pretense – away –
>
> Say if it's really – warm at noon –
> Whether it's Buttercups – that "skim" –
> Or Butterflies – that "bloom"?
> Then – skip – the frost – upon the lea –
> And skip the Russet – on the tree –
> Let's play those – never come! [26]

Yet it would be a mistake to attribute to Emily Dickinson a progressive, reasoned disillusionment with the world of nature as her examination of it became more penetrating. All of the attitudes discussed above were held throughout this period. They represent not successive intellectual positions but alternative reactions to a single problem.

However, precisely because she had a mind that characteristically worked through metaphor, Emily Dickinson was alert to the distinction between object and symbol. If nature as symbol had in the end no more vitality than a painted sun tacked up on one's bedroom wall, nature itself could still exercise an attraction so powerful that only a faith in immortality, independent of nature, could compete with it.[27] One advantage that could be derived from recognizing an unbridgeable gulf between man and nature was that one could be free to examine nature on its own terms.[28] But for Emily Dickinson of 1860 such detachment from nature, such independence from the need to make or to find nature spiritually significant, was not possible, nor would it be until she had found a basis for faith in immortality that was independent of the natural order. The poem quoted below, written in 1859, poignantly expresses her helplessness, disillusionment, and yearning as she confronts a natural world that she loved and that could not help her:

These are the days when Birds come back –
A very few – a Bird or two –
To take a backward look.

These are the days when skies resume
The old – old sophistries of June –
A blue and gold mistake.

Oh fraud that cannot cheat the Bee –
Almost thy plausibility
Induces my belief.

Till ranks of seeds their witness bear –
And softly thro' the altered air
Hurries a timid leaf.

Oh Sacrament of summer days,
Oh Last Communion in the Haze –
Permit a child to join.

Thy sacred emblems to partake
Thy consecrated bread to take
And thine immortal wine! [29]

The general implication of the poem seems to be that the poet, while aware through the "testimony" of nature itself that no evidence of immortality is to be found there, wishes for the last time to reexperience the moments in which nature had seemed through her "communion" with it to offer proof of immortality.

Intuition and personal perception were not the only instruments, however, that she considered making use of in her attempts to examine nature for evidence of immortality, but she quickly realized that her subject was not susceptible to scientific or mathematical inquiry:

> My figures fail to tell me
> How far the Village lies –
> Whose peasants are the Angels –
> Whose Cantons dot the skies – [30]
>
> Low at my problem bending,
> Another problem comes –
> Larger than mine – Serener –
> Involving statelier sums.
>
> I check my busy pencil,
> My figures file away.
> Wherefore, my baffled fingers
> * Thy perplexity? [31]

. . .

Thy perplexity/Thine extremity

Yet she saw in the comparative anatomist's attempt to deduce a total structure from limited evidence,[32] in the astronomer's to perceive and to trace the motions of bodies hitherto unseen,[33] a concern with problems of perception, measurement, and definition with which she could identify, despite the discrepancy, grotesque for any poet, between the terminology of science and the objects to which it referred.[34] Certainly her sympathy was great for the concern, the care, and the discipline with which the scientist conducted his investigation. And simply as a member of the Amherst community, Emily Dickinson would have presumably shared the general respect for science that Presi-

* On this and all subsequent occasions when poems are quoted for which the Johnson edition supplies variant readings, the word or words in question will be immediately followed by an asterisk and repeated below the poem separated by a slash (/) from the variant reading or readings. When an entire line has a variant reading, that line will be preceded by an asterisk.

dent Hitchcock had brought to Amherst.[35] Moreover, the conclusions reached through scientific investigation had the advantage of relative certainty; if through the poet's intuition the ascent of the dead to heaven could be observed and "tracked" and charted, her fears that she had made the wrong choice in deciding to suffer and humble herself in time so that she could be exalted in eternity would be set at rest. And even if she could not yet find the evidence to justify this hypothesis, she could appreciate the mentality that demanded verifiable knowledge and would not stop at faith:

> "Faith" is a fine invention
> When Gentlemen can *see* –
> But *Microscopes* are prudent
> In an Emergency.[36]

So she wrote Samuel Bowles in a poem that undercuts her more sentimental excesses, adding in the same letter "That *Bareheaded life* – under the grass – worries one like a Wasp." [37] The "Emergency" was very likely the death of her aunt Lavinia on April 17, 1860, an event which deeply affected Emily Dickinson.[38] The letter to Bowles cited above, as well as another letter enclosing a poem,[39] questions the arbitrary way in which the living are struck down and gives no hint that the dead will be rewarded. "I cant explain it, Mr. Bowles" she wrote. But if she could not explain death she could examine it, and the "Microscope," the instrument for intense scrutiny within the narrowest of limits, was the means she chose, turning it upon her experience and upon her consciousness of her experience.

No critic can help noticing Emily Dickinson's preoccupation with death, and a number of them have attempted to find a basis for it in specific events in her early life. Whicher and Chase, both using the poem "I never lost as much but twice" [40] as evidence, cite the effect upon her of the deaths of Leonard Humphrey and Benjamin Newton, and assume the third "loss" to refer to the Reverend Charles Wadsworth's departure for San Francisco.[41] Johnson, on the other hand, locates the significant experience in an earlier event, the "shattering impression" left with Emily Dickinson after seeing her friend Sophia Holland shortly before Sophia's death,[42] and, to show how this experience continued to affect her, he cites a letter Emily Dickinson wrote six years later in which she describes to Jane Humphrey her attempt to imagine herself lying in state, "a little white gown on, and a snowdrop on my breast."[43] In his discussion of "I heard a fly buzz when I died"[44] Johnson gives great weight to this formative experience. "It is of course because Emily Dickinson had from childhood felt an unusual sensitivity about such events," he writes, "that she is here uniquely able to give reality to the moment."[45] The letter to Jane Humphrey was, however, written with the intention of consoling Jane for her father's death, and it reflects not the continuance of a genuine trauma but the irritating and competitive egotism of the bedside visitor who soothes the invalid by dwelling on the magnitude of her own ailments. It is an extremely tactless letter, as Emily Dickinson seemed momentarily to realize – at one point in it she wrote "I'm a naughty, bad girl to say sad things, and make you cry" – but she did, nonetheless, mail it.

The inferences which Whicher and Chase draw from Poem 49:

> I never lost as much but twice,
> And that was in the sod.
> Twice have I stood a beggar
> Before the door of God!
>
> Angels – twice descending
> Reimbursed my store –
> Burglar! Banker – Father!
> I am poor once more!

are at first sight more tenable. Lacking the advantage of the chronology established by Johnson in his edition of the poems, neither Chase nor Whicher could have known that the poem was written no later than 1858 and hence could not possibly refer to Wadsworth's departure for California in May of 1862. Yet a close reading of the poem itself reveals that while the first two "losses" are losses through death – and presumably do refer to Newton and Humphrey, the third loss is one of a different order, a loss not "in the sod," for which the previous losses are used as the best analogy.[46] Thus the poem's emphasis is not on the deaths of Newton and Humphrey *per se* but upon the magnitude of her present loss. To do the poem the injustice of paraphrase: Only twice have I felt a deprivation at all comparable to what I feel now – and both times that was through the death of someone close to me. Both times I was reimbursed, after Humphrey's death by Benjamin Newton and after Newton's death by the firm conviction that all I had lost would be restored to me in the afterlife. Now I have lost this conviction and can only beg that power which has both enriched and robbed me to reimburse me once more.

To spend time attacking the interpretations of Emily Dickinson's biographers and critics would be unfair to the reader were it done only for the pleasure of an academic quarrel. But to understand her poetry on death, to avoid confusing statements of metaphor with statements of fact, it is necessary to disentangle it from the incidents of biography. Few of these poems are recollections or elegies, and the few that are betray one cultural and extra-personal influence that can be safely ascribed to her poetry on the dead – the influence of the "graveyard" school of poetry, the most vulgar and ludicrous aspect of that cult of sentimentality which Mark Twain, whose satire is in itself proof of the cult's wide popularity, ridiculed through the immortal poetess Emmeline Grangerford, artist of "And Thou Art Gone Yes Thou Art Gone Alas," and so much resembling "Emilie" Dickinson that one would be tempted to assume imitation did not chronology forbid. One need only compare Miss Grangerford's "Ode to Stephen Dowling Bots, Dec'd.," whose "spirit was gone for to sport aloft/In the realms of the good and great" with Poems 53 and 78, for example, to substantiate Chase's contention that "the intellectual life of Emily Dickinson and her young friends . . . was also susceptible to a thoroughly vulgarized sentimentality." [47] One need only imagine Emmeline's self-portrait entitled "Shall I Never See Thee More Alas" of

a woman in a slim black dress, belted small under the armpits, with bulges like a cabbage in the middle of the sleeves, and a large black scoop-shovel bonnet with a black veil, and white slim ankles crossed about with black tape, and very wee black slippers, like a chisel, and . . . leaning pensive on a tombstone on her right elbow, under a weeping willow, and her other hand hanging down her side holding a white handkerchief and a reticule. . . .[48]

as an illustration for the following poem to see that convention rather than experience initially directed Emily Dickinson to choose death as a poetic subject:

> Where I have lost, I softer tread –
> I sow sweet flower from garden bed –
> I pause above that vanished head
> 　　　And mourn.
>
> Whom I have lost, I pious guard
> From accent harsh, or ruthless word –
> Feeling as if their pillow heard,
> 　　　Though stone!
>
> When I have lost, you'll know by this –
> A Bonnet black – A dusk surplice –
> A little tremor in my voice
> 　　　Like this!
>
> Why, I have lost, the people know
> Who dressed in frocks of purest snow

Went home a century ago
Next Bliss! [49]

The same convention was probably also responsible for her practice of sending "occasional" poems or, as Emmeline called them, "tributes." [50] The tradition of the "tribute" was certainly known in Amherst. Emily Dickinson's aunt, Lavinia Norcross, addressed this poem, quoted in part in Leyda, I, 11, to her sister, Emily, shortly after their mother's death in 1829:

> . . . What if her frail & earthly form
> Lies in its dark & narrow bed
> What if the heart once beating warm
> Lies low among the silent dead
>
> O look not there! but raise thine eye
> To higher climes where angels are
> Where pleasures never bloom to die
> Sister—our mothers happy there

Small wonder that Emily Dickinson had to learn to distinguish between emotion and sentiment! That Emily Dickinson's work reflects as well as repudiates the limited resources of her culture has been amply discussed by Chase,[51] and it is clear that such sentimental excesses as the above should be used to condemn the milieu rather than the poet. What distinguishes Emily Dickinson from her contemporaries is not her independence from such conventions but her ability to refine them. In respect to the major subjects of her poetry – death, nature, immortality – the conventional response is reduced, in the sense that the metallurgist "reduces" the ore, to personal vision, and the agency, the alembic as it were, is the careful reference of convention to observed fact.

She was not, however, so scrupulous a follower of the principles of scientific inquiry during these first few years of her poetry. Poems 187, "How many times these low feet staggered" and 216 "Safe in their alabaster chambers," both

37

written in 1860, are the first in which the dead do not serve
merely as the point of departure either for the poet's
affirmation of her own ultimate immortality or for her
concern that she might not attain it. In either case, as
shown in the two poems below, the dead are no more than
stock figures, and death is significant only in terms of what
the poet can expect to gain from it. As an artistic statement,
neither of the poems can be taken seriously, but as demonstrations of Emily Dickinson's alternative feelings about
immortality they are revealing:

> Taken from men – this morning –
> Carried by men today –
> Met by the Gods with banners –
> Who marshalled her away –
>
> One little maid – from playmates –
> One little mind from school –
> There must be guests in Eden –
> All the rooms are full –
>
> Far – as the East from Even –
> Dim – as the border star –
> Courtiers quaint, in Kingdoms
> Our departed are.[52]
>
> .   .   .
>
> Bless God, he went as soldiers,
> His musket on his breast –
> Grant God, he charge the bravest
> Of all the martial blest!
>
> Please God, might I behold him
> In epauletted white –
> I should not fear the foe then –
> I should not fear the fight! [53]

Immortality rather than death then is the point of
reference of these early poems; her reflections on death do
not condition but are conditioned by whatever attitude

toward immortality is dominant at the time that they are composed. Death is merely, as the popular poetry she read demonstrated clearly, the most appropriate phenomenon through which her attitudes toward immortality could be dramatized. For anyone as concerned with the possibility of immortality as was Emily Dickinson, death was the crucial event, and the vision of the dying – and next to that the observations of those who watched them die – were the furthest outposts of human consciousness, the logical vantage points from which to attempt to *see* and therefore to verify the existence of immortality. Regardless of the effect upon her of the death of any specific person, death was inevitably one of the major subjects of her poetry. Indeed the very fact that her early poems treat death so sentimentally appears to indicate that convention and logic rather than personal experience were the principal influences upon her choice of death as a suitable poetic subject. When one compares the best of her early poems upon the dead, "She bore it till the simple veins" with a later poem, "The last night that she lived," the advance from a stereotyped response to a complex emotion that is intimately apprehended and is rendered with precision and thoroughness is evident:

> She bore it till the simple veins
> Traced azure on her hand –
> Till pleading, round her quiet eyes
> The purple Crayons stand.
>
> Till Daffodils had come and gone
> I cannot tell the sum,
> And then she ceased to bear it –
> And with the Saints sat down.
>
> No more her patient figure
> At twilight soft to meet –
> No more her timid bonnet
> Upon the village street –

But Crowns instead, and Courtiers –
And in the midst so fair,
Whose but her shy – immortal face
Of whom we're whispering here? [54]

. . .

The last Night that She lived
It was a Common Night
Except the Dying – this to Us
Made Nature different

We noticed smallest things –
Things overlooked before
By this great light upon our Minds
Italicized – as 'twere

As We went out and in
Between Her final Room
And Rooms where Those to be alive
Tomorrow were, a Blame

That Others could exist
While She must finish quite
A Jealousy for Her arose
So nearly infinite –

We waited while She passed –
It was a narrow time –
Too jostled were Our Souls to speak
At length the notice came.

She mentioned, and forgot –
Then lightly * as a Reed
Bent to the Water, struggled * scarce –
Consented, and was dead –

And We – We placed the Hair –
And drew the Head erect –

And then an awful leisure was
Belief * to regulate – [55]

. . .

lightly/softly   struggled/shivered
Belief/With nought, Our faith

In Poem 144 it is precisely the easy assumption of the last
two stanzas that vitiates the emotion established in the first
part of the poem. The poem drifts from an individual
experience stated with the confidence that it will call up of
itself the requisite emotion to a stock situation toward
which our response is overtly supplied. What begins as
emotion ends as sentiment. At the outset the poet writes
from what has been felt, but she slides over to what is
hoped, and must support her uncertainty through a series
of conventional symbols; thus the occasion of the poem is
genuine, but its resolution is not. In contrast to Poem 1100,
the dominant emotion is not the inevitable product of the
situation from which it is made to arise.

This impulse to apply a facile conclusion to a complex
experience is typical of much of Emily Dickinson's early
work; fortunately, and it is this that distinguishes her
poetry from the contemporary poetry on which she drew for
subject, she is not able to rest content with such conclusions. The same conflict that was noted in her poetry dealing with nature – the conflict between the wish to find in it
evidence of immortality and the need to remain faithful to
her own observations about nature – is present in her early
poetry about death. Thus we can expect to find, alongside
of the optimistic poems of the type quoted above, poems in
which the fate of the dead is a problematic one, where
reward is not certain but dependent upon an arbitrary
judgment: [56]

> My wheel is in the dark!
> I cannot see a spoke
> Yet know it's dripping feet
> Go round and round.

My foot is on the Tide!
An unfrequented road –
Yet have all roads
A clearing at the end –

Some have resigned the Loom –
Some in the busy tomb
Find quaint employ –

Some with new – stately feet –
Pass royal thro' the gate –
Flinging the problem back
At you and I! [57]

But the uncertainty of fate makes observation, aided,
perhaps, by the poet's intuition, only the more imperative,
even though, paradoxically death is an experience which
yields of itself no evidence, which can be interpreted only
in terms of the preconceptions one brings to it. Using, as
she so often does, the sea to symbolize the flux of time
within which both living and dead sail, and the land to
symbolize the destination on the other side, Emily Dickinson in the two poems below expresses her uncertainty and
her sense that the poet's eye and the flight of his imagination are the only means by which that mystery may be
penetrated:

Whether my bark went down at sea –
Whether she met with gales –
Whether to isles enchanted
She bent her docile sails –

By what mystic mooring
She is held today –
This is the errand of the eye
Out upon the Bay. [58]

· · ·

Once more, my now bewildered Dove
Bestirs her puzzled wings

> Once more her mistress, on the deep
> Her troubled question flings –
>
> Thrice to the floating casement
> The Patriarch's bird returned,
> Courage! My brave Columba!
> There may yet be *Land!* [59]

Yet even observation of the dead grants no evidence but only estimate.[60] The sole evidence we have is of their departure not their destination,[61] and the signs of death "A throe upon the features –/A hurry in the breath –/An extasy of parting" [62] are themselves ambiguous, suggestive equally of torture and of exaltation. Thus the microscope, the "fine invention," with which the prudent supplement their faith reveals no more than did the preconception it was to supplant; one could indeed *see* the *Ding an sich,* but except in terms of a prior belief one could not know what it was one had seen.

This sense of the discrepancy between the appearance of an object and the meaning of it was for Emily Dickinson at no time more graphically and grotesquely apparent than in the presence of death. Few verses reveal more sensitivity to the Christian paradox or are more receptive to its ironies than is the initial stanza of Poem 184:

> A transport one cannot contain
> May yet, a transport be –
> Though God forbid it lift the lid –
> Unto it's Extasy!

But then the ironic mode, depending as it does on two discrete lines of vision converging upon the same object, was a natural one for Emily Dickinson when she contrasted human grief with the joy of those who have assumed the perspective of eternity – i.e., those who have been "transported," or when she compared human corruption with the incorruptibility for which corruption was the prerequisite. "She was mute from transport –/I – from agony –" [63] the poet remarks, watching, as it were, herself crossing that gulf, the gulf that is symbolized in many of her other poems by darkness or water, between the living and the dead. In another poem, she seizes upon the irony inherent in this situation to analyze the limitations of human perception and language and to mock the presumption of human grief:

A throe upon the features –
A hurry in the breath –
An extasy of parting
Denominated "Death" –

An anguish at the mention
Which when to patience grown,
I've known permission given
To rejoin it's own.[64]

Still, when we examine all of Emily Dickinson's poetry in these early years we must conclude that irony represented for her a momentary respite from her vacillations between hope and despair, rather than a stratagem consciously chosen to provide her with a secure vantage point from which to dominate and to fuse the contradictions she perceived and felt in her experience. Her irony in these poems is a means of mastering the conflict caused by the mystery of her fate, not a means of penetrating that mystery, and the question of her fate is for her a far too important one to allow her to succumb for long to the temptation of balanced detachment. The antidote for such uncertainty was not irony or resignation but discovery, no matter what the risk. "I would go, to know!" she writes in 1859.[65] To verify immortality through her own perception would be to verify the power of her intellect and of her talent as well. Her wish to be the privileged initiate into mysteries that lie in a world not ordinarily susceptible to human consciousness and not bound to the cycles of time may have been motivated as much by a need to assure herself of her intrinsic

44

superiority to the rest of Amherst as it was to assure herself of ultimate recognition in Heaven. The poetry itself may express a desperate need for faith, but the writing of it, as we can see in the poem below, is an act of pride, a pitting of the resources of human consciousness against the obscurantism of God:

Just lost, when I was saved!
Just felt * the world go by!
Just girt me for the onset with Eternity,
When breath blew * back,
And on the other side
I heard recede the disappointed tide!

Therefore, as One returned, I feel,
Old secrets of the line * to tell!
Some Sailor, skirting foreign * shores –
Some pale Reporter,* from the awful doors
Before the Seal!

Next time, to stay!
Next time, the things to see
By ear unheard,
Unscrutinized by Eye –

Next time, to tarry,
While the Ages steal –
* Slow tramp the Centuries,
And the Cycles wheel! [66]

. . .

felt/heard   foreign/novel
blew/drew   Reporter/"reporter"
the line/"the Line"
Slow tramp the Centuries/Tramp the slow centuries

Like many of Emily Dickinson's poems, this poem reflects the attempt, and the failure of the attempt, to establish some conclusive estimate and judgment of the meaning of death. It is an essentially "scientific" poem in that the poet's aim is to discover the evidence that will allow her to advance from hypothesis to axiom. Death is treated as an objective fact that is to be explored, described, and assessed, and the poet does not rest content merely with repeating conventional hypotheses about death but gives us a notation of her attempts to make such an assessment. Like any scientific investigator she is limited by the appropriateness and the range of the technology available to her, and some of her poetry during this period is, as we have seen, concerned with the examination and criticism of the efficiency of the various instruments – intuition, faith, tradition and convention, consciousness, the senses and the scientific apparatus that extends them – through which our judgments of this vital phenomenon, death, might be made. Far from disregarding the limits of judgment, as Yvor Winters charges, she was continually sensitive to and frustrated by them. Only in respect to the more conventionally religious poems,[67] where the poet is willing to depend on faith alone, is it possible to agree with Winters' criticism,[68] and surely it is obvious to Winters that in the Christian religion, and in any other system in which faith is the ultimate moral act, the "limits of judgment" are precisely the limits which one should not respect. Emily Dickinson's respect for them is an accurate index of her independence, integrity, and heresy.

We are fortunate that Emily Dickinson's faith was so fragile and that her integrity prevented her tentative conclusions from becoming final ones. A thesis on "The Concept of Death in Emily Dickinson's Early Poetry" would be dispiriting and disillusioning for both writer and reader, for Emily Dickinson was not, regardless of what she might have felt herself to be, an original or profound thinker. During this period her general statements about death (and, for that matter, about immortality) were banal: Death is at worst the refuge of the weary and oppressed,[69] at best the agency through which the lowly shall be at last raised on high.[70] In short, her early poetry on death,

46

derived largely from the popular "graveyard" poetry of the type Twain satirized, shares the intellectual limitations of such poetry.

This assertion that Emily Dickinson's considered and conclusive generalizations about death and immortality are neither stimulating nor significant (in this she is the precise opposite of the one other major American poet for whom death was such a compelling theme, her contemporary, Walt Whitman) is made not to belittle her poetry but to shift our attention from Emily Dickinson the thinker to Emily Dickinson the reactor, for her statements about death and immortality are far less meaningful than are her reactions to these subjects when she realizes a definitive statement cannot be made. Her best poetry does not, as Whitman's does, reconcile opposites or resolve contradictions through an intellectual system; it delineates the role and interplay of opposites as the components of an intense and complex emotion. Her poetry, then, is dramatic rather than reflective, and its center of interest lies not in the concepts or projected states of experience – death and the human fate after death – that form its ostensible subject, but in the inner life of the protagonist, in the reverberations set up within her consciousness when she contemplates areas where consciousness cannot enter. Indeed by her greatest creative period, the years 1861 to 1864, Emily Dickinson was no longer treating death only as an objective fact, a phenomenon to be investigated, but also as the most accurate metaphor through which to objectify one of her most characteristic states of feeling.

This open identification, made in her later poetry, of death with her emotional life raises the question of whether, behind the earlier poems in which death is significant only to the extent that immortality is still not assured, there is not a deeper attraction toward death itself; for in some of the poems written at this time [71] death appears to be sought not for the immortality which may succeed it, but for its own sake:

47

Ah, Necromancy Sweet!
Ah, Wizard erudite!
Teach me the skill,

That I instil the pain
Surgeons assuage in vain,
Nor Herb of all the plain
Can heal! [72]

Certainly, as an examination of the poem "How many times these low feet staggered" [73] reveals, death, because of the uses to which it can be put, has its temptations. Through it the meek, acquiescent "housewife," who in life never complained of her burden of drudgery, can achieve an impregnable indolence. The dead woman's rebellion is total, unqualified by any dependence upon the forces which provoked it. The indifferent strength with which she confronts the living who view her corpse mocks and refutes the views they held of her when she was alive, and their very situation of helplessness before her now is the mirror-image of the condition she knew in life. The autonomy, the independence that the housewife was denied in life are conferred here not by immortality but by the very act of dying. Passivity and negation become the modes of supreme assertion, and the "indolence" of the housewife is, in an ironic reversal of the root meaning of the word,[74] the vital assertion and exercise of her power:

Try – can you stir the awful rivet –
Try – can you lift the hasps of steel!

Mockingly the poet, in sympathy with the dead woman who need not herself deign to mock, urges the living to try their strength against the strength death has bestowed here. Through dying, the act which would seem to be the ultimate expression of reticence, self-effacement, suppression, withdrawal – the very tactics which the housewife had selected for dealing with the world around her – the victim can at last gain the attention of the living, return

48

their indifference, and surpass and overthrow their power. Victim in life, in death, the agency through which the meekest of us automatically humbles and abashes the most proud, she becomes the victor.

Despite the fact that the occasion for the poem is the death of the housewife, the poem itself is not one of speculation about the fate of the departed, nor does the speaker, either through observation of the dead or identification with the dying, attempt to transcend the limits of human consciousness. The poem is directed at the living, not the dead, and its protagonist is the poet, one of the living, as she examines a particular stratagem for dealing with the restrictions and oppressions that are inevitable to the extent that one lives within a framework of social relationships. The poem does not deny the value of life but is critical of the conditions under which so much of living must be done, and the figure whose experience and fate directly elicit the emotion of the poem is, significantly, not a generic figure such as a "woman" or "person" but a "housewife," a figure presented in terms of status and occupation. The distinction made in the poem between the dead woman and the living voice that addresses a larger audience with a series of mocking imperatives shows us that this housewife is not to be identified with Emily Dickinson the poet. The solution, the turning to death to master life, that was the only one available to the housewife, the poet's *alter ego,* is one which the poet herself is able to reject because of the opportunity given to her by her art for expression, assertion, freedom, and power. For both poet and housewife, however, the culture, the demands and expectations which defined the culture were the same, and thus the poem does reflect her attitude toward the society within which she felt obliged to live.

In this poem dying appears to be an aggressive act, one that will confound and abash the living, and that will, as the last two stanzas remind us, arouse them to express with guilt and remorse the affection they now realize they had for too long withheld. They are reproached and rebuffed by someone they can no longer frighten or punish. And as they note how the house has fallen into disuse since the house-wife's death, how:

> Buzz the dull flies – on the chamber window –
> Brave – shines the sun through the freckled pane –
> Fearless – the cobwebs swing from the ceiling –

they will, within the terrible limitations of their capacity to sympathize and appreciate, recognize her importance to them at least as a functionary if not as a human being.

If immortality is the sphere in which the meek and the neglected come into their own, death is the means through which they retaliate. It is the last threat of the child who knows he is too small to kill, who, since he cannot withdraw his love from the parents he resents, must attempt to manipulate them through it. It is the one act of revenge which carries no danger of retribution. But when Emily Dickinson, or rather the child, "Emilie," asks in a series of rhetorical questions:

> On such a night, or such a night,
> Would anybody care
> If such a little figure
> Slipped quiet from it's chair –
>
> So quiet – Oh how quiet,
> That nobody might know
> But that the little figure
> Rocked softer – to and fro –
>
> On such a dawn, or such a dawn –
> Would anybody sigh
> That such a little figure
> Too sound asleep did lie
>
> For Chanticleer to wake it –
> Or stirring house below –
> Or giddy bird in orchard –
> Or early task to do? [75]

She is prudently masking revenge with self-sacrifice, aggression with submissiveness. Elsewhere she is more forthright, reserving her most explicit threat for those who try too strenuously to console her with their religious doctrines:

> Talk with prudence to a Beggar
> Of "Potosi," and the mines!
> Reverently, to the Hungry
> Of your viands, and your wines!
>
> Cautious, hint to any Captive
> You have passed enfranchized feet!
> Anecdotes of air in Dungeons
> Have sometimes proved deadly sweet! [76]

This protagonist is not a timid child but a sullen, resentful member of the disenfranchised. But in the end her threat, like the child's, is one not of assault, but of self-destruction.

The captive, the beggar, the prisoner, the household drudge, – all of these are images of the oppressed and helpless. For such people death is their sole weapon of assertion and offense and their sole means of compelling affection and recognition. At the same time, for all of these figures death represents an escape, a release from suffering, drudgery, and persecution:

> This covert have all the children
> Early aged, and often cold,
> Sparrows, unnoticed by the Father –
> Lambs for whom time had not a fold. [77]

A few of the poems expressing a wish for death derive from a more specific complaint against the conditions of life in Amherst; the attempts of insensitive people to break through the privacy essential for the practice of her art. It is a world of casual rather than malicious cruelty, of the wanton destruction of the schoolboy robbing birds' nests or the institutionalized barbarism of the hunter tracking down his quarry – cruelty accepted or condoned by society;

and hence the society will offer no relief from it. Using again the bird as image of the poet, she finds only in death a refuge where the harried sensibility can rest inviolate:

> Never the treasures in her nest
> The cautious grave exposes,
> Building where schoolboy dare not look,
> And sportsman is not bold.[78]

Yet the more one examines Emily Dickinson's poetry of the years 1858 through 1860, the less one is convinced that death itself is an important theme for the poet. Death is the ostensible subject of some poems [79] and it is a part of the *content* of a great many of them, but it is never in itself the center of interest. Either, as in the majority of her poems, "Death [is] but our rapt attention/To Immortality" [80] – that is, that death and the dead are scrutinized only because they necessarily mark the limits of our perception when we look for evidence of eternity from our standpoint in time – or, when the poet's attention seems to be limited to death alone (more precisely, to the act of dying), death is examined as a possible mode of response to the pressures and restrictions of living. Hence in these latter poems it is not death but the life against which dying is raised as a strategy and an alternative that is the poet's real subject.

Within the privacy of her room Emily Dickinson was not reticent about revealing in her poetry her attitudes toward the world in which as time went on she increasingly declined to participate. This choice, this closing of the valves of her attention, though probably precipitated by the events of 1861 and 1862, the years of the Reverend Charles Wadsworth's conjectured second visit [81] and of his departure for California, was not initiated then; it is the extension of a strategy for dealing with the world at large that she had begun to form and to articulate in her poetry by the end of 1860. Always sensitive to infringements on her privacy – and one should remember the extent to which New England reticence is a result of New England curiosity [82] – Emily Dickinson decided early to adopt a protective coloration, to put on the mask of the happy or the penitent child and to hide her unhappiness or resentment. "Mirth," she wrote, "is the Mail of Anguish –/In which it Cautious Arm." [83] By this formal acquiescence to the role expected of her, she abandoned the possibility, remote as it was, of being respected by either her family or her community as a serious artist, but she avoided the risk of an open break that as a single woman of thirty in the Amherst of 1860 she could not afford to make. Nearly twenty years later, in 1879, Europe watched with amazement as Ibsen's Nora, fed up with playing skylark and squirrel and Capri maiden in Torwald's house, opened the front door and left. Emily Dickinson's maneuver, characteristic in its double impulse of retreat and compromise, would be to take refuge behind the door of her bedroom, but to leave the door ajar. [84] As early as 1860 she had come to the conclusion, influenced by what experiences of rejection and misunderstanding we do not know, that the sympathy of the world at large was to be mistrusted and feared and that one must masquerade before it "Lest anybody spy the blood/And 'you're hurt' exclaim!" [85] It is a peculiar yet typically Puritan type of self-reliance, a self-reliance *faute de mieux,* the inverse and source of Emerson's affirmation of the powers of the self, that Emily Dickinson exhibits here. Nora's decisive act is based on the conviction that the self can establish a viable relationship with the world through action. For Emily Dickinson the self can only endure in a world with which it cannot, except through art, find a meaningful connection. She affirms life but not living. "To be alive – is Power" [86] but to live is to suffer, and the way to stay alive is to endure and to hide one's suffering from the world that caused it, lest vitality be compromised.

The world that Emily Dickinson pictures in these poems is a prison from which one could not escape except through death, [87] and a tyranny against which the only effective act of resistance is to die. Her alternatives to dying were a rigorous stoicism that would at terrible cost preserve her integrity, or a propitiation, through supplication and through the subordination of her own impulses to rebel, assert, or challenge, of the tyrant Himself. Her prevailing sense of helplessness during this early period before she recognized that her art was the mode through which she would triumph over conditions of living – that:

> No Rack can torture me –
> My Soul – at Liberty –
> Behind this mortal Bone
> There knits a bolder One –
>
> You Cannot prick with saw –
> Nor pierce with Cimitar –
> Two Bodies – therefore be –
> Bind One – The Other fly – [88]

forced her to the latter choice. Much as she admired the stoicism of the housewife in Poem 187 ("How many times these low feet staggered"), she does not herself always have sufficient faith in her own inner resources or apprehension of her own artistic power to sustain the pressure of suffering. As she knew:

> . . . the stillness is Volcanic
> In the human face
> When upon a pain Titanic
> Features keep their place – [89]

The confidence, characteristically qualified, with which she wrote Austin in 1851 that "Fathers real life and *mine* sometimes come into collision, but as yet, escape unhurt!" [90] and the bravado behind her letters of the early 1850s discussing her attitude toward religion and her contemporaries who practiced it [91] have been replaced by a sense of deprivation and weakness, expressed in the frequent use of the pilgrim, the beggar, and the child as the representatives of her verse,[92] and by a strategy of wariness and frugality,

54

like a tiny animal whose only defense is to make itself inconspicuous, to minimize its demands on a hostile environment, and to fill these few essential needs with circumspection.[93]

Toward the world she is cautious; toward the forces that control it and are responsible for it she is propitiatory, assuming the roles of child,[94] or beggar,[95] or faithful worshipping pilgrim,[96] all three being images of helplessness, of poverty of resources, and of dependence on the largesse of authority. These poems, defective as they are artistically, do express the extent to which she felt incapable of coping with "real life" and thus imply a deeper sense on her part of alienation and estrangement. But she was not yet ready to take the assertive, indeed aggressive step that would transform alienation into uniqueness, and estrangement into a dramatic ritual of isolation, and that would make her one of the centers of attention of Amherst for at least the last fifteen years of her life. The young Mabel Loomis Todd, recently moved to Amherst, described her as follows in a letter she wrote her parents in November of 1881:

I must tell you about the *character* of Amherst. It is a lady whom the people call the *Myth*. She is a sister of Mr. Dickinson, & seems to be the climax of all the family oddity. She has not been outside of her own house in fifteen years, except once to see a new church, when she crept out at night, & viewed it by the moonlight. . . . Her sister, who was at Mrs. Dickinson's [Susan Gilbert Dickinson] party, invited me to come & sing to her mother sometime. . . . People tell me that the *myth* will hear every note – she will be near, but unseen. . . . Isn't that like a book? So interesting.

No one knows the cause of her isolation, but of course there are dozens of reasons assigned.[97]

The precise date of Emily Dickinson's decision to formalize her sense of isolation by refusing to see most visitors and by wearing white is impossible to determine, but in 1863, probably in March, Samuel Bowles wrote Austin Dickinson "to the Queen Recluse my especial sympathy – that she has 'overcome the world'." [98] But well before this time her dominant impulse was indeed to court the favor not of this world but of the power that was behind this world and that might reward and compensate her in the next. It is this guarantee she seeks in the poems alluded to above, and it is precisely because this poetry arises from wish instead of feeling that it is so unsatisfactory. These poems in the voice of "Emilie" are essentially incantations, are magic rather than art, efficacious attitudes rather than emotions refined and cast, as, indeed, she indicates in one of the few forthright poems of this period when, unable to find God expressing Himself in nature through the neat analogies Professor Hitchcock may have taught her to expect, she audaciously accuses Him of a similar sly attitudinizing:

> To hang our head – ostensibly –
> And subsequent, to find
> That such was not the posture
> Of our immortal mind –
>
> Affords the sly presumption
> That in so dense a fuzz –
> You – too – take Cobweb attitudes
> Upon a plane of Gauze! [99]

To call the "Emilie" poems insincere would be misleading, for the desperation from which they proceed is genuine enough; it is the position in which the poet must place herself to ward off this desperation that is artificial, but beneath her acts of humility lies a sense of humiliation, and consequently of resentment. Suppressed by the poet as she confronts and tries to propitiate both God and man, this resentment, described in Poem 175 through the image of the dormant but appalling Vesuvius,[100] lies just below the surface. For the most part these early poems deal each with one side of this conflict rather than with the total conflict itself. Side by side are poems of penitence and defiance, boldness and self-deprecation, devotion and resentment. It is not

surprising that Emily Dickinson should have felt humili-
ated at having to sue for help from the power responsible
for her misery, a power that appeared to require from the
suitor an attitude of infantile dependency and a style banal
and bloodless.[101] Of all the poems written during this
period that present the poet speaking directly to God, only
in Poem 49, the famous "I never lost as much but twice"
does she plead like a lawyer before a court instead of like a
serf before the lord of the manor. In this poem the poet is
able to state with dignity before God a brief but precisely
articulated complaint. She is a petitioner still, but one re-
sourceful and intelligent enough to draw up a bill of griev-
ances, to cite past precedent as an argument before the
Judge, and she is scrupulous – and courageous – enough
to remind Him that since He is omnipotent, He is also the
responsible agent, that He is "Burglar" and "Banker" as
well as "Father." In this enumeration of God's attributes
she moves from accusation, to assessment, to respectful en-
treaty,[102] reminding the court that under God, precisely
because there is no separation of powers, the court is
morally obliged to reimburse her. The multiple and contradictory aspects of God revealed in this poem anticipate
the difficulty Emily Dickinson would have in arriving at a
fixed and consistent conception of God and of her attitude
toward Him. If much of Emily Dickinson's early poetry is
understood as the expression of successive attempts and
failures to construct such a position, and if the resentment
that underlies so many of her early poems of devotion to
God and the suspicion, fear, and skepticism behind those
which joyously affirm and exult in immortality are kept in
mind, her vacillations and apparent contradictions become
more comprehensible.

Yet, since to rebel against the conditions of this world
was to rebel against the maker of it, thereby risking the loss
of the one compensation, immortality, that was tantalizingly
held before her, Emily Dickinson was understandably in-
clined toward finding some justification for the neglect, the

misery, and the sense of restriction and subjugation that seemed to characterize such a great part of the experience God had chosen to allot to her. And if, as the price of immortality, she was to submit to her fate and accept it, she would have to free herself from these feelings of humiliation and resentment that her attempts at submission aroused and that in fact precluded any genuine acceptance. Her poetry shows us that she tried to justify suffering, or at least justify reconciling oneself to suffering, in several ways. For one, she turned to what was perhaps the most traditional argument, the one which Emerson in his essay, "Compensation," characterized as "orthodox" [103] and which he wrote the essay to refute, the argument that the suffering we endure on earth will be made up for in heaven, an assumption that underlies the great majority of Emily Dickinson's early poetry on immortality [104] and which is explicitly stated in several of her poems that attempt to establish the function of suffering in the universal order: [105]

> Tho' I get home how late – how late –
> So I get home – 'twill compensate –
> Better will be the Extasy
> That they have done expecting me –
> . . . Transporting must that moment be –
> Brewed from decades of Agony! [106]

> • • •

> I shall know why – when Time is over –
> And I have ceased to wonder why –
> Christ will explain each separate anguish
> In the fair schoolroom of the sky –

> He will tell me what "Peter" promised –
> And I – for wonder at his woe –
> I shall forget the drop of Anguish
> That scalds me now – that scalds me now! [107]

The extension of this argument, hinted at by the reference to Christ as a schoolmaster in the poem quoted above,

was that suffering was employed by God as a kind of peda-
gogical device, a negative example that would make one
appreciate future bliss all the more; it was an argument
that had the advantage of being fortified by reference to the
analogous pattern in nature – the appreciation of spring
depending on the contrast with winter, of day depending
on the contrast with night – so long, of course, as one believed that God taught us through natural analogies.[108]
Any such reasoning had to be tentative, however, so long as
immortality was an hypothesis and not an axiom. Hence at
one moment Emily Dickinson can assert confidently that
God's discipline is a sign that she will be eligible for "pro-
motion" – "Who never lost, are unprepared/A Coronet to
find!"[109] at another, make a more detached and more
qualified assessment that is not without undertones of irony
and of criticism of God's method of education – "*If* pain
for peace prepares/Lo, what 'Augustan' years/Our feet
await!"[110] and at still another can bitterly characterize
this technique where God forces his pupils:

> To learn the Transport by the Pain –
> As Blind Men learn the sun!
> To die of thirst – suspecting
> That Brooks in Meadows run!

as "the Sovereign Anguish," and "the signal wo!"[111] The
schoolroom has turned out to be the same old prison.

Thus the hypothesis that suffering was God's means of
sharpening the appreciation of the students He had selected
for the immortality that He would confer on them did not,
when followed out, lead to a conception of the relationship
of man to God that was any more palatable than, or in the
end very much different from, the one this hypothesis was
established to supplant. It did indeed, in contrast to the
more "orthodox" explanation, make human suffering comprehensible in terms of logic, where before it could merely
be accepted on the basis of trust alone; but both the trust
and the logic were still too dependent on an immortality in

which the poet could not wholeheartedly believe and which she by no means felt assured of, and, worse still, this logic did not alter at all the image of the human being of whom complete submission was demanded, who in life would suffer no less by virtue of his submitting, who was not merely to believe "he loveth that chastizeth" but to love the chastizer. The required meekness, no matter what the inheritance it was required for, was impossible for Emily Dickinson to adopt, whether as a pupil or as prisoner. When she attempted it, it galled her pride and vitiated her art. As an artist she could not be genuinely convinced of her own insignificance, though as a human being within the finitude of mortal life she was deeply aware of the limitations of her power, and this very awareness made her appreciate the more her principal resource – her consciousness – and made her more determined not to sacrifice it. "God," she wrote to the Hollands in September of 1859, "was penurious with me, which makes me shrewd with Him." It was a battle of wit against force, and in the same letter [112] she shows that her wit can strike back by reproving the "Banker" for His miserliness. "How many barefoot shiver," she writes, "I trust their Father knows who saw not fit to give them shoes."

One of the most anthologized of Emily Dickinson's poems, and one that is generally held to be representative of her best work and of her characteristic attitude (though when originally published anonymously it was assigned to Emerson), [113] is Poem 67, the famous "Success is counted sweetest," written in 1859 and chosen by the poet for submission to Higginson in 1862.[114] It affirms that the consciousness learns best from negative example and that a life of renunciation and deprivation is one to be chosen by an intelligence that is superior because it is dedicated to understanding rather than reward and because its ambition is to establish a true definition rather than to participate in a public triumph. The poem differs significantly from those poems on suffering that we have examined earlier: Here the protagonist is an active and independent learner, a student, not a pupil; here suffering exists not to demonstrate God's superiority or to prepare us to appreciate His future benevolence by contrast, but to increase our comprehension of experience. God may wish to test our faith and fortitude through making us suffer, but we can use suffering to augment our most specifically human resource, the consciousness. In this way suffering can be explained and justified without reference either to the possibility of immortality or to God Himself. From being a state of humiliation, suffering is raised to an act of dignity. Whicher has described very well the logic by which Emily Dickinson converted the passive state of suffering and deprivation into a vital function in mortal life:

To her deeper scrutiny it appeared that opposites did not destroy each other but brought each other into being. . . . All that could be known at all was known by antithesis. Without the eternal interplay of contradiction there could be no experience. Whatever was negative, therefore, became a contribution to the positive. . . . The defects of God's universe that Emily so sharply noted were from this standpoint potential beneficences.[115]

One can indeed call this philosophy a philosophy of compensation, but it is difficult to agree with Whicher's assertion in the same chapter that "Emily, however, like Emerson before her, was Compensation's child." The function of Emerson's essay is to demonstrate the essential justice of nature; the function of Emily Dickinson's thought – and of the art through which it was expressed – was to find an area in which the need for self-assertion could be met in a universe firmly ruled by an authoritarian God. Emerson's compensation refers to a natural law of balance, an inevitable restitution by nature for losses incurred and an inevitable "tax," as Emerson put it, on profits derived. What Emily Dickinson saw was not Emerson's equitable polarity but cosmic usury where "For each exstatic instant/We must an anguish pay . . . For each beloved hour/Sharp pittances of years." [116] Against such exorbitant rates she protested. For her, the potential compensation gained from adverse experience is achieved through the insight of the creature, not as a consequence of the natural law of the Creator. The insight was that adverse experience could be converted by the mind to the mind's enrichment, provided that one had the capacity to perceive this paradox. Whether this paradox was established by God to test the intelligence of His creation or whether it represented a chink in the armor of His supposed omnipotence did not really concern her; her first task was to survive. For Emily Dickinson what is involved is not a law of compensation as evidence of a just and balanced universe but an ability to compensate, an attribute of mind whose possession defines the superior intelligence. To Emerson's statement that "every sweet hath its sour; every evil its good" [117] Emily Dickinson replied in effect that every evil was a test of the capacity of the intelligence to turn it to account. This is the outlook of a mind that is alert for and sensitive to paradox, that conceives and evaluates in hierarchies, and that is deeply concerned with the determination of status.

Here then was a sign by which the superiority of one's intelligence or perception – or to use the word which Emily Dickinson preferred because it did not discriminate, or indeed differentiate, between the two – of one's "consciousness" – could be confirmed, and a way of coping with life through which that superiority would be demonstrated. Such a means of verifying one's status and justifying one's conduct had several advantages: It made submission to suffering, neglect, and deprivation a choice of the intelligence rather than an act of abnegation and an admission of helplessness; it preserved and reinforced that sense of exclusiveness and uniqueness that she had revealed as early as 1849 when she refused to profess membership in the Congregational Church; [118] it encouraged her to believe that her private and eccentric vision was correct and should be cultivated; and it transferred the source of her superiority from an external force that inflicted suffering to an internal resource that proved itself through converting suffering. If God was still Father and Burglar, He was, if Emily Dickinson could mint her own currency, not necessarily the only Banker available.

To use consciousness, for which the evidence was clearly identifiable, rather than grace as the criterion for membership in an "elect" must have appealed to this woman who had scrutinized the skies and flowers of Amherst, Massachusetts, for evidence of the immortality that a staunchly Congregationalist community was always ready to assure her existed. Instead, the elect knew and revealed themselves through their readiness to base their lives on the fundamental truth that they alone had the capacity to apprehend – that attainment is achieved through consciousness, not through acquisition. They know that knowledge is taught not by experience but by what experience fails to provide, that:

> Water is taught by thirst.
> Land – by the Oceans passed.
> Transport – by throe – [119]

and hence they understand that possession precludes attainment. The "purple Host" and the one "defeated – dying" in "Success is counted sweetest" do not represent a choice between the familiar alternatives of contemplation and action, however, for the poet knows that these choices are not proper alternatives. Contemplation *is* the significant action. To contemplate is to win, insofar as on earth we can win at all. To act, to possess through action, is, because of the very way in which we derive knowledge, to prohibit knowledge, hence, because we cannot possess what we cannot identify, to lose.

No such strategy for obtaining "success" was needed with respect to Heaven; for Emily Dickinson apparently believed that one's attainment of immortality did not depend upon moral law or on God's arbitrary selection, but would be the result, if it occurred at all, of a higher and as yet unverified natural law that differed only in degree from the laws discovered by Kepler and Newton and that, like these laws, was potentially deducible through careful observation. The question of divine judgment, the alternatives of salvation and damnation, are not posed in the poetry she wrote at this time, and the possibility that Heaven might be denied to her specifically is not considered.[120] If Heaven exists, it is open to all, a democracy of courtiers rather than an elite composed of the elect:

> One dignity delays for all –
> One mitred Afternoon –
> None can avoid this purple –
> None evade this Crown! [121]

Consequently her concern with heaven is intellectual rather than moral; it is a place to be discovered rather than earned. It is difficult to imagine a more heretical view of immortality than this one, or one more at variance with her Puritan heritage. The profound overtones that made the possibility of salvation play such a meaningful part in Puritan experience, the dogmas of original sin, of grace, and of pre-destination are discarded, and the role of God is reduced to that "general principle of confused motion" of an "empty, idle, and almost unconscious sort" that Calvin rebuked as characteristic of sophist thought.[122] When Calvin wrote that God was accounted omnipotent "not because he can indeed act, yet sometimes ceases and sits in idleness, or continues by a general impulse that order of nature which he previously appointed; but because, governing heaven and earth by his providence, he so regulates all things that nothing takes place without his deliberation" [123] he was anticipating, and warning against, precisely the conception of the function of God that Emily Dickinson's early poetry assumes.

Divorced from its moral basis, and unverifiable by any evidence so far available to the poet's consciousness, immortality, for Emily Dickinson, is a product of wish-fulfillment fantasy rather than of religious faith, a compensatory device or compensation as "orthodox" for the psychiatrist of today as for the preacher Emerson cited.[124] Far from being the "flood subject" of her poetry at this time, immortality is the manifest content of it, the true subject being the conditions and tensions in her own life for which immortality is to serve as an antidote. Her statement to Higginson "You mention Immortality. That is the Flood subject," [125] a quotation upon which both Johnson and Anderson have leaned heavily in their discussions of Emily Dickinson's major themes, is really more appropriate to her poetry of 1866 when the letter was written than it is to the period under discussion here,[126] when the variety of attitudes she takes toward immortality reflect her vacillations between wishing and perceiving, and when the real issues her poems are concerned with are not immortality and death or salvation and damnation but confinement and liberty, impotence and power, submission and assertion, neglect and recognition. These themes arise, just as do those poems in which she developed her theory of the attainment of success through the extension and refinement of consciousness, from her deep dissatisfaction with the conditions under which she had to live as woman and artist in Nineteenth Century New England, as a dependent child within her family, and as a human being under God. The real question she asked was not "will I be crowned in Heaven" but "by what strategy can I fill the needs of the inner life in a world in which neither God nor man appears to recognize, support, or sustain it," or, to put the question more simply, "how is the poet to live?"

Though Emily Dickinson had not, in 1860, made the formal renunciation and adopted the dramatic devices of wearing white and of speaking through the language of flowers and ferns on silver trays, of leaving her door ajar for conversation uncompromised by corporeal presence, the reticence, the sense of isolation, the mistrust of the outer world, the feelings at once of exclusiveness and helplessness, of disdain and fear – in short, the complex of opposing feelings which this act of renunciation expressed and unified within a single symbolic action – are evident in the poetry of these early years of her career. Already, too, she had made the decision to rely exclusively on her inner resources, to make perception rather than wealth or power or prestige or conformity, whether to the wishes of God or of man, the standard by which she would measure her worth. That her poetry is, at its best, a testament to the ability of the human consciousness to distill a plenitude of riches from which would seem to be a paucity of experience, that it illuminates how the imagination can enrich and surmount the conditions of a drastically circumscribed life is evident to any reader. If, as well as "Poetry" [127] she read "Self-Reliance," she would have found in Emerson's statement that "society everywhere is in conspiracy against the manhood of every one of its members" [128] an affinity with her own feelings and a support for her own convictions.

However, for Emily Dickinson, Emerson's statement localizes the conflict too narrowly: God, she felt, as well as society, is a part of this conspiracy. Untouched by the transcendentalist assumption of sympathy, even of identity between God and man, she retained from the Puritan conception of life a sharp sense of the struggle between Divine will and human pride. If she could not share the optimistic belief of the transcendentalists that democracy was a cosmic law as well as a secular institution, she was sufficiently a child of her time to resent deeply the tyranny of an absolute God and to believe that as an individual she possessed sufficient power to outwit Him. By 1860 she had begun her own movement of resistance against God and man, a campaign of guerilla warfare, subversive and underground, that countered brute and blatant power with covert wit. To transform her position from that of desperate resistance to open triumph, from rebellion to revolution, she needed and she yearned for, the support of some foreign

66

power, equal if not superior to her adversary, some prince who would break the long, long seige of her castle and who, with her as queen, would establish their own inviolate and inviolable kingdom. Early in 1860, the Reverend Charles Wadsworth chose to visit Amherst.[129]

There dwelt, there trode the feet of one with whom she deemed herself connected in a union, that, unrecognized on earth, would bring them together before the bar of final judgment, and make that their marriage-altar, for a joint futurity of endless retribution.

Hawthorne, *The Scarlet Letter*

Chapter 3

The fact that the dates of Emily Dickinson's love poetry and of her descriptions of the growth and destruction of love and the effect of love's ending coincide with the dates of Wadsworth's visit to Amherst and his transfer to California is an intriguing one. But even if, as is argued in this chapter, the famous "Master" letters are drafts of letters actually sent to Wadsworth, we cannot be certain that his was the figure that occasioned and is incorporated in much of the poetry Emily Dickinson wrote from 1860 through 1862. Though I believe internal evidence strongly indicates that these poems and drafts of letters were in fact inspired by Wadsworth, I make this assignment not to renew controversies or solve mysteries but to end the tiresome disputes and inquiries that have neglected Emily Dickinson's poetry for the simpler and more prurient pleasures involved in reducing the facts of her art to the facts of life. For what it is worth, I think Wadsworth was "the man," and it will be worth something if, this hypothesis accepted, we can, as serious students and admirers of Emily Dickinson, go about our real business of trying to define the "life" of which her art is both the expression and the result. After all, in the end the identity of this figure matters far less than his presence in so much of Emily Dickinson's work and what that presence tells us about the bent, the needs, and the characteristic deployment of Emily Dickinson's imagination. To demonstrate the probability that Wadsworth was the man involved, and to avoid the stylistic enervation that results from continual qualification and hedging, I have argued affirmatively from what is in fact a working hypothesis.

"One must distinguish biography from literary biography, distinguish between the study of the empirical person who wrote poems and that undeniable 'personality' present in poems which makes them recognizable as written by the same person" [1] wrote Austin Warren in his review of the Johnson edition of Emily Dickinson's poems. Undoubtedly he had the Reverend Charles Wadsworth in mind, for no reader of Johnson's edition can help but wonder whether the coincidence of Emily Dickinson's most intense period of poetic activity with Wadsworth's visit or visits to Amherst and his departure for California is only coincidental. That this great outburst of poetry in 1861 and 1862, 452 poems or nearly one-fourth of the total number of poems for which a definite year can be assigned, was generated by some crisis in the poet's life has been assumed by the biographers and critics of Emily Dickinson fortunate enough to have had the advantage of Johnson's chronology.[2] Even Anderson, the critic most reluctant to link the content of Emily Dickinson's poetry to the facts of her life, has noted that there may be a connection between Wadsworth's departure and Emily Dickinson's intensified commitment to her art, and finds it unfortunate "that a relationship of such potential significance should remain so dark." [3]

But Anderson's regrets are far outweighed by his unwillingness to make use of even the limited external evidence concerning the relationship between Wadsworth and the poet available to us and by his stern refusal to draw upon the poet's statements in her art. What is distinct for Warren, Anderson finds to be disjunct. Yet Charles Wadsworth would seem to have played a profound and extensive part – a part "cast" by Emily Dickinson in a drama of her own making – in the poetry written in this period. It is useful, therefore, to review the principal arguments critics have raised against earlier attempts to place Emily Dickinson's poetry within a biographical context and to establish the position the present study will take.

Both Chase and Whicher warn against the temptation to forget that life and art, fact and imagination, though they may be reciprocal, are not identical. George Whicher states the problem with his customary clarity and judiciousness:

We need not doubt for a moment that Emily Dickinson's poems record minutely and truthfully a love and a sorrow deeply felt by a most sensitive nature. It is one of her triumphs that they do so with matchless poignancy. But in dealing with the biography of the writer of these vividly personal lyrics we must guard against the temptation to make her life fit the pattern suggested by her poems. From time out of mind poets have been privileged to round out the imperfect arcs of fact.[4]

There is no quarrel here with the assertion that art does not hold the mirror up to history, or with the implication that the Wadsworth depicted in Emily Dickinson's poetry would be unrecognizable to the Charles Wadsworth who, when he had already been settled for three years in the safety of San Francisco, was described in 1865 by Samuel Bowles as first among the "orthodox" preachers.[5] There are, as we shall see, strong indications that at least once Wadsworth was confronted with the image Emily Dickinson had made of him, and that he was offended by both the attempt and the execution. We are not interested in Wadsworth, however, but in the "personality" that needed – and in why it needed – to make use of him, in the ends to which he was put, and, because of its effect upon Emily Dickinson's poetry, in the persistent attempt of the poet's imagination to fashion a rival God from such intractable material. The personality to whom Warren referred in the statement with which this chapter opened, and the one to whom we must refer when trying to answer the question which originally prompted this book – "What was Emily Dickinson like?" – will be found in the life congruent to these poems, in the sensibility that found the arcs of fact imperfect, the passions that demanded their extension, and the imagination that joined each to each and fixed the circle's scope. Her admonition to Higginson, the very one critics cite when they object to attempts to understand the poet through her work, that "When I state myself, as the Representative of the Verse – it does not mean – me – but a supposed person" is an assertion of wit, mischief, and exasperation, but not one of fact. What other advice could she give to a man who, asking the same question we have above, was dense enough to believe that daguerreotypes supplied likenesses more reliable than the verses he had already received? What else *could* she say, since Higginson's request for a portrait was, she knew at once, a dead giveaway, and the imperceptive answer he would give indeed had implicitly already given, to her reply "Could you believe me – without" [6] a foregone conclusion?

Why repeat Higginson's error at this late date and assume that the woman in white he saw in Amherst in 1870 [7] was a "truer" Emily Dickinson than the "supposed person" he had been encountering in poetry since 1862? To be sure, this person was not the Emily Dickinson Amherst knew, as the poet herself again and again delights to tell us, but she is the best evidence we have of the mind that created her for she is that mind's very embodiment. In this letter she is drawing for Higginson the same firm distinction between the private and public self that she drew for the "citizens" – a term invariably used with contempt – of Amherst who knew her only as Squire Dickinson's eccentric daughter, and, with her characteristic blending of irony and rectitude, is insisting to each that the self he cannot see is the true one. Thus, to derive the nature of the poet from the figure she portrays in her poetry is to exhibit somewhat greater faith and, a quality more esteemed by Emily Dickinson, greater perception, than did the first of her critics. We will find the Emily Dickinson we have reason to wish to know, not in the annals of Amherst, painstakingly winnowed by Leyda, though this information can help direct our search and keep us from straying out of bounds, but in the picture she projected, larger and truer than life, through her poetry. She knew this too, and the finest and most subtle irony in this letter to Higginson occurs when, after denying his request in that passage with its faint echo of doubting Thomas, she proceeds to paint an exquisite verbal portrait, and then asks him "Would this do just as well?" [8] As if her whole life were not a demonstration of her answer!

The more cogent arguments against any attempt to relate the statements of Emily Dickinson's poetry to the facts of her life are concerned less with denying that poetry is a form, even a superior form, of autobiography than they are with preventing the reduction of poetry to biography pure and simple. Chase has cautioned the critic against such simplemindedness:

Though lack of concrete evidence makes it difficult to estimate with much particularity Wadsworth's influence on the life of our poet, it was surely extensive. But it is, of course, a very superficial understanding of her life which makes the Wadsworth connection absolutely crucial – which says, in effect, that Emily Dickinson became a recluse because of her frustrated love for a married man, that she dressed in white in order to be the priestess at the altar of love, and that she became a poet in order to write a "letter to the world" conveying the interesting facts in spiritual language, about her love life. However commendably "human" such an attitude toward Emily Dickinson may be, it involves a libel upon her, by underestimating her both as a woman and as a poet. It also involves a libel on poetry, by underestimating the complexity of experience out of which good poetry comes, the difficulty with which it is written, and the reasons why it is written. Emily Dickinson wrote poetry before she met Wads-

73

worth; the path towards her ultimate seclusion already stretched before her.[9]

One must respect the motives behind this warning. It would indeed be libelous to reduce Emily Dickinson to the stock figure of the bereaved lover whom she presented in her earlier and more derivative poems. Moreover, she knew both from her own attempts to "research" nature and from the observations the citizens of Amherst made about her that truth was scarcely confined to, and certainly inadequately defined by, the data to which the scientist, the biographers, or just the gossip was privy. Indeed the discrepancy between external fact and internal truth, the axis on which a number of her poems turn, is truly *axiomatic* to her thought. It is the axis of irony when the poet's perception is contrasted to the blindness of the rest, and of paradox when she sees that the corpse is the bed in which revelation will resurrect the spirit.

Emily Dickinson assumed that the data of biography, as well as of meteorology and botany, were insufficient and misleading, and that the poet was distinguished by his ability to perceive and to construe. Anderson, sharing the low esteem in which Chase, Miss Dickinson, and this writer hold the reduction to biography of the complexities of art and of the experience from which art is generated, advises the critic to take what seems to be the next logical step, to study the poetry without reference to biographical data. His fullest statement of his argument deserves attention since it is concerned primarily with the poetry under consideration in this chapter and since the method employed in this chapter is the one against which the argument is apparently directed:

The range of this poetry, covering all the motions of the heart in its progress through the profoundest of human experiences, has tempted biographers to seek a parallel love affair in her actual life. . . . But the external evidence remains fragmentary in the extreme, and the dilemma is only increased by the recent dis-

74

covery and publication of three unsent love letters in her handwriting, echoing the phraseology of the poems and addressed to
an unidentified "Master." Whether the problem is ever solved or
not, it remains a strictly biographical one. It is precarious enough
to use creative writings to reconstruct a love affair in the artist's
life. It is even more dangerous to reverse the process and use the
conjecture as a guide to the poems, for this tends to divert attention from their intrinsic value to their usefulness in filling out a
supposed pattern. The reader with this interest uppermost is frequently attracted to inferior poems because he is moved by the
"autobiographical crisis" he thinks he can piece out from the
fragmentarily sketched narrative, rather than by the poem as a
work of art.[10]

Let us agree that the love affair Anderson has also
observed in Emily Dickinson's poetry is not an exact
reflection of any relationship she had in her life and that a
work of art is of necessity greater than the sum of the
impulses, circumstances, and materials out of which it is
composed. It is greater than they, but it is not completely
detached from them. Thus the alternative to a strictly
parallel relationship between art and biography is not, as
Anderson would seem to limit it to being, the absence of
any relationship at all; it is a relationship that is at the very
least tangential, at the most, concentric. Moreover, since
poems are not manna nor readers *tabulae rasae,* the poems,
as a body of work, cannot be considered in isolation;
something must be brought to bear upon them if we are to
speak of the poems at all and not merely transcribe them.
The argument that the poem must be appreciated and
confined solely within its own verbal structure, would, if
followed out, lead us even beyond absurdity, for, taken
literally, it would strike us dumb. In actual fact Anderson
adroitly observes that vital and elusive distinction between
deriving generalizations and imposing them, and while he
has little to say about biographical influence, he frequently
supports his generalizations by referring to literary, intellectual, and in particular Christian influences. One could

even argue that his preference for certain poems is determined by their appropriateness to the thematic patterns on which his study is based. However, the point here – and it is one with which his book as a whole if not his statement above demonstrates agreement – is that a work of art is created out of occasions and is not entirely distinct from them, and that if the occasions are kept properly subordinate so that poems are studied as works of art rather than artifacts, a knowledge of occasions may be useful. After all, the difference in outline observed when occasion and poem are placed one against the other is a map drawn by the artist's impulse. The poet may, in the common phrase, rise above occasions, and through his art he may momentarily free himself from them; but his art is never freed *of* them, and the manner and form in which he turns his occasions to account bear the artist's characteristic imprint.

Unfortunately the extreme fastidiousness with which in New England relatives respected the privacy and the wishes of their deceased,[11] together with Emily Dickinson's failure during her lifetime to achieve an importance sufficient for people other than her sister, her few intimate friends, and some of her correspondents to consider her letters worth preserving,[12] has made it extremely difficult to establish the extent and nature of her actual relationship with Wadsworth. It is thanks only to the confluence in Victorian New England of a cult of sentiment with a tradition of parsimony that we have as many letters as we do, and on the subject of Wadsworth nearly all of them, with the exception of three drafts of letters in Emily Dickinson's handwriting,[13] are silent. The facts we do have, derived from Emily Dickinson's correspondence and from a few other nonliterary sources, are scant but they merit recapitulation.

In all probability Wadsworth and Emily Dickinson did not meet before Emily and Lavinia's visit early in March of 1855 [14] to Philadelphia, where their hosts, the Colemans,

76

were members of the Arch Street Presbyterian Church, of which the Reverend Charles Wadsworth was the pastor.[15] It would seem that at this time, or on another occasion for which all evidence has been lost, she heard Wadsworth preach and that he impressed her in a way that none of the ministers of Amherst appear to have done. She obviously did not hide her admiration or her desire to hear or at least read more sermons by the same man, for in January of 1858 Mrs. Eudocia Flynt, a close friend of Emily Dickinson's correspondents the Norcross sisters and of Eliza Coleman, though not of Emily Dickinson herself, wrote in her diary "sent E. Dickinson Mr Wadsworth Sermon – preached in Phil – ." [16] The one letter from Wadsworth to Emily Dickinson that survives – it is an undated reply to a letter, now lost, describing some heartfelt "trial" and "affliction" so obliquely that the Reverend's compassion was equalled by his bewilderment – may have been written around this time if the affliction referred to was Austin's attack of typhoid fever in the fall of 1858.[17] Wadsworth's tone, though sympathetic, is a rather formal and entirely pastoral one: "I am very, very anxious to learn more definitely of your trial, and though I have no right to intrude upon your sorrow yet I beg you to write me, though it be but a word." [18]

We can assume that she complied, for a correspondence more extensive than the fragment we possess must have preceded Wadsworth's first visit to Emily Dickinson in Amherst, a visit which took place in the spring of 1860.[19] Beyond the few details Emily Dickinson wrote to Wadsworth's friend James D. Clark over twenty years later,[20] nothing is known about this meeting, but the intensity of its effect upon her perhaps can be inferred not only from many of the poems she was to write for the following two years but also from a letter to Catherine Scott Turner, the girl who in 1859 Emily Dickinson had admitted to her "select society." [21] In this letter to her widowed friend, which Johnson dates "summer 1860?" Emily Dickinson uses the imagery she had worked out as early as 1858 in her famous "I never lost as much but twice," where riches and poverty stand respectively for love and loss:

I *have* been a Beggar, and rich tonight, as by God's leave I believe I am, The "Lazzaroni's" faces haunt, pursue me still! . . . There is a subject dear – on which we never touch, Ignorance of its pageantries does not deter me – I, too went out to meet the "Dust" early in the morning, I, too in Daisy mounds possess hid treasure – therefore I guard you more – You did not tell me you had once been a "Millionaire." 22

This letter, in addition to assuring us of Emily Dickinson's virgin state, indicates to us that she is presently – "tonight" – in love. It is not a letter of condolence – Catherine Scott Turner had been a widow since 1857 – but a reaction to the news that her friend had indeed been married,23 and it is an assertion that in spirit, the "wealth" that really counted, if not in experience, Emily Dickinson had not lagged behind. Here, just as in the love poetry she was writing at this time, she makes the emotion subordinate to the status it confers. Her confession that she is in love is, then, really a declaration that she has not been outclassed.

To be sure, this single letter does not identify Wadsworth as the donor of these riches. A stronger case can be made if the three "Master" letters, first published by Millicent Todd Bingham in 1955, were addressed to Wadsworth.24 The letters, actually drafts of letters, Johnson assigns, on the basis of handwriting, to the years 1858, 1861, and 1862. The first opens "I am ill, but grieving more that you are ill" and is sincere, sympathetic, proper, and in no way passionate or agitated. In it Emily Dickinson makes clear that she is in correspondence with the recipient. While there is no internal evidence that would lead one to assure this "Master" letter was intended for Wadsworth, neither the date nor the tone of the letter contradict this assumption, and there is good reason to believe that the two had been in correspondence around this time.

The second of the three letters to "Master" reveals a

more complex relationship and a far more intense emotion. It is written to someone outside of New England, someone from whom the writer sought "a thing called 'Redemption' – which rested men and women," for whom she "forgot the Redemption [in the Redeemed – I did'nt tell you for a long time, but I knew you had altered me – I] ²⁵ and was tired – no more," someone to whom "To come nearer than presbyteries – and nearer than the new Coat – that the Tailor made . . . – in holy Holiday – is forbidden me." These lines, with their echo of Revelations 7:13–14, clearly associate the recipient with the ministry and imply that, until Heaven, the formal occasions of the Church are the only ones where their meeting may be sanctioned. Later in the same letter she asks if he could come to Amherst that summer, arguing "[Would it do harm – yet we both fear God –]." She goes on to say, using the same images of death and immortality she has established in poetry, that once having seen him, she can rest content until they meet in eternity. The general tone of the letter is pleading and pathetic; she apologizes for her inability to repress a longing she is not responsible for – "God made me – . . . Master – I did'nt be – myself. . . . He built the heart in me – Bye and bye it outgrew me – and like the little mother – with the big child – I got tired holding him." Since we know that Emily Dickinson did see Wadsworth in the spring of 1860 and that she had previously turned to him for spiritual guidance, it seems likely that the meeting alluded to in this letter, the one to which the writer came for "Redemption" and left with an aroused and passionate love which she did not reveal and which she recognized was forbidden during her lifetime, was with the same man.²⁶

The third and last of these drafts, opening with the lines "Oh, did I offend it – [Did'nt it want me to tell it the truth]," makes it clear that some version of the second letter was sent and that its message was understood and rejected. Again Emily Dickinson refers to a meeting, presumably the same one, describing it here as "that awful parting" where she never flinched "but held her life so tight he should not see the wound," a meeting at which she was once borne "unto [royal] wordless rest." Though the reply has been lost – perhaps it was burned at Emily Dickinson's request with the other letters she saved until her death – it must have been severe in tone and devastating in effect. His rejection has left her amazed ("Wonder stings me more than the Bee. . . . Wonder wastes my pound, you said I had no size to spare"), wounded ("I've got a Tomahawk in my side but that dont hurt me much. . . . Her master stabs her more – "), contrite (*"this* Daisy – grieve her Lord . . . but must she go unpardoned – . . . Master – open your life wide, and take me in forever, I will never be tired – I will never be noisy when you want to be still. I will be . . . your best little girl – nobody else will see me, but you – but that is enough – I shall not want any more – "), and abject ("Daisy . . . kneels a culprit – tell her her [offence] fault – Master – if it is . . . small eno' to cancel with her life, [Daisy] she is satisfied – but punish [do not] dont banish her – shut her in prison, Sir – only pledge that you will forgive – sometime – before the grave, and Daisy will not mind – She will awake in [his] your likeness.") .

Another phrase in the letter, where she suggests that her provincial lack of delicacy may have been responsible for the offense she obviously had not expected to provoke ("perhaps her odd – Backwoodsman [life] ways [troubled] teased his finer nature (sense) ") would seem to fit Wadsworth, a resident of Philadelphia, rather than Samuel Bowles, who would not be likely to scorn the culture of the Amherst Valley. Moreover, her plea "teach her, preceptor grace – teach her majesty" is more appropriate when directed to a minister, especially when we recall the context in which Emily Dickinson customarily employs regal imagery, than to an editor. And while Bowles could certainly have taught her deportment, he was not qualified to lead her toward "grace."

If some variation of this draft was sent to Wadsworth, Johnson's tentative date of early 1862 should probably be pushed back into 1861, since no reference is made to Wadsworth's decision to move to California, and that decision was announced in the Philadelphia papers in January of 1862.[27] Other letters written during the latter half of 1861 also allude to some critical event during this period, and, as we shall see, the poetry written during that year is far more specific concerning the nature of that crisis. The "terror – since September – I could tell to none" mentioned in a letter to Higginson dated April 25, 1862 might refer either to the rejection itself or some knowledge on her part of Wadsworth's transfer prior to the public announcement. In the fall of 1861 Susan Gilbert Dickinson wrote to her sister-in-law "If you have suffered this past Summer I am sorry," [28] and Emily Dickinson herself, apologizing for her refusal to see her close friend Samuel Bowles when in October, 1861 while recovering from sciatica he called at the Dickinson house, wrote "Perhaps you thought I did'nt care – because I stayed out, yesterday, I *did* care, Mr. Bowles . . . but something troubled me – and I knew you needed light – and air – so I did'nt come." [29]

Was Wadsworth's visit in 1860 fortuitous or fatal? The question compromises anyone who would agree to either or both assumptions, but it directs us toward the harsh and often diametric relationship that art and life insist upon displaying one to the other. One can say, to paraphrase Voltaire, that if life had not presented a Reverend Charles Wadsworth Emily Dickinson would have had to invent him, and then add that to a great extent she did. Certainly the man who in 1852, when the twenty-two year old Emily Dickinson was beginning to experiment in poetry, was capable of saying that "the steam engine is a mightier epic than the *Paradise Lost*. The magnetic telegraph is a lovelier and loftier creation of true poetry than Spenser's *Fairy Queen* or Shakespeare's *Tempest*" [30] could not have been the creation who inspired Emily Dickinson to write some of her finest poems. And Wadsworth's reaction, when confronted some time in 1861 with the Wadsworth Emily Dickinson had made of him, was to deny the likeness.

And well he might have. The implication of the closing statement of the last of the "Master" letters – "I will be . . . your best little girl – nobody else will see me, but you – but that is enough – I shall not want any more – and all that Heaven only will disappoint me – will be because it's not so dear" – that in Emily Dickinson's mind her minister had superseded the God they were both born to serve, makes the offense Wadsworth took understandable and pardonable. To forget, as Emily Dickinson had already confessed to doing, the redeemer in the redeemed was idolatry; to abet her to do so would have been sacrilege. It was not necessary for a minister to read of Chaucer's Prioress, or of Dimmesdale for that matter, to know how easily Amor can be confused with Caritas or to recognize how subtle is the line that lies between them, and Emily Dickinson's poetry shows that she did not cross that line in ignorance. Out of Wadsworth's professional solicitude, his rightful and righteous refusal to share in what Emily Dickinson openly called "The Sweetest Heresy," [31] and his decision, presumably made for professional reasons, to accept the offer of the Calvary Church in San Francisco, Emily Dickinson constructed a drama of passion, transgression, defiance, punishment, damnation, and despair, assimilating, as Hawthorne may have taught her to do,[32] the conventions of medieval romance within a Calvinist framework, and transforming Wadsworth's departure for California from an act of choice to a defeat in the lists.

We cannot know what deep needs and fears, themselves the products of experiences inaccessible to us, led Emily Dickinson to bestow this intense and unwanted love upon the Reverend Charles Wadsworth, and caused her to reject a heavenly father she had found to be forbidding, tyrannical, omnipotent, and obtuse for an earthly one of whom twenty years later she could still say "Heaven might give him Peace, it could not give him Grandeur," [33] a "father" who was forbidden her by both divine and secular law and who was the loyal servant of the very God she had elected him to replace. But it was a choice of failure as well as of defiance, of punishment and damnation along with assertion and liberty. For this poet deeply committed to a Calvinist tradition that galled her spirit even as it channeled it, Wadsworth's transfer to California was merely the outward and visible sign of the retribution that was inevitable from her first moment of apostasy. When she chose to love and to deify Wadsworth, she must have, at a level deeper than her deepest consciousness, chosen the consequences of suffering, exile, damnation, and despair as well.

Why she did so we can only speculate, but a deep sense of guilt must have predicated such a choice. Certainly by 1860, and independently of Wadsworth's effect, Emily Dickinson had concluded that her superior perception, or "consciousness" not only distinguished her from the insensitive mass of mankind but also was the instrument by means of which she could preserve her dignity and integrity in the face of a demanding God so jealous and envious of human perception that He had ordained isolation as both the reward and condition of the artist's life. The very act of writing a poem – an action that would come to be so vital for Emily Dickinson that she would consider only those who did it to be truly alive – was, because of the commitment and testament to human perception involved, a counterthrust against the one force that, to the living who agreed to forego what was vital in life, held out the promise of an un-evidenced immortality. Thus in an ordered, though dictatorial, universe the audacity of these poems would have to call forth its retribution, and Emily Dickinson, by choosing Charles Wadsworth, made sure that it did.

But those of us who are aware of the great distance that lies between a maiden lady's fantasies about a married Philadelphia preacher and the achievements of Emily Dickinson's imagination recognize that Wadsworth could not be important as a source of the poet's artistic power or as an influence upon it, for that power was not his to give; he was but the efficient cause of the way that for a while her power was deployed. Wadsworth matters because some four hundred and fifty poems, now placed in a random order that sets poems of suffering beside poems of joy, and poems of devotion next to others that are almost blasphemous in their bitterness, are resolved into a coherent sequence once we piece together from the inferences, allusions, and metaphoric language of the "Master" letters the fantasy that Emily Dickinson made of him. Wadsworth, then, does not supply the inspiration for these poems so much as he does the "plot" of them, a plot consistent with the Emily Dickinson who before Wadsworth ever came to Amherst yearned for an antidote and antitype to the only God she knew. It is a plot that begins in 1860 with a love that is ecstatic, defiant, liberating, ennobling, and banal, and it ends sometime in 1862 with an ecstasy from another source, that experience of divine forgiveness which both Emily Dickinson and her Puritan ancestors designated "grace." In the interim the poet moves from defiance, condemnation, punishment, exile, and damnation, to contrition and despair, from agony and isolation to a deep emotional paralysis, and then to the painful resumption of a life without hope of salvation or rescue, a life in which only the exercise of consciousness sustains her.

No such mood is hinted at in the love poems Emily Dickinson wrote in 1860, the first year in which love poems appear; and a number of love poems assigned by Johnson to 1861 are likewise untroubled by any hint of separation, rejection, or fear. These poems, which must have been written after Wadsworth's visit and before his reply to some version of the second "Master" letter, share the smug and rapturous tone of the letter that Emily Dickinson wrote to Catherine Scott Turner in the summer of 1860 when she announced that she too was "rich tonight." [34] They are statements, at once effusive and insipid, of the intoxication of love,[35] of the fidelity of her devotion,[36] and of her readi-

ness to sacrifice herself for her beloved,[37] sentiments that are
also expressed in the last two letters to "Master."[38] The
language of these poems, however, is strained rather than
intense, and the poet does not explore, manipulate, or extend her imagery to project an individuated emotion but
slaps together a few stock symbols:

> Come slowly – Eden!
> Lips unused to Thee –
> Bashful – sip thy Jessamines –
> As the fainting Bee –
>
> Reaching late his flower,
> Round her chamber hums –
> Counts his nectars –
> Enters – and is lost in Balms.[39]
>
> . . .
>
> Did the Harebell loose her girdle
> To the lover Bee
> Would the Bee the Harebell *hallow*
> Much as formerly?[40]
>
> . . .
>
> Least Rivers – docile to some sea.
> My Caspian – thee.[41]
>
> . . .
>
> Forever at His side to walk –
> The smaller of the two!
> Brain of His Brain –
> Blood of His Blood –
> Two lives – One Being – now –[42]
>
> . . .
>
> Say – that a *little life* – for *His* –
> Is *leaking – red* –
> *His little Spaniel* – tell Him!
> *Will He heed?*[43]

What is significant about these poems is not their content – the morbid undertones of the poet's expressed eager-
ness to sacrifice herself and to submerge and even obliterate

her personality in the beloved derive from literary convention rather than pathology – but precisely their extreme dependence on convention, their substitution, as in the early poems on death, of convention for feeling. They are, these poems to the supposed great love of Emily Dickinson's life, expressions of the idea of love rather than the experience of it, products of fancy rather than imagination. In the absence of belief Emily Dickinson had turned to incantation; here in the absence of emotion she turns to sentiment, and in the absence of a relationship from which emotion could come, to melodrama. In these poems love is not so much felt as it is insisted upon, and the poet insists upon her love because of the dilemmas it would seem to solve and the status it might bring:

> He put the Belt around my life –
> I heard the Buckle snap –
> And turned away, imperial,
> My Lifetime folding up –
> Deliberate, as a Duke would do
> A Kingdom's Title Deed—
> Henceforth, a Dedicated sort –
> A Member of the Cloud.[44]

The imagery of limitation – "He put the Belt around my life," of dedication, and, less overtly, of death ("My Lifetime folding up") – contrasts with the images of expansion and of eternal life that Emily Dickinson usually associated with immortality, but the imagery of royalty and investiture has been transferred from the divine to the earthly father and lover. In her statement to Wadsworth, "I used to think when I died – I could see you – so I died as fast as I could" [45] the intense self-sacrificing dedication expected of any true lover is echoed. She was quite aware that the choice of Wadsworth involved a conscious shifting of loyalty from God to man:

> *One Life* of so much Consequence!
> Yet I – for it – would pay –

My Soul's *entire income* –
In ceaseless – salary – [46]

. . .

A solemn thing – it was – I said –
A Woman – white – to be –
And wear – if God should count me fit –
Her blameless mystery –

. . . And then – the size of this "small" life –
The Sages – call it small –
Swelled – like Horizons – in my breast –
And I sneered – softly – "small"! [47]

Here the opposition between the white robes of immortality
and the bridal gown of an earthly marriage, a marriage in
this case of the spirit rather than the flesh, is clear. Certainly when she wrote in 1860 "I'm 'wife' – I've finished
that –/That other state" [48] she was announcing not a literal elopement but a rejection of the submission God demanded for submission of a more pleasing kind, though one
not, as a comparison of the language of the "Master" letters
with her earlier poems celebrating her meekness and docil-
ity to God makes clear, entirely dissimilar. Indeed it is safe
to say, and logical, considering the importance Wadsworth
attained in her mind, that she invested him with the attributes of God and transferred to him not only her devotion
but her humility as well. If, being a mortal, he could not
confer grace, he could, through the very grandeur she believed him to have, dignify her with the glory of having
been chosen by him.[49]

But most of the poems she went on to write in 1861 emphasize the brevity of this glory, the sickening return to a
mundane world, and the poet's discovery that she has forfeited an immortal estate for the imitation of heavenly
bliss. Wadsworth is "an Amethyst remembrance," [50] fittingly the jewel of regal color, or, an image usually used to
denote God, the sun, whose momentary illumination of the
morning has left only:

> . . . a *new necessity!*
> The *want* of *Diadems!*
>
> The Morning – *fluttered* – *staggered*
> *Felt feebly* – for her *Crown* –
> Her *unannointed forehead* –
> *Henceforth* – Her *only* One! [51]

Heaven itself becomes "the interdicted Land" [52] that was "too common – to miss –/Too sure – to dote upon" [53] once the poet comprehends that the price of her evanescent love has been to be excommunicated from those to be granted immortality. At this stage, however, her reaction is less to repent or regret than to stand by the choice she has made. "To fill a Gap/Insert the Thing that caused it – " she caustically advises an imaginary well-wisher obtuse enough to think she can be consoled for the man she has been deprived of, "You cannot Plug a Sepulchre –/With Air." [54] Elsewhere she speaks of ". . . the Pearl –/That slipped my simple fingers through," [55] and in still another poem contrasts and prefers her brief status as a woman in love to her earlier roles of child and pilgrim:

> The Sackcloth – hangs upon the nail –
> The Frock I used to wear –
> But where my moment of Brocade –
> My – drop – of India? [56]

It is evident from Emily Dickinson's poetry that she preferred to make God the villain and the two lovers equal as victims. The offended minister of the "Master" letters is soon replaced by the star-crossed lover exiled because some divine law has been violated. The lover has not sailed to California to a better job but been "wrenched/By Decalogues – away – ." [57] Elsewhere, the image of an unpredicted eclipse is used to denote both the magnitude of her loss and the direct, specific instance of divine intervention outside of the natural order of events that forced the two to part.[58] The real obstacle that divides them is not a physical one that can be overcome but a moral one that is paradoxically at once imperceptible and unassailable, "A Cobweb – wove in Adamant – ," a word that describes the attitude of the weaver as well as the material of the web. The image is extended to evoke the coyness of courtship, the veil of the virgin bride, and the princess of medieval romance, imprisoned in the giant's castle and guarded by the fierce dragon of the moral law:

> I had not minded – Walls –
> Were Universe – one Rock –
> And far I heard his silver Call
> The other side the Block –
>
> I'd tunnel – till my Groove
> Pushed sudden thro' to his –
> Then my face take her Recompense –
> The looking in his Eyes –
>
> But 'tis a single Hair –
> A filament – a law –
> A Cobweb – wove in Adamant –
> A Battlement – of Straw –
>
> A limit like the Vail
> Unto the Lady's face –
> But every Mesh – a Citadel –
> And Dragons – in the Crease – [59]

While the underlying image here is one of enforced virginity, the "law," the particular section of the Decalogue involved, is apparently the First Commandment rather than the Seventh, for the poems that deal with the offense for which the lovers have been punished refer to idolatry and not to adultery. In a poem written with someone who "served Heaven" in mind – and the Reverend Charles Wadsworth would be a likely candidate – she explains why they must be parted in heaven as well as on earth:

Nor could I rise – with You –
Because Your Face
Would put out Jesus' –
That New Grace

Grow plain – and foreign
On my homesick Eye –
Except that You than He
Shone closer by –

They'd judge Us – How –
For You – served Heaven – You know,
Or sought to –
I could not –

Because You saturated Sight –
And I had no more Eyes
For sordid excellence *
As Paradise

. . .

excellence/consequence [60]

In a number of poems the heaven of love, "a Counterfeit –/
We would not have Correct – " [61] is preferred to the
heaven sacrificed for it, the "invitation – Your's reduced/
Until it showed too small –." [62] As aware of the resem-
blance of Amor to Caritas as the medieval courtly lover, she
chooses to serve the religion of love and raises secular love
to a holy state through investing it with religious imagery.
Thus the meeting of the lovers is equated with communion,[63] the lovers themselves are the congregation of
their heretic church,[64] and the love they celebrate is the
source of glory, the profane counterpart of grace. The
convention of the suffering and faithful courtly lover [65] is
assimilated to the martyrology,[66] and equated with the
prototype of passionate action and suffering, Christ's passion at Calvary.[67] In this respect she is more of a medieval
poet than a metaphysical one, and it is unfortunate that her
affinities in spirit with the earlier tradition have been
neglected for the more obvious ones in "compound man-

ner" with the metaphysicals.[68] Unlike the medieval poet, however, she responds more to the heresy than to the symmetry involved in this opposition of God to God and heaven to heaven, and she does not delude herself that symmetry holds throughout, no matter how great her wish may be to equate the love she has chosen with the love that as a creature of God she has been commanded to give. She is aware that her rival god is not Apollo but a mortal man. In 1862 she could write that in the service of Love "To fail – is Infidel" [69] and affirm that her own faith, less perishable than God's power, would last until ". . . the Heavens – disband –/And Deity conclude –" [70] but she knew that for this profane fidelity the grave was the only bed and the only permitted heaven.

There are a few indications that this jealous God who demands love but works by power will be so moved by the lovers' loyalty to one another that, reminded of His foremost child, He will reward them with a marriage sanctified in Heaven. Certainly God's rewards to the Christian martyrs showed that He valued highly one's ability to endure the pain He had inflicted. In the famous "There came a day at summer's full" the poet explicitly states that the lovers, though they have participated in a communion which rivals the orthodox sacrament, will:

> . . . rise –
> Deposed – at length, the Grave –
> To that new Marriage,
> Justified – through Calvaries of Love – [71]

and she uses the word *justify* in the precise theological sense of the action by which one is or is made acceptable to God as righteous or worthy of salvation. But elsewhere she clearly regards her loyalty to Wadsworth, or to the "image" that, in more than one sense of the word she made of him, as unjustifiable in the eyes of God, and she anticipates that at the Last Judgment these unrepentant lovers, faithful to their own religion, will be sentenced to an eternal death.

91

The occasion of the poem below would seem to be the pronouncement of this sentence:

> Like Eyes that looked on Wastes –
> Incredulous of Ought
> But Blank – and steady Wilderness –
> Diversified by Night –
>
> Just Infinites of Nought –
> As far as it could see –
> So looked the face I looked upon –
> So looked itself – on Me –
>
> I offered it no Help –
> Because the Cause was Mine –
> The Misery a Compact
> And hopeless – as divine –
>
> Neither – would be absolved –
> Neither would be a Queen
> Without the Other – Therefore –
> We perish – tho' We reign – [72]

As early as "Success is counted sweetest" Emily Dickinson had learned to convert the punishments and humiliations of a tyrannical God to her own account. To fashion and flaunt a banner of the very stuff designed for penitential gowns was the act and proof of rare intelligence, unquenchable spirit, and fine economy. It was precisely by the endurance of pain that she could defy her torturer. She recounts how, after God had employed all His instruments of judgment – exile, engines of torture, the gun, the dungeon:

> They summoned Us to die –
> With sweet alacrity
> We stood upon our stapled feet –
> Condemned – but just – to see –
>
> Permission to recant –
> Permission to forget –

We turned our backs upon the Sun
For perjury of that –

Not Either – noticed Death –
Of Paradise – aware –
Each other's Face – was all the Disc
Each other's setting – saw – [73]

Here the choice is clearly of love and not of Heaven, of the
one whose face "would put out Jesus'," [74] and who himself
granted a heaven that was "a Counterfeit –/We would not
have Correct –." [75] By committing herself to:

The power to be true to You,
Until upon my face
The Judgment push His Picture –
Presumptuous of Your Place – [76]

she is choosing death, or "setting," forsaking eternal life,
and is willing to accept the fact that with respect to secular
faith martyrdom is strictly its own reward.

For Emily Dickinson it was reward enough. Though in at
least one poem she envies those who have not been
"doomed," [77] have not hopelessly compromised their
chances for eternal life, she prefers the status of "Queen" [78]
or "Empress" [79] of Calvary, rivaling the Son at the same
time she defies the Father, and using, with a sacrilege that
must have been deliberate, the conventional trope of the
marriage of the Lamb as the central image for a poem that
celebrated a forbidden and secular communion. This
"Acute Degree" is indeed a "Title Divine," but a title that
will never be recognized in any ceremony of coronation,
and a wedding "without the swoon/God sends us Women –."
One can understand why late in 1861 she could write to
Samuel Bowles "The hallowing – of pain – makes one afraid
to convalesce –" [80] and enclose a poem in which, in the very
act of asking Christ's merciful intervention she presumes her
own suffering to differ only in degree.[81] Pain itself, though
applied with the calculation and ingenuity of a Master
Inquisitor:

A Weight with Needles on the pounds –
To push, and pierce, besides –
That if the Flesh resist the Heft –
The puncture – cool[l]y tries –

That not a pore be overlooked
Of all this Compound Frame –
As manifold for Anguish –
As Species – be – for name – [82]

is actually the very agency of status, an unintended gift
from a God too imperceptive to appreciate its utility.
"Power," she wrote, "is only Pain –/Stranded, thro' Discipline," [83] and discipline she had learned, and learned to
use, long before these lines were written.

By 1874, in a poem that, like many of the poems of 1862,
does describe a parting and a preference for the departed
over immortality, Emily Dickinson was able to write "He
will refund us finally/Our confiscated Gods –" [84] but even
at this late date the capital "H" for "he" is awarded not to
God but to the person God has driven from her. In 1861 she
was less optimistic. "God keep his vow to 'Sparrows,'" she
concluded a poem sent to Samuel Bowles, "Who of little
love – know how to starve," [85] bitterly assailing both God's
miserly refusal to give the living more than "crumbs" of
Divine love and the emotional poverty and naivete of the
sparrows who accept starvation.

At the same time the disciplined intellect, for whom
ambiguity was the greatest torture, could take a grim
satisfaction in the cold, unequivocal finality of its fate:

The Truth, is Bald, and Cold –
But that will hold –
If any are not sure –
We show them – prayer –
But we, who know,
Stop hoping, now –

· · ·

> Others, Can wrestle –
> Your's, is done –
> And so of Wo, bleak dreaded – come,
> It sets the Fright at liberty –
> And Terror's free –
> Gay, Ghastly, Holiday! [86]

The firmness of so terrifying a conclusion could itself be satisfying. As an artist she could appreciate the purity of pain and through a supreme effort of her habitual irony could counteract her suffering through her aesthetic appreciation of its integrity, could declare, "I like a look of Agony,/Because I know it's true –." [87] With a chilling disengagement she was at times able to observe her own pain in disciplined detachment and convert agony to art, as if, emotionally dead, autopsy were the last pleasure available to her and the poetic diagnosis the one vital activity accessible:

> I breathed enough to take the Trick –
> And now, removed from Air –
> I simulate the Breath, so well –
> That One, to be quite sure –
>
> The Lungs are stirless – must descend
> Among the Cunning Cells –
> And touch the Pantomime – Himself,
> How numb,* the Bellows feels! [88]
>
>   •   •   •
>
> numb/cool

But this readiness to dissect the emotions, this preference for clarity, comprehension, and precision over the contentment available only to the imperceptive, was not, it would seem from her poetry, the attitude with which in life she responded to this emotional crisis; rather it was the one through which she became able to assimilate that crisis into poetry. She was, after all, anatomist and not surgeon, and since she was the patient too, could not, when the anesthesia wore off, forget her mortal illness.

Her sense that her election of a mortal lover to replace the love owed to Heaven had doomed her to an eternal death, a death for which her life, isolated from the man for whom eternal life had been sacrificed, was the temporal prototype, affects all her poetry in this period. In contrast to the poetry written before 1861, death is no longer considered as a phenomenon from which immortality might be inferred or even as a means of assertion against the onerous conditions of mortal life, but as a sentence which has been irrevocably handed down [89] or a fate whose certainty is in grim contrast to the "seesawing" of the living soul.[90] Death is no longer desirable as the agency through which immortality may be conferred; hence all her statements where the dead are envied are ironic ones. The characteristics with which death is imbued – the "Liberty," [91] the "Holiday," [92] the "Cordiality" [93] (the associations with the heart, with warmth, with medication show with what careful irony the word has been chosen by one who assumes herself to be incurably moribund) – are precisely those which her punishment, death itself, has denied her. Death does not afford these rewards; for the fortunate, faithful souls it is the prerequisite for them. But for Emily Dickinson no hope of immortality mitigates the horror of death; and life, so close to death that the difference is one limited to degree, assures her that dying will be not an escape but a continuation. In this period the sense of the Christian paradox is lost, and is replaced, in speaking of death, by irony that is used not to disguise death's horror but to control it.

Even before this time Emily Dickinson had concluded that nature did not provide sufficient evidence of immortality to allay either her anxieties about it or her resentment against God's failure to provide more substantial proof of it. Now when the poet looks at nature, the intimations she finds are of death:

There's a certain Slant of light,
Winter Afternoons –
That oppresses, like the Heft
Of Cathedral Tunes –

Heavenly Hurt, it gives us –
We can find no scar,
But internal difference,
Where the Meanings, are –

None may teach it – Any –
'Tis the Seal Despair –
An imperial affliction
Sent us of the Air –

When it comes, the Landscape listens –
Shadows – hold their breath –
When it goes, 'tis like the Distance
On the look of Death – 94

It is ironic that the significance of that momentary "Slant of light" lies precisely in its disappearance, that what it illuminates is the prospect of darkness, and that God uses intimations of His presence only to confirm that He is alienated from the observer. His "light" is the "Seal" He has affixed to His sentence, and the sentence is "Despair." Thus the cathedral tunes, a sign to the devout to assemble in mutual faith and in mutual hope for salvation are for the poet an oppressive counterpoint to the sign the light has granted her. The setting, *after*-noon, i.e. after that period of the zenith that Emily Dickinson so often associated with the eternal radiance of the immortal estate, and the season of winter, always associated in her poetry with death, are carefully chosen; even on the visual level they combine to create an atmosphere of bleakness that light cannot dispel.

In other poems as well nature is informed by the poet's preoccupation with death and by her heightened consciousness of the evanescence of earthly beauty. But now nature sends no messages, except its indifference, and is a sign not of spiritual but of mortal fact:

> Of Bronze – and Blaze –
> The North – Tonight –
> So adequate – it forms –
> So preconcerted with itself
> So distant – to alarms –
> An Unconcern so sovreign
> To Universe, or me –
> Infects my simple spirit
> With Taints of Majesty –
> Till I take vaster manners *
> And strut upon my stem –
> Disdaining Men, and Oxygen,
> For Arrogance of them –
>
> My Splendors, are Menagerie –
> But their Competeless Show
> Will entertain the Centuries
> When I, am long ago,
> Some * – Island in dishonored Grass –
> Whom none but Beetles * – know.[95]

. . .

manners/attitudes   Some/An   Beetles/Daisies

Here the intimations of nature are infections, not revelations. If the northern lights momentarily seem to transmit to the poet a sense of her own capacity for power and freedom, she is quickly reminded of the transiency of human life and human achievement. The motion of the poem is from freedom to limitation, a descent from the aurora borealis to "Some – Island in dishonored Grass –/ Whom none but Beetles – know," and the poem culminates in her awareness that, in contrast to the aurora, the universe is so concerned with her that the very grass of her grave will be dishonored.[96] If nature instructs the spirit at all, she does so only by revealing her beauty to be fitful and deceptive. The rainbow is an "eccentricity," beautiful not because it manifests the Covenant, but because, knowing it will vanish, we so endow it. "Delight is as the flight –" [97] the poet tells us; the atypical aspects of nature are beautiful, but the true face of nature, the face which speaks to us, is the empty sky. Even her poems about sunsets, the subject of the majority of poems written about nature at this time, are limited to description or emphasize the brevity of the sunset's beauty.[98] From none of them is a deeper lesson drawn or inferred.

Since by 1861 Emily Dickinson had already concluded that, despite the assumptions of Emerson, nature offered no reliable evidence of the character or disposition of the supernatural world, it is not surprising that one finds a decline in the number of poems of which nature is the subject and that many of the ones she does write are only descriptive. But an examination of her earlier poetry would not lead one to anticipate that one of its principal themes – the poet's struggle to protect the integrity of her life and work from a society that is at once inquisitive and unresponsive – would be discarded. True, she is aware and no less contemptuous of the imperceptive, provincial people of Amherst, but now she views them from the prospect of an exalted estate gained through love, where she is outside "the Circuit of the Rest." [99] They are inferiors, but they no longer have the power to oppress her; that power, as we have seen, is reserved to someone far greater, if no less petty in His jealousies or contemptible in His obtuseness. Once Wadsworth, or more properly the creation he inspired, appears, the world of Amherst dwindles from antagonist to setting, to the drab backdrop against which Emily Dickinson's inner drama of passion, defiance, and punishment is played. The situation – the disparity between the internal life where, in another context, Emily Dickinson located "Meanings," [100] and the meaning ascribed to her by "the rest" who knew no better than to judge by appearances – was still productive of irony, but the poet's knowledge of her new "wealth" allows resentment to yield to amused mockery and a posture of deference. She will "deal occasional smiles/To lives that stoop to notice mine –/And kindly ask it in –." [101] She has "An Orleans in the Eye/ That puts it's manner by/For humbler Company." [102] Such politeness stems not from a loss of the arrogance that informs so much of her earlier poetry but from the relative security of her new estate. It is one thing to hope for an inheritance; it is quite another to know that one has acquired a kingdom. In the latter instance, one can afford to be polite. True arrogance, that attitude with which the indifferent dead confront the helpless and importunate living, she now reserved for God. In the long interval between mortality ("the Dial life") and judgment, she can subsist on arrogance, and when at last the grave is opened God will be greeted by a stare of "cool – concernless No –," [103] a stare too insolent for the humble Miss Dickinson who until late in 1860 could only hope to become a Queen, and which was, while alive, beneath her dignity once she had become one.

Emily Dickinson's sense of the superiority she gained by choosing romantic passion over bourgeois felicity is most clearly expressed in a poem that both Chase and R. P. Blackmur have condemned as obscure:

> More Life – went out – when He went
> Than ordinary Breath –
> Lit with a finer Phosphor –
> Requiring in the Quench –
>
> A Power of Renowned Cold,
> The Climate of the Grave
> A Temperature just adequate
> So Anthracite, to live –
>
> For some – an Ampler Zero –
> A Frost more needle keen
> Is necessary, to reduce
> The Ethiop within.

Others – extinguish easier –
A Gnat's minutest Fan
Sufficient to obliterate
A Tract of Citizen –

Whose Peat life – amply vivid –
Ignores the solemn News
That Popocatapel exists –
Or Etna's Scarlets, Choose – [104]

Their evaluation of the poem, or at any rate their sense of
its intention, rests on two false assumptions, that the poem
consists only of its first four stanzas, and that it is "on one of
the dominant Dickinson themes, the obituary theme of the
great dead." [105] The last stanza, not available to Blackmur,
since the complete poem was not published until 1947,[106]
but accessible to Chase, whose book, *Emily Dickinson*, appeared in 1951, makes clear through the word toward which
the entire poem is directed, the final imperative, "Choose,"
that the poet is presenting her audience with irreconcilable
and inescapable alternatives, and that she is justifying her
own choice. In this poem the power of love is measured in
terms of what it can resist. For "some," and certainly the
poet is one of these, it can resist the grave itself, and she
boasts of her superiority to "Others," the pedestrian lovers
of Amherst whose affections are of such low intensity that
"A Gnat's minutest Fan" can blow them out. But the
poem's principal intention, as the last word indicates, is to
present possibilities rather than to assert and defend the
poet's commitment to a particular position; while the
choice she has made is clear in the first two stanzas, she is
aware that "Peat life," not incandescent, is "amply vivid,"
and that to merit the attentions of "Renowned Cold" is a
dubious distinction. The imagery of heat, far from being
the product of automatic writing Blackmur claims it to
be [107] is worked out with great care. The opposition of
peat to volcanic life is not used to lure us into a rash acceptance of the romantic notion of sacrificing ourselves for

passion but to make us aware, and wary of, the consequences of following the passionate impulse. The volcano, unique, commanding, powerful, is as destructive as it is beautiful; the peat, while undistinguished and homely – it is merely one piece of turf from a larger bog, just as the "Citizen" is one unit of a "tract" or area of land – does have a useful and accepted place in the social order, for it keeps the domestic hearth alight. Yet to choose this life, one must ignore a more "solemn," more profound knowledge of the intensity with which it is possible for each one of us to live. Here, as elsewhere, Emily Dickinson feels that knowledge and the distinction that the possession of knowledge confers are worth their price, but she admits the price. In one sense – that the poem assumes one's ability to choose one's lot and calls on its audience to do so – it is reminiscent of the repeated imperatives of the transcendentalists, but Emerson would never assume that knowledge cost so much and would have felt that what Emily Dickinson defined as alternatives could in fact be, and in essence were, synonymous.

To read the first stanza correctly it is helpful to recall the convention that the effect of the departure of one lover was to bring about the spiritual death of the other, a logical extension of the commonplace that to lovers their love was life. Critics who have misread this stanza have ignored both this convention and the distinction Emily Dickinson makes in the first two lines between "Life" and "Ordinary Breath," taking literally what was meant as metaphor, and, conversely, interpreting the word *went* in line one as a metaphor for dying when it means simply what it says. The occasion of the poem is the lover's departure and its effect, one analogous to death, upon the poet. "Life" in the first line refers to that aspect of *her* life that he took with him, leaving her but life enough "just adequate/So Anthracite, to live – ." Thus the poem is not an elegy, and we need not picture Emily Dickinson weeping at yet one more indecipherable Amherst headstone. It is a debate, and a resolution, both of which are caused by the final separation of the lovers, and death is one of the metaphors, extended through the familiar antithesis of frost and fire, through which the debate is rendered. Less about passion than about status, less about private suffering than about the principle into which suffering provides an insight, the poem moves swiftly from an individual to a universal plane. It is public not personal, hortatory not revelatory. The poet is not overheard but confronts her audience directly.

Initially Emily Dickinson chose to write of death because the "graveyard" poets demonstrated that it was a fashionable and proper subject for the aspirant poetess. In her early poetry that choice had been reinforced by her deep need to determine whether she could reasonably expect the infinite power and glory of an immortal estate to compensate for her circumscribed life. After the deliberate rejection of immortality she believed herself to have made by committing to Wadsworth the adoration properly reserved to God, death took on a new significance. No longer merely the necessary interval before and catalyst for immortality, it was the fate to which she had willingly, albeit fearfully, consigned herself, and which metaphorically speaking had been hers ever since God had shown His displeasure by banishing Wadsworth to San Francisco. Now its importance lay in being the only trysting place these condemned lovers had left. In earlier poems death had been devoutly wished for as the only place from which one could spy out the secrets beyond the grave. Now the secret was out, for her at least; her choice of Wadsworth, and of damnation had seen to that, and even in the absence of this literary convention, her scrupulous sense of the ratio of time to eternity would have been enough to make her feel that she was all but dead already.

But in this context death takes on a mixed coloration. Normally considered to be the antithesis to life and the supreme example of isolation, for this coy mistress, forbidden to meet her lover either on earth or the other side of paradise unless she recanted the love that would make their meeting meaningful, death was the means and the grave the only bed where these lovers, aside from their brief appearance before the bar of judgment, could be reunited. It is not surprising to find in some of her poems that once earthly love has been assigned the values of Caritas, death becomes the condition of life, and that darkness, while retaining its conventional significance of damnation, is at the same time the "light" of the earthly paradise the lovers have chosen, and that imagery associated in earlier poems with immortality should be transposed to the tomb. In this "light" one of her more obscure stanzas becomes comprehensible:

> What need of Day –
> To Those whose Dark – hath so – surpassing Sun –
> It deem it be – Continually –
> At the Meridian? [108]

The moment of her lover's actual death – as opposed to the "death" to which the lovers had been sentenced – would be the only time in mortal life that the poet could express her love without censure, as the various poems, all written in 1862, that depict a deathbed reunion make clear.[109]

The poem "More Life – went out – when He went" has already shown us that by 1862 Emily Dickinson had moved from the exploration of death as a poetic subject to its exploitation as a metaphor for describing an emotional state in which the inner life suffers deprivation and paralysis. In other poems written in the same year she examines the appropriateness of this metaphor.[110] This death, a death of the heart for which Emily Dickinson often substituted the theological term "despair," a term peculiarly appropriate considering the conditions under which she had "died," had none of the compensations, bitterly qualified as they might be, of the death of the body that might lead to immortality. Because she and the lover, of whom Wadsworth was the inspiration, could be reunited in the grave, death could be considered to be the resurrection of the heart but not of the spirit. It is therefore essential to determine whether in a given poem the poet uses death in a literal sense or as the objective correlative of a present state of feeling, as fact or as metaphor. Otherwise, as is evident when considering "More Life – went out – when He went," metaphor is mistaken for either fantasy or biography; poems that are articulate delineations of a state of feeling are misconstrued as phantasmagoria (Winters' error); and the poet's therapeutic attempt to surmount, control, and reorder an experience that threatens to overwhelm and disintegrate the psyche are misinterpreted as hysterical outbursts and morbid hallucinations forced into the meters of Watts' *Christian Psalmody*.

One should also distinguish between poems like "More Life – went out – when He went," poems manipulating the conceit that the loss of love equals the loss of life, and the many poems in which the metaphor is used not because it is the logical extension of a literary convention but because in point of fact it represents how the poet feels. When Emily Dickinson writes:

> Rehearsal to Ourselves
> Of a Withdrawn Delight –
> Affords a Bliss like Murder –
> Omnipotent – Acute –
>
> We will not drop the Dirk –
> Because We love the Wound
> The Dirk Commemorate – Itself
> Remind Us that we died.[111]

she is not expressing deeply masochistic impulses, nor is she under any delusion that she is dead; she is attempting to rise above her unhappiness by exploring a paradox. Intellectual fascination with the contradictions in feeling – that we do not wish to forget what is painful to us – and image – that, "dead" we remind ourselves of our death by the living act of holding the knife that killed us, and thus remain alive precisely by recalling that we are not – supersedes and disciplines the feeling itself. One feels, reading this intellectual exercise, that the poet is drawn more to the dexterity of her "conceit" than to her emotion; when Emily Dickinson actually writes about pain and despair her vocabulary is very different; adjectives of status like "acute" and "omnipotent" are replaced by "leaden," "cool," and "numb." In "I felt a Funeral, in my Brain," Emily Dickinson overtly states what is implicit in many of her other poems, that death is what "it," the feeling out of which the poem is generated, is like:

> I felt a Funeral, in my Brain,
> And Mourners to and fro
> Kept treading – treading – till it seemed
> That Sense was breaking through –
>
> And when they all were seated,
> A Service, like a Drum –
> Kept beating – beating – till I thought
> My Mind was going numb –
>
> And then I heard them lift a Box
> And creak across my Soul
> With those same Boots of Lead, again,
> Then Space – began to toll,
>
> As all the Heavens were a Bell,
> And Being, but an Ear,
> And I, and Silence, some strange Race
> Wrecked, solitary, here –
>
> And then a Plank in Reason, broke,
> And I dropped down, and down –
> And hit a World, at every plunge,*
> And Finished * knowing – then – [112]
>
> . . .
>
> plunge/Crash –   Finished/Got through –

We are a long way from the graveyard or "the great dead." Even the objective correlative of the funeral is discarded as, in its progress, the poem moves from the mind trying to repel catastrophe to the mind overwhelmed by it. The initial attitude is one of enforced numbness, a protective device against a feeling that, when it forces its way to consciousness, has, paradoxically, the effect of extinguishing consciousness, just as, in the dramatic situation the poet uses as metaphor for her feeling, sound adds to sound only to culminate in silence. The funeral ritual, reluctantly admitted at the outset, *is* at least a ritual, a way in which one tries to deal with feelings that threaten to destroy one. And it fails. The mourners move on; the real crisis of the poem follows with the speaker abandoned, isolated even from the silence of her isolation.

A number of poems written around this time recount an experience of extreme shock in which the personality is all but irreparably shattered. Lightning is the image used to describe the onslaught of this crisis, but it is characteristic of Emily Dickinson to qualify the comparisons she makes. Like any country child she knew that lightning never strikes twice, and kills but once; but "We – who have the Souls –/Die oftener – Not so vitally –" [113] she wrote with her usual quick apprehension of analogies and tidy eye for distinctions:

> It struck me – every Day –
> The Lightning was as new
> As if the Cloud that instant slit
> And let the Fire through –
>
> It burned Me – in the Night –
> It blistered to My Dream –
> It sickened fresh upon my sight –
> With every Morn that came –
>
> I thought that Storm – was brief –
> The Maddest – quickest by –

But Nature lost the Date of This –
And left it in the Sky – [114]

Lightning and death are inadequate metaphors; the experience that is both cause and substance of the poem is one outside of the natural order.

Her use of this image in two poems that refer so clearly to a critical and devastating moment in her life makes one wonder whether the usual interpretations given to another poem written at the same time and employing the same image are justified. The poem, the well-known "He fumbles at your Soul," [115] Whicher takes to be an expression of the effect of Wadsworth's sermons,[116] a view accepted without question by Johnson [117] and considered plausible by Chase.[118] As in the poems cited above, Emily Dickinson draws attention to lightning's destructive power – in this poem it "scalps your naked Soul" and in the one above, of which only the final two lines were quoted, it "scalps a tree" – but here she is more concerned with the "imperial" force that directs destruction, that toys with its victim as the pianist toys with his keyboard. The imagery of the poem confronts us with a curious, indeed grotesque but not un-Dickinsonian synthesis of the parlor recital and the Deerfield massacre. The poet tells us that all other "etherial" blows she had sustained were intended preludes to this one. In a descending order of probability, Chase suggests several ways in which this poem might be interpreted. "Yet 'he' might be God bestowing the ravishment of grace, a lover consummating their love, the cosmos encroaching upon her unto death, or even Death himself." [119] But there are no "degrees" of death, in any literal sense, and death's target is the body not the spirit; and to call this force the "cosmos" scarcely clarifies the meaning of the poem. Nor does it seem justifiable to impute to Emily Dickinson such a degree of sexual sophistication as Chase's second interpretation would presume. As for the remaining suggestion that the poem describes the "ravishment" of grace, it is true that

Emily Dickinson could have found a precedent for describing grace in terms of an overpowering sweetness for which the effect of music could serve as an analogy, though the equation is one more characteristic of Whitman.[120] The principal argument against this interpretation – that when Emily Dickinson did experience what she considered to be grace she described it in very different terms – will have to be deferred until the following chapter. But if the referent is God rather than Wadsworth, and the occasion is the same one for which, in poems written at the same time, lightning is her usual metaphor, the poem is consistent both to itself and with those around it.

Other poems reinforce the impression that 1862 was the year of an emotional crisis so profound that Emily Dickinson could not always rely on the means by which she usually was able to surmount and control critical tensions and conflicts. "I told my Soul to sing – " she writes, describing an ineffectual defense against what she herself says could be "Madness":

> She said her Strings were snapt –
> Her Bow – to Atoms blown – [121]

Alert to grotesque discrepancies between appearance and reality, cause and effect, and proud that in such a deceptive universe she, at least, was not to be fooled, Emily Dickinson notes how little it takes – to be sure, in the way the majority define magnitude – to cause that finely articulated network of forces in tension, the poet's consciousness, to go haywire. After all, she had spent years acquiring a master mechanic's knowledge of her own workings. She knew how "A Small Leech – on the Vitals –/The sliver, in the Lung –/ The Bung out – of an Artery –"[122] could be enough to throw that delicate, that painfully and precisely adjusted mechanism out of whack, how a shrewd hit could let energy, hitherto harnessed and channelled, flare out crazily, shudder the stricken frame, and then run down:

The Brain, within it's Groove
Runs evenly – and true –
But let a Splinter swerve –
'Twere easier for you –

To put a Current * back –
When Floods have slit the Hills –
And scooped a Turnpike for Themselves –
And trodden * out the Mills – [123]

. . .

a Current/the Waters   trodden out/blotted out –,
                                          shoved away

The analogy can be carried further. In another group of
poems Emily Dickinson describes the consequent state,
when the machine is spent. The transition is from seizure to
coma, or from hysteria to a state that is almost catatonic, "a
Languor of the life/. . . When the Soul/Has suffered all it
can –" [124] that only a physiologist or physician could distinguish from death. In this state when the consciousness is
broken, the suspension of faculties is so complete that the
power to perceive, and with it the ability to discriminate
and define, is lost in respect even to time; and sensation,
retracted to its narrowest span, registers only pain:

Pain – has an Element of Blank –
It cannot recollect
When it begun – or if there were
A time * when it was not –

It has no Future – but itself –
It's Infinite contain
It's Past – enlightened to perceive
New Periods – of Pain [125]

. . .

time/Day –

To feel identity dissipate and the discrete categories of
time dissolve was for Emily Dickinson not an experience of
transcendental awareness but a sign that the consciousness,

110

the instrument by which the poet lived and through which she stood forth against both God and citizen, was threatened with destruction. Nothing could be more foreign and more distasteful to her than Whitman's urge to merge and incorporate, and she would have resented his insistence that identity, if one understood it, vindicated democracy, for the more she looked around her the more she understood no such thing. Toward society her approach is fastidious and aloof – even the Civil War gets scarcely a nod, and this from the daughter of a prominent lawyer and ex-Congressman – and her attitude is thoroughly aristocratic. Toward the world at large her impulse is to measure and define in order first to comprehend and then to preserve her integrity by mapping out her precise position within the eternal and the infinite. In her mind the knowledge of identity was inseparable from the knowledge of one's limitations. Indeed, awareness of one's limitations, or, to use her word for defining the range within which the consciousness could enlighten its mortal center, of one's "circumference," *was* consciousness. Hence, if "Captivity is Consciousness –/So's Liberty." [126] To put it another way, to be free, one first had to know where one stood.

In the poem above, the light of consciousness is dim, is all but extinguished; even the heavily monosyllabic vocabulary has a stripped, ruthless simplicity. Irony and metaphor are beyond the power of this weakened vision of the world as an undifferentiated blur of pain. And for Emily Dickinson this state was one near death; she knew the life of the mind lay in its capacity to perceive and to discriminate, and that it was essential, if she was to be a poet, to recover these powers. The most famous of her poems upon pain describes the first motions of the prostrate consciousness toward recovery:

> After great pain, a formal feeling comes –
> The Nerves sit ceremonious, like Tombs –
> The stiff Heart questions was it He, that bore,
> And Yesterday, or Centuries before?

The Feet, mechanical, go round –
A Wooden way
Of Ground, or Air, or Ought –
Regardless grown,
A Quartz contentment, like a stone –

This is the Hour of Lead –
Remembered, if outlived,
As Freezing persons, recollect the Snow –
First – Chill – then Stupor – then the letting
    go – [127]

The method to start oneself toward recovery, a method as
mechanical and ultimately as effective as artificial respira-
tion, is through participation in a structured and repetitive
action, something that in "I felt a Funeral, in my Brain,"
the speaker is not yet able to do. Whether the therapeutic
action is a funeral ceremony, or some other ritual, or is
merely the mechanical round of domestic routine does not
matter; the shattered sensibility needs motion and order
regardless of the context. Thus the central tension in the
poem is between images of motion and form and images of
immobility and dissolution. At the same time the opposing
images are curiously parallel. The meaningless circularity
of the "round" – possibly the resumption of domestic tasks
and manners – imitates the very formlessness it is counter-
acting, and likewise the black figures in rigid posture on the
mourners bench, to whom the nerves that "sit ceremonious,
like Tombs – " are compared, emulate the darkness and
immobility of the dead (the simile and the suggestion in
context of cerements beneath the word *ceremonious* reinforce the comparison) as the mourners observe a ritual
which, paradoxically, keeps the dead alive and intact. The
nerves too resist death through a formal imitation of it.
They take the posture of the tombstone, but they point
toward the quick as well as toward the dead, for though
they are motionless, they are taut and erect, ready to re-
spond. And the basic development of the poem is from

potential to kinetic energy. Hence the central images of freezing and thawing are, in addition to the associations with death that they have acquired from earlier poems, particularly appropriate here. The transition from the initial to the final state begins in the first stanza when the protagonist, hitherto passive and static, is able to question. The question – whether it is she or Christ who has suffered this apparent death – reflects the power pain has to destroy one's consciousness of even the elemental distinctions of time and person. But the question itself is a mode of resurrection, for the very act of questioning arises from a vision of alternatives and hence leads to an obligation to perceive, discriminate, define, and choose. As the stanza ends, vitality has begun to reassert itself, and in the intellect circulation has begun to be restored. In the second stanza activity increases, but the range of consciousness, the circumference, is still confined to the action itself. Where it takes place, what is outside it – "Ground, or Air, or Ought – " does not matter, for beyond this small area of life that has been generated by an action apparently purposeless in itself, category gives way to blank indifference. The dead are indeed "regardless," and the thwarted suicide, discovered in drugged sleep, undoubtedly prefers "contentment" to being walked endlessly up and down the hated room he cannot yet see. Still the stiff heart, though cramped and chilled, was rescued before being frozen. The poem is retrospective; the time has been "remembered" and "outlived." The very act of memory, involving the analysis and structuring of experience, is part of the act of rescue, and the final stage in the restoration of the vitality of consciousness is the creation of the poem itself.

Thus for Emily Dickinson the creation of poetry is a vital activity in the fullest sense.[128] Against the "regardlessness," the stillness and indifference, the lack of differentiation that characterize chaos, she sets perception, motion, and order. The mind's weapon against the paralysis of despair is its capacity to define and to subordinate despair to the form the mind imposes upon it. The soul in despair cannot select its own society, but it can select the words through which to describe its plight. When the world appears as chaos the formal order of poetry may be as artificial, as arbitrary, as the postures of mourning or the busywork of household tasks and genteel manners, but the imposition of order is itself a purposeful and salutary act.

In comparison with "Pain – has an Element of Blank – ," quoted earlier,[129] the poem below shows the poet's increased ability through the practice of her art to assert her mind against an experience that has threatened to overwhelm it. The former poem reflects such an experience; this one, as the poet tries to discover form and meaning in the spiritual vacancy in which she finds herself, grasps and structures experience:

> The difference between Despair
> And Fear – is like the One
> Between the instant of a Wreck –
> And when the Wreck has been –
>
> The Mind is smooth – no Motion –
> Contented as the Eye
> Upon the Forehead of a Bust –
> That knows – it cannot see – [130]

It takes a fine eye indeed to spy paradox and irony in the void, and it takes the thrift, resourcefulness, and economy of one well trained in the domestic virtues to convert a profound sense of futility into the nourishment by which the spirit is revitalized.

Through definition, the poet attempts to comprehend both her own state and the general concept of despair. In contrast to "After great pain," there is a sharp sense of motive and control on the part of the speaker, who demarcates the stages of her crisis for her own intellectual purposes. With respect to this poem and to the poems that

Emily Dickinson wrote in 1861 and 1862, one can use the speaker's distinction between the onslaught of the crisis [131] and its aftermath. The "contentment" that typifies the latter stage would indicate it to be preferable if the poem were like earlier and more facile ones that turn on the conventional paradox of the contented corpse; but this poem concerns a living death that leads to no immortality. "Contentment" here involves the absence of both tension and hope, a state of feeling that is langorous, seductive, and deadly. "Quartz," the adjective with which "contentment" is modified in "After great pain," calls up simultaneously the delicate play of light across the pure and intricate crystal and the hard, inert face that generates no light itself. Here the same noun is qualified with even greater complexity. Though the eye is again "regardless," the mind's contentment is not that of marble – otherwise the last line of the poem would be unnecessary – it is contented because it can at least know, even if the only data the eye can give is that the eye is blind. Or is it? The final line contradicts the image in the act of completing it, for the perception of blindness is a form of sight, or of insight, that is, sight in its truest sense. What the mind "sees" is the subject of the first stanza, that it has moved from one state to another, hence that it *is* at least somewhere.

To say that it is in despair may be correct, theologically speaking, since the poet describes herself as one for whom "the Heavens were stitched – ," but the word also suggests a universe in which alternatives, though they are precluded for the person in question, do exist, whereas the state Emily Dickinson is trying to define, and through defining surmount or at least hold in check within the categories of language and the formal structure of poetry, is one quite literally indescribable, a state in which one can *see* nothing, can only perceive that one is in it. To render it, she needs images of infinite void, images like midnight or the endless, formless expanse of the open sea:

But, most, like Chaos – Stopless – cool –
Without a Chance, or Spar –
Or even a Report of Land –
To justify – Despair.[132]

Elsewhere she tries through language, through the employment of consciousness, to describe a sense of being exiled at
the extreme range of consciousness:

I saw no Way – the Heavens were stitched –
I felt the Columns close –
The Earth reversed her Hemispheres –
I touched the Universe –

And back it slid – and I alone –
A Speck upon a Ball –
Went out upon Circumference –
Beyond the Dip of Bell – [133]

But a state that by definition lacks characteristics of its own
can be described only through analogy and defined only
through opposition. "It was not Death," she writes with a
chilling pose of naivete that emphasizes how close the parallel is, "for I stood up,/And all the dead, lie down." And
yet:

The Figures I have seen
Set orderly, for Burial,
Reminded me, of mine –

As if my life were shaven,
And fitted to a frame,
And could not breathe without a key,
And 'twas like Midnight, some – [134]

In spirit, whether we use the word in the precise religious
sense or in the broader sense of the extra-physical aspects of
being alive, Emily Dickinson felt she was as good as dead
already. She is

As far from pity, as complaint –
As cool to speech – as stone –
As numb to Revelation
As if my Trade were Bone – [135]

But she is aware that she is drawing analogies, not writing equations. Emily Dickinson certainly appreciated the difference between a figure of speech and a statement of fact, though she did not share the common view about which was the closer to the truth. In the verses below, the poet does not find the normal proofs of life sufficient evidence that life exists. The moribund spirit, the center of consciousness, has now so faint a connection with the living flesh that the poet can scarcely perceive the bond. Even her fingers, in which morning glories, ironically the flowers of immortality, are held, seem to be branches of some other limb:

I am alive – I guess –
The Branches on my Hand
Are full of Morning Glory –
And at my finger's end –

The Carmine – tingles warm –
And if I hold a Glass
Across my Mouth – it blurs it –
Physician's – proof of Breath – [136]

To understand how Emily Dickinson answered the question implicit in this and other poems – "Am I alive or dead?" one needs to know how she defined life as well as the concepts of perception, consciousness, and "circumference" upon which her definition was based. Certainly her definition is not the conventional one – the "physician's proof" is obviously not enough – and one should expect that her poems about the absence of "life" will be the most informative. As early as 1858 in "Success is counted sweetest" she had believed that knowledge was to be gained only through the absence of the subject to be known, that indeed absence was the price, or as she put it in 1866 "Perception of an object costs/Precise the Object's loss." [137] Long convinced that the contradiction between observed fact and essential truth was a universal condition of which only the poet was aware, she found that the common view of life defined it in form but not in essence. Like the physician's proof, hers involved motion, but for the motion of blood and lungs, manifest in breath, she substituted a two-fold motion of consciousness: its sweep, like a lighthouse beam's, in full circle through total darkness; and its extension from center to circumference, both motions being manifest in vision. This activity is the truly vital one.

The figure is of further aid. As Emily Dickinson saw it, the lighthouse keeper lived by virtue of his light, a logical consequence of the assumption that death is characterized by the obliteration of consciousness. The radius of the beam defined the magnitude of perception; the beam's circumference described the area within which objects were potentially accessible to the consciousness; and the beam was the agency, the only one, by which they could become accessible. Through the act of seeing what lay in the beam's path one became aware of the self as discrete, as distinguished from the nonself, as having a form. Through the consequent acts within the consciousness – analysis, classification, differentiation, and ultimately naming – what one saw made one aware of oneself as a dynamic process of response, comparison, and comprehension; one became aware of the self as agent as well as object. It is the possession of this sense of identify that distinguishes the living from the dead, but if the light goes out, its keeper is conscious only of being blind, and the distinction breaks down. Or almost does. One still has the evidence of the muscles as one moves through total darkness, through what is "most like Chaos – Stopless – cool –/. . . like Midnight, some –," [138] the locale of Emily Dickinson's poems presently under discussion.

In a poem recounting the beginning of her emergence from despair, the central image of which is the appropriate one of a leavetaking, she describes a similar adjustment to darkness:

> We grow accustomed to the Dark –
> When Light is put away –
> As when the Neighbor holds the Lamp
> To witness her Goodbye –
>
> A Moment – We uncertain step
> For newness of the night –
> Then – fit our Vision to the Dark –
> And meet the Road – erect –
>
> And so of larger – Darknesses –
> Those Evenings of the Brain –
> When not a Moon disclose a sign –
> Or Star – come out – within –
>
> The B[r]avest – grope a little –
> And sometimes hit a Tree
> Directly in the Forehead –
> But as they learn to see –
>
> Either the Darkness alters –
> Or something in the sight
> Adjusts itself to Midnight –
> And Life steps almost straight.[139]

Like the halting, mechanical steps in "After great pain" this motion in darkness preserves at least a minimal sense of identity and permits the speaker to remain "erect." The difference between living and dead becomes one of stance or posture, but only in the most superficial sense is it one of attitude. In other poems she considers the postures of prayer,[140] of domestic duties, of social conventions[141] – the movements by which for the mass of mankind living is defined and to which it is limited – to be varieties of a painful, wearisome therapy that keeps her physically alive

119

and gives to others an assurance of life and sanity sufficient
to prevent them from prying:

> Therefore – we do life's labor –
> Though life's Reward – be done –
> With scrupulous exactness –
> To hold our Senses – on – [142]
>
> . . .
>
> At leisure is the Soul
> That gets a Staggering Blow –
> The Width of Life – before it spreads *
> Without a thing to do –
>
> It begs you give it Work –
> But just the placing Pins –
> Or humblest Patchwork – Children do – *
> To still it's noisy Hands – * [143]
>
> . . .
>
> spreads/runs   do/may
> still it's noisy Hands/Help it's Vacant Hands –

In the final line, though not in the variant to it, the echo
in the word *still,* of the soul's awful leisure manages to
suggest that the soul is drawn to as well as repelled by the
possibility of the body's extinction. It is not surprising that
Emily Dickinson was at times reluctant to recommit herself
to a life deprived of all essential meaning and of the
possibility of recompense in eternity, or that momentarily a
complete death might seem tempting even to one who
could not "once look up – for Noon." [144] The poem below,
though superficially resembling "How many times these
low feet staggered" [145] in its depiction of dying as a gesture
of pride, proceeds from a despair so deep that resignation and a mild envy, masked by the flat, objective tone
of the statement but implicit in the care with which the
progress of death is detailed, have replaced the resentment
of the living that is the central mood of the earlier poem.
The poet raises the possibility, and it is never more than
that, that in a life of defeat there is one final moment where

pride and courage might assert themselves. Ironically the assertion is made through imitation, a defiance and mockery of death possible only at the point of death, where the corpse at last gives back as good as she has got:

> 'Twas warm – at first – like Us –
> Until there crept upon
> A Chill – like frost upon a Glass –
> Till all the scene – be gone.
>
> The Forehead copied Stone –
> The Fingers grew too cold
> To ache – and like a Skater's Brook –
> The busy eyes – congealed –
>
> It straightened – that was all –
> It crowded Cold to Cold –
> It multiplied indifference –
> As Pride were all it could –
>
> And even when with Cords –
> 'Twas lowered, like a Weight – *
> It made no Signal, nor demurred,
> But dropped like Adamant.[146]

· · ·

Weight/Freight –

But Emily Dickinson sternly rejected suicide. It was the recourse of the gnat she said in one poem,[147] and there as elsewhere that insect is used to typify the average citizen. The poet, while she may envy this creature whom nature permits to dash his brains out against her window, knows she is of another species, one upon whom the canon 'gainst self-slaughter is binding. "We cannot put Ourself away," she stated flatly in the same poem where she had described her precise performance of "life's little duties," "As a completed Man/Or Woman – When the Errand's done/We came to Flesh – upon – " [148] Still, when what is left of life is adherence to the forms and prohibitions by which others have defined it, and when one's identity is in consequence

121

nothing but the aggregate of the conventions one observes, then death, or rather the results of dying, could seem desirable. The poet investigates this possibility:

> For Death – or rather
> For the Things 'twould buy –
> This – put away
> Life's Opportunity –
>
> The Things that Death will buy
> Are Room –
> Escape from Circumstances –
> And a Name – [149]

A careful shopper and shrewdly conscious of the limits of mortal judgment, she is characteristically prudent and cautious in her appraisal of this bargain:

> With Gifts of Life
> How Death's Gifts may compare –
> We know not –
> For the Rates – lie Here – [150]

Emily Dickinson was a good enough Latinist to appreciate the profound difference involved when "circumstance" was substituted for "circumference" to define the limits within which life had to be lived. If these limits were no longer set by the penetrations of one's own exploring consciousness but were imposed by "circumstances" – literally the things set around one – then life bore little prospect of liberty and the narrow grave was indeed wider than the "narrow Round." [151] To be sure, the grave could no longer be seen as the gateway into the absolute freedom of eternity and infinity, but it at least guaranteed the relative freedom of privacy and the dissolution of the restrictions within which life on the formal level was by definition lived; and no other life was open to her if the lightning of God had indeed blasted the consciousness and left but its frame to function. Entombed in "circumstances," she adjusted herself to a darkness almost indistinguishable from death and yet at the same time welcome to one who in the light had perceived so much of pain, frustration, and helplessness.

It seems strange at first to think that a poet whose deepest wish is to surmount limitations of the flesh and the restrictions of divine laws and human conventions and who characteristically affirms the power of her imagination to do so should wish to exchange the liberty of consciousness for the prison of either the inner or the outer grave.[152] But in Emily Dickinson the instinct for liberty is always qualified by the need for limitations, and restriction is not the opposite of freedom but the condition necessary for it. Her most vital assertions and extensions of consciousness are made to extend boundaries, never to break them, and it is precisely the state of total freedom, when all boundaries break down and one is left with "stopless" Chaos, when one "lets go" of every restriction, that is most terrifying to her. Such total freedom, she discovered in 1862, aroused not exultation but despair. The "Demurer Circuit"[153] of prison life – the poet reminds us that the less modest circuit she had attempted with Wadsworth had led her to this prison – is preferable; it has a "Geometric Joy," pure if circumscribed, analogous to the indestructible crystalline purity of "quartz contentment."

To Emily Dickinson some "house," some sheltering framework, was as necessary for her spirit as for her verse. Even outdoors her setting is the village, or the meadows and fields near it, or her own formal garden rather than "nature" or the open road. In her poetry "wilderness" connotes terror, waste, and destruction,[154] rather than the source of any vital strength. She is a rural poet but not a primitive one. She likes her land domesticated, surveyed, and with a proper deed of ownership, and above all she demands a roof over her head. Her concern with lines of authority, with laws, transactions, and structures of power, reveals a mind deeply committed to a civilized life if disdainful of a prosaic one. "I dwell in Possibility –/A fairer House than Prose –" [155] she wrote in 1862, but it was still a house, a structure that shelters as well as encloses, and it is fairer than the house of prose not because one can more easily leave it but because it has a better view of the world outside. But better any house, even one without windows, than existence in the wilderness – an opinion Hester Prynne would never have shared – especially after one remembered what one had seen there. "A Prison gets to be a friend –" [156] she wrote, also in 1862, presumably before her announcements later in that year that she had taken up a new residence.

The move from prison to possibility was not an easy one and, as the next chapter will show, required outside help. It was the last of the many moves Emily Dickinson made in 1861 and 1862, from the magnificent domain of love to which she thought Wadsworth had given her title, to the cell of the prisoner awaiting judgment, to the grave itself, the transition, as she described it, "From Dungeon's luxury of Doubt/To Gibbets, and the Dead – ." [157] The first reluctant steps toward a return to life from this numbing yet seductive emotional paralysis are described in "After great pain, a formal feeling comes." Her hesitancy to "live" arises from her awareness that a resurrection of the spirit involved the revival, the "thawing," of a consciousness that had acquired a connoisseur's sensitivity to the refinements of pain and conflict, and would make her acutely aware of what she wanted desperately to forget, that she was condemned to a life deprived of love on earth and reward in heaven. She describes what a return to life is like in the poem below, a poem whose meaning becomes much clearer when seen in the framework of the psychic drama in which she had cast the "supposed person," her "representative of the Verse." What is the use, she asks, of resurrecting the soul in time when its eternal "Sentence" of death, banishment from immortal life, still stands? The poem combines three stages of the crisis that we have seen treated separately elsewhere: the initial blow, the paralytic effect, the initial reawakening. In the penultimate stanza the sensations and emotions previously established are linked to the moral transgression and punishment that provoked them, and the images of life and death in the final stanza have a theological as well as an emotional significance:

'Twas like a Maelstrom, with a notch,
That nearer, every Day,
Kept narrowing it's boiling Wheel
Until the Agony

Toyed coolly with the final inch
Of your delirious Hem –
And you dropt, lost,
When something broke –
And let you from a Dream –

As if a Goblin with a Guage –
Kept measuring the Hours –
Until you felt your Second
Weigh, helpless, in his Paws –

And not a Sinew – stirred – could help,
And sense was setting numb –
When God – remembered – and the Fiend
Let go, then, Overcome –

As if your Sentence stood – pronounced –
And you were frozen led
From Dungeon's luxury of Doubt
To Gibbets, and the Dead –

And when the Film had stitched your eyes
A Creature gasped "Repreive"!
Which Anguish was the utterest – then –
To perish, or to live? [158]

The poems that describe her first tentative reemergence into a circle of life wider than the prison house of circumstance that succeeded the grave remind one, in their emphasis upon the painfulness of renewed perception, of how

Plato's cavedwellers were overwhelmed by their first sunlight. The poet knows that not nature but her anticipation of suffering transforms the robin's song into a shout and the daffodils' yellow into a lance of light; yet when she says of the birds' singing that ". . . all Pianos in the Woods/Had power to mangle me – ," [159] the images of yellow, music, and pain recall the stunning music and scalping lightning of God's initial blow.[160] To her nerves, erect but protected no longer either by ceremony or the darkness of the tomb, nature is no paradise of uncorrupted and harmonious life but a mindless glare, jangle, and babble, a cacaphony of sound and garish color that the average country sentimentalist associates condescendingly and exclusively with urban life. She describes an Amherst where

> Wild flowers – kindle in the Woods –
> The Brooks slam – all the Day –
> No Black bird bates his Banjo – [161]

and

> The Birds declaim their Tunes –
> Pronouncing every word
> Like Hammers – [162]

But this racket and jangle were, she knew, the projections of her own discordant spirit upon the natural world. A less intrusive but far more disquieting aspect of nature, precisely because it could not be dismissed as a projection of the observing mind, was nature's indifference to her, for this indifference revealed how great a gulf there was between her inner state and the external world. Any impression of rapport with nature, that it shared or even mocked her suffering, was illusory. Simply stated, nature did not give a damn, or, as she put it with that irritating grandiloquence she sometimes used to give dimension to her private grief, "Auto da Fe – and Judgment –/Are nothing to the Bee – ." [163] As an audience before whom she could parade her private Calvary, nature was a washout.[164]

It was not for sympathy, however, that Emily Dickinson chose to reexpose herself to man and nature – though she sometimes resented the fact that none was available – but, as Anderson's perceptive analysis reveals,[165] for the "mastery" of environment that one gains by an accurate perception of it. For a woman of such pride, pity did not assuage pain but incremented it.[166] To surmount pain Emily Dickinson made use of the only means she trusted, not prayer but poetry. "I dreaded that first Robin, so,/But He is mastered, now," [167] she wrote, and by "now" she meant at the very moment of writing the line, the moment when experience, accurately comprehended, is subordinated to the artist's analysis and structure of it. It is a mistake to assume that for Emily Dickinson the purpose of art was restricted to communication – the facts of her life are sufficient evidence of that. Art was power, a power arising not from the poem's ability to move its reader but from the very act of its composition. Consciousness *was* mastery – though, because of a paradox now quite familiar to us, one could master only what one did not have – and "comprehension," as Emily Dickinson stated when she wrote "The Brain – is wider than the Sky – ," [168] is a word to be taken literally; it involves not merely apprehension but containment and possession. Therefore, "The One who could repeat the Summer Day – /Were greater than itself – though He/Minutest of Mankind should be – ." [169] Only God is, it would seem, proof against the brain's aggrandizement:

> The Brain is just the weight of God –
> For – Heft them – Pound for Pound –
> And they will differ – if they do –
> As Syllable from Sound – [170]

The final simile is an extraordinarily complex and telling one; the consciousness, and hence the soul and, in any essential definition of the word, the individual, is inferior to God, for each syllable includes only a fraction of the total

127

range of sound. Moreover, each syllable is also finite. At the same time the syllable is the instrument by which sound is articulated. Thus, while the mortal soul is inferior to its source in range both through space and time, it is more perceptive and more intelligent.

If consciousness meant so much, no less than life itself, and could do so much, speak for – if not to – the infinite and make sense out of the supernatural, one can see why Emily Dickinson was in the end willing to take the painful steps to restore it, and one can also see why, as she developed this mystique, her commitment to poetry would become so deep and so extensive that by July of 1862 she could write Higginson "My Business is Circumference – ." [171] Perhaps even before then, though it must have been during that same year, she decided that while she could not avoid God's judgments and punishments, she could have the satisfaction of putting them in better English:

> I read my sentence – steadily –
> Reviewed it with my eyes,
> To see that I made no mistake
> In it's extremest clause –
> The Date, and manner, of the shame –
> And then the Pious Form
> That "God have mercy" on the Soul
> The Jury voted Him –
>
> I made my soul familiar – with her extremity –
> That at the last, it should not be a novel Agony –
> But she, and Death, acquainted –
> Meet tranquilly, as friends –
> Salute, and pass, without a Hint –
> And there, the Matter ends – [172]

The poet improves upon the "sentence" as she answers the question asked at the close of Poem 414, " 'Twas like a Maelstrom, with a notch," – why live again when under sentence of death? Familiarity with fate breeds not contempt but a mutual respect. Between the poet and death there is hostility but not fear. The posture they bear toward one another resembles friendship, but their attitude, the best attitude man is capable of having in the face of death, is that of two enemy officers, or gentlewomen, who have met on a neutral ground where both hostility and respect are attributes of professional honor. Neither God nor death can be "comprehended" in the sense that the rest of experience can be, but, as the line "The Brain is just the weight of God" indicates, the individual soul can raise itself to an equal status by directly confronting them. Thus the poet reads her sentence not in the hope of finding loopholes – God leaves none – but to substitute understanding, and hence rational discourse, for terror, and what better vehicle was there for applying a rational and dispassionate analysis to contentions and questions of authority and right than the legal language which, along with the lawyer's propensity for determining and defining the answers to these questions, she had acquired from her father? Moreover, to make the soul familiar with its "extremity" – the word, like "Matter," is a triple pun,[173] the other two referents being the body itself and the greatest peril that the soul could face, i.e., damnation – was, we realize when we recall how she defined her trade, circumference, what Emily Dickinson conceived to be the poet's business.

Since her careful perusal of God's ways of judgment had revealed that "mercy" was not an attribute of God but a form invented by the jury, not the judge, perhaps because they felt the need for better public relations, one could scarcely expect Emily Dickinson to be grateful to a God whose justice was so absolute, whose jealousy so extreme, whose punishments were – and here one remembers the maelstrom with the notch – a mixture of blind fury and cunning, calculated contrivance. She could, of course, pray, as the good jurors of Amherst were all too likely to tell her, and in one poem she impatiently replied to them:

Of Course – I prayed –
And did God Care?
He cared as much as on the Air
A Bird – had stamped her foot –
And cried "Give Me" – [174]

Her description of prayer recalls a later land-surveyor, the
indefatigable K. and his telephone calls to the Castle:

Prayer is the little implement
Through which Men reach
Where Presence – is denied them.
They fling their Speech

By means of it – in God's Ear –
If then He hear –
This sums the Apparatus
Comprised in Prayer – [175]

Her own prayer, composed when life seemed to be the
narrowest of prisons, for "the liberty to die – " [176] was
refused her, though " 'Twere better Charity," the divine
love imputed to God but which here He conspicuously fails
to manifest, "To leave me in the Atom's Tomb –/Merry,
and Nought, and gay, and numb –/Than this smart
Misery." [177] At times, indeed, God's refusal to grant re-
quests seems to be motivated by malice rather than indifference, or by a brutal pleasure gained from the exercise of
His power. She recalls how God tantalized Moses with a
glimpse of the promised land and then denied him entrance
to it "As Boy – should deal with lesser Boy –/To prove ability," [178] and when her own request for immortality is denied
because the highest price she can offer for it, "Being"
is too paltry for the seller to consider, God is compared
to a supercilious Merchant who asks with deliberate condescension and cruelty " 'But – Madam – is there nothing
else –/That We can show – Today?' " [179] To this question,
there was indeed an answer. Precisely because she was ban-

ned from immortality, the poet was potentially in a position to comprehend it, not by any effort of her own consciousness but by God's willingness to allow the radius of consciousness this ultimate extension. To ask this last favor she counts not on God's mercy, charity, or even justice, but rather, as the result of her shrewder appraisal of His character, His taste for sadistic teasing and bullying, His delight in asserting His power by revealing and then withholding His favors:

> To One denied to drink
> To tell what Water is
> Would be acuter, would it not
> Than letting Him surmise?
>
> To lead Him to the Well
> And let Him hear it drip
> Remind Him, would it not, somewhat
> Of His condemned lip? [180]

Yet her very ability to make such a request indicates the speaker's substantial recovery from the terror, despair, and leaden resignation with which successively she had reacted to God's judgment. And in other poems written in 1862 the speaker, having regained her equilibrium – the image is hers – [181] can accept her loss and her defeat [182] and even advise her comrade in crime to resign their fate to God.[183] Though the prospect of salvation is no less remote, her defiant apostasy has been replaced by a yearning for the immortal life. Her hope that others who have experienced despair have subsequently been saved, expressed in the poem "Did you ever stand in a Cavern's Mouth – " [184] at least raises the possibility of repentance. In one poem she can even envisage the possibility of a life in which immortality had not been denied, a life in which:

> . . . the Days – could every one
> In Ordination stand –

And Majesty – be easier –
Than an inferior kind –

No numb alarm – lest Difference come –
No Goblin – on the Bloom –
No start * in Apprehension's Ear,
No Bankruptcy * – no Doom –

But Certainties of Sun – *
Midsummer * – in the Mind –
A steadfast South – upon the Soul –
Her Polar time – behind –

The Vision – pondered long –
So plausible * becomes
That I esteem the fiction – real – *
The Real * – fictitious seems –

How bountiful the Dream –
What Plenty – it would be –
Had all my Life but been * Mistake
Just rectified * – in Thee [185]

                    . . .

start/click
Bankruptcy/Sepulchre, Wilderness
Sun/Noon
Midsummer/Meridian
plausible/tangible – , positive
real/true
Real/Truth
but been/been one, bleak
rectified/qualified

The imagery in both the version that Johnson has chosen
and in the variant readings is revealing, particularly
when we recall other poems in which images of royalty, of
riches, and of the solar and seasonal cycles have been used.
In this poem the poet recognizes that the "majesty" she has
chosen is inferior and more arduous than the "Majesty" she
has willfully sacrificed. Noon, midsummer, and meridian
are all equated – they are alternatives – as images of some
kind of apogee, the perigee being alternatively winter,

bankruptcy (the opposite of wealth), sepulchre (the opposite of immortality), and wilderness (the opposite of order and, by extension, of Ordination). But the poet makes quite clear that this hope is fictitious, is a "Vision," of a "life" that is more vital than the life she is living. "I think To Live – may be a Life/To those allowed to try" [186] reads the alternative version of the opening lines of this poem.

Forbidden this attempt, she could, by recalling her thesis that knowledge and possession are mutually exclusive, find in her "death" the compensation that it at least had taught her to appreciate and in this sense perceive eternal life. In the final stanza of a poem written in 1862 that recounts her "first well Day – since many ill – " the poet asks hopefully:

> My loss, by sickness – Was it Loss?
> Or that Etherial Gain
> One earns * by measuring the Grave –
> Then – measuring the Sun – [187]
>
> . . .
>
> Etherial Gain One earns/seraphic gain, One gets –

But she is too wary of the mind's capacity to force its prejudices upon an indifferent and untestifying nature, and is too scrupulous and fastidious intellectually to abide with a conventional view she had previously discarded, that suffering was God's method of instruction. Such conjectures were products of fancy, not imagination, were deceits rather than insights, and intensified one's suffering instead of compensating for it:

> Conjecturing a Climate
> Of unsuspended Suns –
> Adds * poignancy to Winter –
> The Shivering * Fancy turns
>
> To a fictitious Country *
> To palliate a Cold –

133

Not obviated of Degree –
Nor eased – of Latitude – [188]

. . .

Adds/gives
Shivering/freezing
Country/Summer – , Season –

That the poem is about the longing of the "dead" (shiver-
ing, cold) for eternal life, that country outside of time
where the sun is not suspended by darkness, is clear to
anyone familiar with the way Emily Dickinson customarily
employs imagery of the seasonal and solar cycles. But the
adverse value given to "latitude" in the final line seems to
conflict with the poet's many complaints against the nar-
rowness, the circumscription of the prison of this life until
one recalls the poet's abhorrence of the undifferentiation,
the infinite "width" that life presents to the person frozen
in despair. If "of" is meant to be a preposition of agency as
well as of possession, the words "latitude," and "degree,"
can be taken in a sense other than the obvious one of
gradation and measurement: "Degree" may stand for the
person of highest rank, and "Latitude" for clemency, for a
flexibility that would permit the rigid and rigorous punishment of "cold" to be obviated. Such conjecture is "poi-
gnant" indeed – Emily Dickinson uses the word with a full
sense of its root meaning – for, numb and deadened to life
as the speaker seems to be, the conjecture that for her, and
because of her own choices of commitment, immortality
has become a "fiction," cuts her to the quick.

It is not difficult, once one has examined closely the
content of the poems of 1862 and tried to find a coherent
pattern and development of theme and attitude within
them to understand why Emily Dickinson wrote so much
during this year. It was a year in which a system of belief
was raised and shattered, a year in which the poet made
and then was forced to relinquish what was perhaps the
most intense and significant emotional commitment of her
lifetime, a year in which she went through successive

states of triumph, defiance, collapse, despair, and resignation. Before Wadsworth's first visit Emily Dickinson's poetry and correspondence had revealed her increasing disaffection as a subject of the earthly kingdom; her subsequent work in 1861 and 1862 recounts the failure of a revolution, a seditious campaign for which the penalty was eternal exile, death without resurrection. In Wadsworth's transfer to California the jealousy – and the omnipotence – of the powers that be seemed clearly visible. Earlier than this Emily Dickinson had come to assume that the price of immortality was the suspension of perception and the endurance of whatever humiliation and loneliness God might contrive to test His candidate; during the course of 1862 she came to feel that the self-styled God of Love proved his devotion through his jealousy and would brook no rival. In addition, it was in this year that she learned – and in the way in which things were best taught, by their enforced absence – how deeply she valued life, both mortal and immortal, and, more precisely, of what "life" actually consisted. It was a year that reinforced, in the harshest way possible, much she had already apprehended of the nature of God and the limitations of man, and suggested how these limitations might be surmounted if not overcome. In 1862 she experienced God's jealousy, His power, and His punishment for those who defied Him. In the same year she was to discover His mercy and His grace.

All weak and diseased bodys have hourly mementos of their mortality. But the soundest of men have likewise their nightly monitor by the emblem of death, which is their sleep, (for so is death often called) and not only their death, but their grave is lively represented before their eyes by beholding their bed; the morning may mind them of the resurrection; and the sun approaching, of the appearing of the Sun of righteousness, at whose comeing they shall all rise out of their beds, the long night shall fly away, and the day of eternity shall never end: seeing these things must be, what manner of person ought we to be, in all good conversation?

Anne Bradstreet, "Meditation LXXI"

The Soul refresht with gracious Steams, behold,
Christs royall Spirit richly tended
With all the guard of Graces manifold
Throngs in to solace it amended
And by the Trinity befriended.

Befriended thus! It lives a Life indeed
A Life! as if it Liv'd for Life.
For Life Eternall: wherefore with all heed
It trims the same with Graces rife
To be the Lambs espoused Wife.

Yea, like a Bride all Gloriously arraide
It is arrai'de Whose dayly ware
Is an Imbrodery with Grace inlaide,
Of Sanctuary White most Faire:
Its drest in Heavens fashion rare.

Edward Taylor, from "The Soule Seeking
Church-Fellowship"

Chapter 4

The sheer amount of poetry that Emily Dickinson wrote in 1862, three hundred and sixty-eight poems,[1] or more than twice the number she would write in any year thereafter, suggests in itself that that year was a pivotal one for her, and inspires one to find the pin on which that pivot turned and the force which swung it. But the effect of reading the poems of 1862 in their sequence in Johnson's edition is to become exasperated that the woman Higginson called "my partially cracked poetess at Amherst"[2] can be so vacillating and inconsistent. There seems to be no central principle here, no progress of the soul, no pattern of moral or intellectual growth. Instead, the soul is now swept to the crest of ecstasy, now dashed into the grave before its time by a God who alternately saves and damns, punishes and rewards. Toward the poet He is successively aloof, solicitous, miserly, munificent, vicious, adorable. He can be her torturer and jailor or her fiancé and bridegroom, and the poet does not seem to know whether she is alive or dead, or alive because she has died to the world – or dead because she is still alive in it. One sympathizes with Higginson's description but must ask whether the confusion and the contradictions encountered in this period of her work result from Johnson's order or from Emily Dickinson's inner chaos. To defend Emily Dickinson's integrity – and hence her sanity – and to show that her sensibility was a coherent and consistent one, it is necessary to retain Johnson's dates but revise his order within a given year. Such a reordering of her poems in terms of their statements and attitudes – the sequence in Johnson's edition is determined by whether the poems are fair copies to recipients, other fair copies, semifinal drafts, or worksheet drafts respectively – reveals that in 1862 Emily Dickinson did not have a crack-up (to return to Higginson's metaphor) but a conversion, and that it was precisely the variety of conversion that both her inclinations and her traditions had prepared her for and against which she had fought so vigorously at Mary Lyon's Seminary in Mount Holyoke in 1848. What happened to her in 1862, fourteen years later, overturning her proudest assumptions and reversing the current of her deepest feelings, was what all true Puritans, Edward Dickinson included, wanted to happen to them: to discover that one had been elected to receive the grace of God.

The term is used here as it was used by Emily Dickinson, in the full theological sense it still had for her neighbors in the Amherst Valley,[3] to denote the central emotional experience of the Christian life. How central it was Perry Miller has made clear in his monumental study of the nature and development of American Puritan thought, *The New England Mind,* where his description of grace reveals how momentous that moment was when the Puritan believed he had experienced regeneration:

The moment of regeneration, in which God, out of His compassion, bestows grace upon man and in which man is enabled to reply with belief, was the single goal of the Augustinian piety. Without it individual life was a burden, with it living became richness and joy. Other people have found other names for the experience: to lovers it is love, to mystics it is ecstasy, to poets inspiration. . . . To the Puritans there was of course only one interpretation. It was the act of communion in which the infinite impinged upon the finite, when the misery of the fragmentary was replaced by the delight of wholeness.[4]

Miller's description echoes many of Emily Dickinson's, who often, to describe grace, made from the abstractions "richness" and "communion" the images of gold and wine. Ecstasy, inspiration – or its etymological touchstone, wind, and by extension wind heard, or music – and love, stem in her poetry, as they do here, from a common source in the universe one sees when one is made regenerate. But the proof of this assertion – that in 1862 Emily Dickinson underwent an experience of grace thoroughly within and consonant with the Puritan tradition – must wait until the meaning of grace and the role the concept played in Puritan dogma are more clearly established:

. . . it meant substantially that there existed a way in which supernal beauty could be carried across the gulf of separation. It was an inward experience in which the disorder of the universe was righted, when at least some men were brought into harmony with the divine plan. . . . It joined God and man, the whole and the particle. God reached out to man with His grace, man reached out to God with his faith.[5]

The ultimate reason of all things they called God, the dream of a possible harmony between man and his environment they named Eden, the actual fact of disharmony they denominated sin, the moment of illumination was to them divine grace, the effort to live in the strength of that illumination was faith, and the failure to abide by it was reprobation.[6]

All commentators assume what even her poetic vocabulary reveals – the recurrence of the terms *election, witness, grace,* and *despair* and the verbs *sanctify* and *justify* are evidence enough – that she was familiar with the basic tenets of Puritan thought, but led by Allen Tate,[7] most critics have found this thought to be but a scaffolding, but wood with the green gone out of it, a few sights or boundaries to keep a would-be transcendentalist from dissipating into the oversoul. The contention here is that her Puritanism, far from being the stock from which she manufactured intellectual supports, was live, firm, and deeply rooted. Certainly her father's words in 1859 when, while his daughter was questioning her father's beliefs and preparing to defy their joint creator, he addressed the celebrants of the two hundredth anniversary of Hadley, Massachusetts, reveal the degree to which the people of the Amherst Valley and the head of the Dickinson household identified with their Puritan heritage and remained committed to the Puritan faith:

And first of all, we should render devout thanks to Almighty God for our ancestry: that the kingdoms of the Old World were sifted to procure the seed to plant this continent; that the purest of that seed was sown in this beautiful valley; that the blood of the Puritans flows in our veins.[8]

Nor was this merely lip-service paid to a heritage outgrown. Edward Dickinson, while all of England was reading Dickens' newest production *A Christmas Carol,* still abjured the gift-giving and mythology of Christmas and "frowned upon Santa Claus – and all such prowling gentlemen – ," [9] as his daughter, Emily, reminded a family friend, years later, when she replied to a letter acknowledging the tribute of a wreath for Edward Dickinson's recent grave. In Amherst itself, numerous revivals in both the college and the community testified to the vitality the Puritan faith retained and were continual reminders to Emily Dickinson that the world she lived in still assumed salvation to be man's chief end, conversion its prerequisite, and grace at once God's attribute and instrument to restore in degenerate mankind the potential to be saved. If, before now, she had not thought that she was lost – and the conviction of original sin is one Puritan assumption conspicuously absent from her early poetry – the failure of her attempt to avoid the galling and onerous conditions God set for those He might elect to be saved had certainly con-

140

vinced her both of God's omnipotence and of her own damnation. The failure of her rebellion was one that could not help but be instructive, and was perhaps meant to be, for God was accustomed to teach repentance by chastisement. The lesson that human love was neither a substitute for nor synonymous with the love God manifested in His grace proved [10] for Emily Dickinson that the articles of Puritan belief were correct; and if her sense of despair at having transgressed them was sinful in its presumption, the feeling of helplessness from which despair arose was the attitude most favorable for regeneration, since God's grace would be most appreciated by those who knew that they could get nowhere without it, and was best comprehended, as Emily Dickinson knew, by those who had it not.

The argument here is that her own experiences, themselves interpreted within the framework of the Puritan ideology that was so deep a part of her background, eventually forced her to accept the relationship of God to man she had resisted, the relationship upon which the concept of grace or regeneration was founded. The fact that she used the terminology and even, as the similarity between the epigraphs from Anne Bradstreet and Edward Taylor and her own poetry indicate, the verbal iconography of Puritanism to depict her own questioning of or rebellion against Puritan ideology, does not, as Tate avers, show her independence of this heritage but her inextricable commitment to it, a commitment that she acknowledged at some time in 1862, not because she consciously adopted the ideology but because, in the best Puritan tradition, she had the experience of being adopted by it, the experience of grace itself.

While a number of poems written in 1862 testify to such an experience [11] and other poems in the same year describe the feeling of emptiness after grace has passed,[12] it is difficult, beyond making the assumption that such poems succeed the ones in 1862 that have been treated in the previous chapter, to determine the date of the experience itself. However, there is a striking difference between her delighted surprise at Mrs. Joseph Haven's unexpected letter early in 1859 – "Your remembrance surprises me. I hardly feel entitled to it. . . . Perhaps tho', sweeter as it is – *unmerited* remembrance – 'Grace' – the saints would call it. Careless girls like me, cannot testify." [13] – and her plea to "Master," tentatively assigned by Johnson to early 1862, "but must she go unpardoned – teach her, preceptor grace." [14] By November of 1862 she hinted to Samuel Bowles that she no longer needed instruction, referring to the select few that "have life" [15] and enclosing the last stanza of a poem justifying spiritual sickness as the means through which the divine Preceptor prepares us for "Etherial Gain." [16] That grace was on her mind is evident from the way in her next letter to Bowles she framed her apology for refusing to come downstairs and greet him: "Forgive me," she wrote, "if I prize the Grace – superior to the Sign." [17] If, as seems likely, grace and its implications are the "Hallowed things" which men and women bandy with a glibness so embarrassing she prefers seclusion – this was her defense to Higginson when he reproached her for "shunning Men and Women" [18] – then the date can be pushed back at least to August of 1862. The contemptuous description of Dickinson piety and the resolute assertion of her own unbelief that she mailed to Higginson on April 25th, 1862 would seem to fix the *terminus a quo*. "They are religious," she wrote, answering his request for a description of her family, "– except me – and address an Eclipse, every morning – whom they call their 'Father.' " [19] But by February of the next year she told Higginson, now stationed in a South Carolina bivouac in command of a Negro regiment, of a different source of darkness:

> Not "Revelation" – 'tis – that waits,
> But our unfurnished eyes –

and, solicitous for his well-being in the midst of war, concluded her letter with a reference that Higginson, the author of the article from which it came, would recognize as being thoroughly Christian: "I trust the 'Procession of Flowers' was not a premonition –." [20]

A number of poems written in 1862 or later describe what had made her change her mind. It was "A Grant of the Divine –," [21] a "Mortal Abolition . . . subject/To Autocratic Air –," [22] "The Heaven – unexpected come,/To Lives that thought the Worshipping/A too presumptuous Psalm –," [23] a moment when "The Silence condescended –/Creation stopped – for Me –," [24] when "My Noon had Come – to dine –," [25] when "Sunrise kissed my Chrysalis –/And I stood up – and lived –," [26] the moment of:

> Eternity's disclosure
> To favorites – a few –
> Of the Colossal substance
> Of Immortality [27]

To describe how she felt the first time she read the woman who became her favorite poet, Elizabeth Barrett Browning, the only appropriate analogy was this same experience of grace:

> I could not have defined the change –
> Conversion of the Mind
> Like Sanctifying in the Soul –
> Is witnessed – not explained – [28]

Several poems recount the experience in terms of the standard Dickinson images of noon and sunrise, of light and life as opposed to spiritual death and blindness. Involved is no vague transcendental influx of apprehension but that "moment of regeneration" [29] which Emily Dickinson, drawing upon the same trope Anne Bradstreet had incorporated in the Meditation that stands as the first epigraph for this chapter, portrayed as the dawn of a new life:

> To my small Hearth His fire came –
> And all my House aglow

Did fan and rock, with sudden light –
'Twas Sunrise – 'twas the Sky –

Impanelled from no Summer brief –
With limit * of Decay –
'Twas Noon – without the News of Night – *
Nay, Nature,* it was Day – 30

. . .

limit/license
the News of Night/Report of Night
Nay, Nature/'Twas further –

. . .

It was a quiet way –
He asked if I was His –
I made no answer of the Tongue,
But answer of the Eyes –

And then he bore me high
Before this mortal noise
With swiftness as of Chariots –
And distance – as of Wheels –

The World did drop away
As Counties – from the feet
Of Him that leaneth in Balloon –
Upon an Ether Street –

The Gulf behind – was not –
The Continents – were new –
Eternity – it was – before
Eternity was due –

No Seasons were – to us –
It was not Night – nor Noon –
For Sunrise – stopped upon the Place –
And fastened it – in Dawn.[31]

In contrast, when recalling the despair which preceded grace, she returned to the images of death and blindness that characterize much of her poetry of 1861 and 1862:

144

I heard, as if I had no Ear
Until a Vital Word
Came all the way from Life to me
And then I knew I heard.

I saw, as if my Eye were on
Another, till a Thing
And now I know 'twas Light, because
It fitted them, came in.

I dwelt, as if Myself were out,
My Body but within
Until a Might detected me
And set my kernel in.

And spirit turned unto the Dust
"Old Friend, thou knowest me,"
And Time went out to tell the News
And met Eternity.[32]

The epigraphs from Edward Taylor and Anne Bradstreet
indicate that the imagery Emily Dickinson employed to
depict the experience of grace was the product of a tradition growing out of her favorite section of the Bible, the
Book of Revelations.[33] These tropes – coronation, the
white bridal gown, the communion sacraments of bread
and wine, and by extension the images of spiritual thirst
and nourishment, as well as the image of light – images
that earlier she had expropriated from their theological
context to endow the earthly lover with eternal glory and to
found and affirm her own heresy – she used in this period
of her life in their original and intended sense, in order to
emphasize the essentially religious nature of this experience.

Her description of God as "Life" and His "News" [34] as
the "Vital Word" suggests and probably echoes the Puritan
term *regeneration,* a word she never used herself. "Grace,"
however, occurs in poems written as early as 1859, though

145

then it denotes merely that "something in a summer's Day" or in a flower that makes nature appear to be more harmonious or more exalted than man.[35] By 1861 the word is used with a more precise sense of its orthodox meaning to describe what God withholds from those "Deformed Men," those suffering the spiritual death, despair, for whom physical death is the only type of grace accessible.[36] A few of the poems in 1862 continue to assert human love against the grace that God refuses as long as the lovers sustain their heresy:

> Nor could I rise – with You –
> Because Your Face
> Would put out Jesus' –
> That New Grace
>
> Glow plain – and foreign
> On my homesick Eye –
> Except that You than He
> Shone closer by – [37]

The word itself (always capitalized) is used much more frequently in 1862,[38] and in the majority of poems it describes a new status granted by God. In one poem she calls it a "Reward for Being," a "Premium," and then, shifting the metaphor to comprise the literal meaning of "election," speaks of grace as a kind of nomination that "The Ballots of Eternity" [39] will confirm. It is the dowry that enables her to be a bride, a dowry whose riches consist of a baptism, but which, unlike the baptism of infancy, is consciously chosen:

> I'm ceded – I've stopped being Their's –
> The name They dropped upon my face
> With water, in the country church
> Is finished using, now,
> And They can put it with my Dolls,
> My childhood, and the string of spools,
> I've finished threading – too –

Baptized, before, without the choice,
But this time, consciously, of Grace –
Unto supremest term – *
Called to my Full – The Crescent dropped –
Existence's whole Arc,* filled up,
With one small * Diadem.

My second Rank – too small the first –
Crowned – whimpering – * on my Father's breast –
* A half * unconscious Queen –
But this time – Adequate – Erect,
With Will * to choose, or to reject,
And I choose, just a Crown – * 40

. . .

term/name
Arc/Eye, Rim (crossed out)
whole Arc/surmise (crossed out)
one small/just one
whimpering/Crowing, dangling
half/too unconscious
A half unconscious Queen/An insufficient Queen
Will/power
Crown/Throne

Anderson argues that the poet's concluding assertion of choice reveals her essential unorthodoxy and leaves us with a ceremony, fused of the rites of baptism and marriage, that "hovers indecisively between heaven and earth" [41] but his argument rests on that rigid interpretation of the doctrine of predestination against which the Arminians rebelled and which the Puritan theocracy found unworkable. In this poem Emily Dickinson is not making an heretical attempt to substitute human choice for Divine favor; she is reiterating what every Puritan knew, that through grace the will is given the power to consent to be saved, that grace affords the possibility not the promise of salvation, and that the regenerate must consciously commit themselves to God lest, having been enabled to make their covenant with Him, they break it and backslide. Nor is Anderson's further argument for the presence of sexual love in this poem – the "submerged sexual implications" of the shift from crescent to arc and diadem – a convincing one. The crown and diadem, completed circles in contrast to the crescent's arc, are often used by Emily Dickinson to indicate the assumption of some higher status, the result either of heavenly or secular love, and here they represent an ingenious fusion of the conventional image of the coronation of the elect with her private symbol of circumference. Thus to put on this crown allows the wearer to perceive from eternity the full circumference, the extension of "existence" whose arc is all that mortal man can see.[42] That this "diadem" of grace has no visible area, not even the location of a point in space, and yet is congruent to the whole of existence is a paradox that must have appealed to her.

There is nothing unique about Emily Dickinson's use of the secular rites of marriage or of coronation to represent the soul's ascension to the immortal estate. Passages from Revelations [43] could have suggested these images to her, and they were the standard tropes by which Puritan culture represented salvation. But her earlier poems that employ such imagery, whether in respect to secular [44] or to divine love,[45] emphasize the desirable and enviable status of those saved (by whatever means) from the lowly life of earth. After her sanctification in 1862 the poet is careful to subordinate her pride in her new status to her gratitude for it:

> The Grace that I – was chose –
> To Me – surpassed the Crown
> That was the Witness for the Grace – [46]

and to guard against the urge to smile back at "Being's Peasantry" by recalling how recently she was among the lost.[47] If possession of this diadem makes her scorn earthly riches and despise the ignorance of those who continue to prefer them, it also makes her aware of how easily grace can be forfeited by just such an excess of human pride:

Who Court obtain within Himself
Sees every Man a King –
And * Poverty of Monarchy
Is an interior thing –

No Man depose
Whom Fate Ordain – *
And Who can add a Crown
To Him who doth continual
Conspire against * His Own [48]

. . .

And/So – , the
No Man depose/Whom fate ordain/[No] Fate depose whom
    Trait [Ordain]
Conspire against/repudiate –

Unlike the imagery of coronation, that of the bride and
the marriage does not appear in any of Emily Dickinson's
religious poems written prior to 1862. The image of the
bride is found for the first time in a poem written early in
1862 and there is definitely used with reference to an
earthly marriage, for the bride is an "Empress" not of
Heaven but of "Calvary," and she is "Royal – all but the
Crown!" [49] but after her change of heart – to use a cliché
particularly appropriate for Emily Dickinson's conversion
during this year – the figure of the bride was used to
express that moment when, to recall Perry Miller's felicitous description of grace, "the finite impinged upon the
infinite." To denote such a moment of communion, commitment, and passage to a higher state, the sacraments of
marriage and baptism and the metaphoric actions of the
acquirement of riches or of the dawning into everlasting
light had traditionally been found to be adequate. Thus
the poet, in a wedding that supersedes any earlier contract
between herself and her earthly lover, is "Baptized – this
Day – A Bride –." [50] In another poem she reinforces the
image of the wedding night by postponing the consumma-

tion of the marriage from the "baptism" of grace to the actual assumption of immortality, equating, as she had done many times before, death with midnight and resurrection with the dawn of an eternal day:

> A Wife – at Daybreak I shall be –
> Sunrise – Hast thou a Flag for me?
> At Midnight, I am but a Maid,
> How short it takes to make it Bride – [51]

But, though a standard trope, this image is not applied in the mechanical fashion of the bees, tombstones, courtiers, and flowers, the staples from which she whipped up her early confections of love, death, and immortality. A late poem, one of the few written after 1864 that uses the figure of the bride,[52] shows that Emily Dickinson was no less aware than Saint Teresa of Avila that the "Bride of Christ" was not a pious tag but an accurate expression of the human heart's yearning for its consummation by divine love. She describes that moment with unashamed and unsubmerged passion:

> The Thrill came slowly like a Boon * for
> Centuries delayed
> It's fitness growing like the Flood
> In sumptuous solitude –
> Its desolation only missed
> While Rapture changed it's Dress
> * And stood amazed before the Change *
> In ravished * Holiness – [53]
>
> . . .
>
> Boon/Light
> Change/Boon/Morns
> ravished/dazzling
> [And stood] before the suddenness
> In simple Holiness

In the last years of her life, when she was already suffering from her final illness, she found a grim irony in the fact

that this ethereal marriage of the spirit required the sen-
suous destruction of the flesh:

> Betrothed to Righteousness might be
> An Ecstacy discreet
> But Nature relishes the Pinks
> Which she was taught to eat – [54]

Revelations had taught her that white was the raiment of
"he that overcometh," [55] whose name will not be blotted
out of the book of life, and the Psalmist added "wash me,
and I shall be whiter than snow." [56] Only in one poem,
Poem 493, where she prays that the soul chosen as bride or
queen will be "a whiter Gift – within –," i.e., be made
sufficiently pure to deserve:

> . . . that munificence, that chose –
> So unadorned – a Queen –

and reaffirms that she has:

> A Gratitude – that such be true –
> It had esteemed the Dream –
> Too beautiful – for Shape to prove –
> Or posture – to redeem!

does she explicitly connect the color with the bridal gown.
Its customary association in her work is rather with death –
snow, frost, winter, the face and shroud of the dead – or
the triumph over death – light, the martyr's robe – and
death itself is "the White Exploit –." [57] The color itself
had in her mind connotations at once of purity and pride,
for the elect and the martyrs who would wear white robes as
the badge of their fortitude and faith, who were, so to
speak, the *crème de la crème*.[58] But the purity meant here
is not that of the virgin bride's innocent passion; it is the
passion of the Christian martyr fired and purged by his
human heart, the terrible purity of the "Soul *at the White
Heat*" (italics hers) :

Refining these impatient Ores
With Hammer, and with Blaze
Until the Designated Light
Repudiate the Forge – [59]

This color, the one which as early as 1862 Emily Dickinson felt to be the right mode for "this Sufferer polite –," [60] was no less important to her than to Melville, though it reflected in her case the Christian mystery and not a Christian enigma, and her practice of dressing in white was a product not of willful or hysterical eccentricity but of a decision to announce (ironically in the midst of the Civil War) her private secession from society through the assumption of a worldly death that paradoxically involved regeneration.[61] If the act was eccentric, the principle it dramatized – that he who loses his life shall save it – was at the very center of the principles by which her Amherst neighbors and their ancestors had professed to live.

"Crowned," "elected," singled out by her Creator for a tremendous and triumphant destiny, she must have taken a secret delight in the timorous and neglected figure that her role of recluse projected and was perhaps designed to project to her neighbors. Whether by design or not, she certainly convinced them; by 1881, when Mabel Loomis Todd arrived with her husband, Emily was known familiarly as "the myth." For her eccentricities "dozens of reasons" were assigned,[62] and in her obituary in the *Springfield Republican* Susan Dickinson stated that "the facts of her seclusion and her intellectual brilliancy were familiar Amherst traditions." [63] This was one of the rare occasions – if we are to believe a less intellecutal but equally strong Amherst tradition – when Austin Dickinson would have been in harmony with his wife, for he felt that Higginson's description of his favorite sister as "a recluse by temperament and habit, literally spending years without setting her foot beyond the doorstep, and many more years during which her walks were strictly limited to her father's grounds" [64] had "hit and revealed her exactly, and with great skill, taste, and good judgment." [65] What Austin's favorite sister said about taste, language, or judgment of the descriptions of herself published in the *Springfield Republican* during her lifetime is unfortunately lost to us, but it must have been tart and barbed. On July 25th, 1878 she had public proof of how she must long have known that others beheld her:

. . . a person long shut out from the world and living in a world of her own. . . . a timid nature; separated from the outside world, devoted to literature and to flowers.[66]

And less than a week later:

. . . a lady of superior culture and education, and who has for many years secluded herself from society for the purpose of indulging in literary tastes and pursuits.[67]

Such effusive condescension did not encourage her to seek out "the Majority" who did not know poetry from prose, or even sanity from nonsense,[68] the men petty traders, scurrying about the surface of the earth without giving a thought to how long they would lie buried under it, the women, catty gossips for whom "To Ache is human – not polite –," [69] solicitous only to get the sweet cream of someone else's misery. Her decision to reverse the normal order of Amherst behavior and keep her eyes open and her mouth shut was, if eccentric, not hysterical, the act of a tactician, and not, as a recent commentator suggests, of a psychotic.[70] If her white gown was bizarre, it was also – and we must remember that her sex prevented her from shipping on a whaler, loafing around Long Island, or building a hut by Walden Pond – expeditious; she could get her work done in peace and without starving. When we recall what Amherst thought of Emily Dickinson we should not forget what Concord often thought of Emerson and Thoreau before their work gave them prestige, or for that matter what they thought of most of Concord; and we might remind ourselves that Hawthorne's experience with public life was a bitter and stultifying one. If we worry about her pattering around the big Dickinson house with a flower in one hand and a freshly sewed fascicle in the other ought we, like Higginson, who was sincerely concerned about the sheltered life she led, to inquire "You must come down to Boston sometimes?", and add "All ladies do," [71] or point to that other artist in white, Mark Twain, as he wows the public from the lecture platform? That gown, that linen suit hang in the racks of props discarded by each of the great figures of American literature who tried to choose a costume for his role and failed to find a perfect fit. For what she wanted on this side of the grave – her art – Emily Dickinson did not choose unwisely.

It was often the Puritan's good fortune to find that the practical and the moral walk hand in hand, not for the reason that man is hypocritical – though the regenerate were no fools and knew they were not meant to be – but because God is intelligent. One should not assume that because Emily Dickinson's retirement was profitable, allowing her to protect her inner life and practice her art in peace, it was merely a maneuver, a mask or *persona,* a complex piece of aesthetic gamesmanship. It came from a genuine religious conviction, but she was enough of a New Englander, to turn it to useful account, and enough of a poet to know that effects are no less genuine for being calculated. "Impregnability," she wrote, "inheres/As much through Consciousness/Of faith of others in itself/As Pyramidal Nerve," [72] and if she could appear impregnable, she might be let alone. Such an "appearance" is, of course, a dramatization, but, in her white gown, reticent, elusive, detached from the world and disdainful of it, she was dramatizing only what she was. She did not repress feeling – a number of her poems describe the turmoil behind her assumed silence [73] – but in the New England of her time where for every laconic Yankee there was another gushing sentimentalist,[74] she had learned to hold herself in check, to reserve herself for her work and her correspondence. Moreover, unlike her silly neighbors so busy in the world they could not see eternity writ large, she had been granted a deeper vision and a fuller promise. She did not follow Edwards into the pulpits of Enfield and Northampton to warn the ignorant "there are black clouds of God's wrath now hanging directly over your heads, full of the dreadful storm, and big with thunder" [75] but she saw to it that posterity would find in her room in Amherst much the same advice:

> How much the present moment means
> To those who've nothing more –
> The Fop – the Carp * – the Atheist –
> Stake an entire store
> Upon a Moment's shallow * Rim
> While their commuted Feet
> The Torrents * of Eternity
> Do all but * inundate – [76]
>
> . . .
>
> Fop – the Carp/Dog – the Tramp
> shallow/fickle
> Torrents/Waters
> all but/almost

For reticence, she had the best of all possible precedents: The mode, silence, in which God communicated His most vital and most arresting word, His grace; [77] and her lofty disdain she considered to be a trial flight of the soul, a rehearsal of the ultimate transcendence appointed to it, a kind of physical conditioning to prepare for the final exercise of her privilege to grasp immortality:

> With Pinions of Disdain
> The soul can farther fly
> Than any feather specified *
> in * Ornithology –
> It wafts this sordid Flesh
> Beyond it's dull * – control

And during it's electric gale * –
The body is a soul –
instructing by the same * –
* How little work it be –
To put off filaments like this
for immortality – [78]

. . .

specified/ratified, certified
in/by –
dull/slow
gale/spell, stay – , might – , act – , span
the same/itself
How little work it be/What little act it be

If not impregnable, she had, through the assurance of
immortality and the support of "Conviction – That
Granitic Base –," [79] a guarantee against destruction by any
forces of this world, and she asserted gently but firmly
her new sense of self-reliance and self-sufficiency:

Reverse cannot befall
That fine Prosperity
Whose Sources are interior –
As soon – Adversity

A Diamond – overtake
In far – Bolivian Ground –
Misfortune hath no implement
Could mar it – if it found – [80]

The inquisitive and the solicitous were deftly turned away
with a polite reminder of their obtuseness, their bad
manners, and their social inferiority and informed that
Emily Dickinson, far from being a gauche, neurasthenic
misfit or social outcast, had made the most brilliant "catch"
of this or any other season:

The Soul that hath a Guest,
Doth seldom go abroad –
Diviner Crowd at Home,
Obliterate the need –

And Courtesy forbids
The Host's departure – when
Upon Himself – be visiting
The Emperor of Men – [81]

One does not have to – and indeed should not – turn
Emily Dickinson into Tennessee Williams' shy, crippled,
and virginal Laura of *The Glass Menagerie* to understand
why Emily Dickinson would describe God in terms of a
gentleman caller or, when the visit was duly reciprocated,
His servant, death, as a courteous, considerate coachman.
Too much has been made of the "subtly interfused erotic
motive (s)" [82] in Emily Dickinson's poetry – she is quite
capable of expressing erotic feelings, whether toward man
or God, with candor and power – and too little of an
equally important mode of intercourse among human
beings and between man and God, good manners. It is
precisely this conjoining of passion with status that distinguished the Puritans from the enthusiasts they detested,
and that separates Emily Dickinson from the Romantic
tradition into which Tate would like to place her work.
True, to the metaphors of a harsher age, the weddings,
contracts, and hard bargains that the Puritans drew upon,
Emily Dickinson did add a touch of Victorian refinement
and sometimes a tone of finickiness or prissiness. By her day
man and God could meet in the front parlor (where man
and Emerson had met in Susan Dickinson's house down the
street) [83] as well as in the bedroom, the bank, and the law
office.

In addition, for anyone so sensitive to etymology as Emily
Dickinson, the "visit" was the metaphor inherent in divine
visitation. God is the "shapeless friend" in her chamber,[84]
the guest for whom "The Soul should always stand ajar," [85]
or, to cite a poem particularly vulnerable to critics who
believe Emily Dickinson to be unconsciously erotic rather
than naïve, the "fire" that came to her "small Hearth." [86]
At times she combined this metaphor of the visitor with

other images habitually associated with grace; the communion sacrament, the spirit's thirst and refreshment, and the apogee of the solar cycle:

I had been hungry, all the Years –
My Noon had Come – to dine –
I trembling drew the Table near –
And touched the Curious Wine – [87]

As the poem proceeds, the "curious wine" is, as it should be, supplemented by bread, the transubstantial bread "so unlike the Crumb/The Birds and I, had often shared/In Nature's – Dining Room –." [88] Any doubt that these references to bread and wine denote a spiritual sustenance not found in the natural world is dispelled by a later poem (1864) in which the poet, allowed by divine favor to be "An Epicure," is granted ". . . a single Crumb/The Consciousness of Thee." [89]

But grace is, to use one of Emily Dickinson's favorite adjectives, evanescent, and though, as she told Mrs. Holland in 1866, drawing again on the rite of communion, "Friday I tasted life. It was a vast morsel," she finished her description of spring, the seasonal equivalent to the soul's visitation by a vital, regenerative principle, by saying "You mentioned spring's delaying – I blamed her for the opposite. I would eat evanescence slowly." [90] In the end, grace, though it visited, did not reside. Momentary plenitude was replaced by an avid hunger for the spiritual fulfillment that grace had promised; the "Sumptuous moment" [91] gives way to "sumptuous Destitution," [92] a condition paradoxical in its essence and contradictory in its effect. "Communion," once established, is broken off, and the poet, simultaneously bereft and grateful, is left to justify her loss, and to resent it.

For the most part, drawing upon the logic she had developed as early as "Success is counted sweetest," that by deprivation we perceive most keenly, and by perceiving possess most surely, Emily Dickinson could argue that this

void that occurred when the "Grant of the Divine . . . /
Withdraws – and leaves the dazzled Soul/In her unfur-
nished Rooms –" [93] was the intentional act of a benevolent God, His method of letting us estimate the bounty of
immortality through sensing the poverty of the mortal
life:

> None can experience stint
> Who Bounty – have not known –
> * The fact of Famine – could not be
> Except for Fact of Corn –
>
> Want – is a meagre Art
> Acquired by Reverse –
> * The Poverty that was not Wealth –
> * Cannot be Indigence [94]
>
>   . . .
>
> The fact of Famine – could not be/Nor fact of Famine
>   could exist –
> The Poverty that was not Wealth/It is that Poverty was
>   Wealth
> Cannot be Indigence/Enables Indigence –

Thus "The Banquet of Abstemiousness/Defaces that of
Wine –"; [95] the pleasure of communion is incidental to its
purpose, to make us aware of the possibilities we may
achieve at the expense of this anterior life. To effect this,
the delights of communion must be evanescent, lest the
experience of regeneration become, as in Emily Dickinson's
life mortal love had for a time become, an end in itself:

> Did Our Best Moment last –
> 'Twould supersede the Heaven –
> A few – and they by Risk – procure –
> So this Sort – are not given –
>
> Except as stimulants – in
> Cases of Despair –
> Or Stupor – . . .[96]

A more complex poem written twelve years later gives a
similar explanation for the departure of grace:

Delight's Despair at setting
Is that Delight is less
Than the sufficing Longing
That so impoverish.

Enchantment's Perihelion
Mistaken oft has been
For the Authentic orbit
Of it's Anterior Sun.[97]

A critic alert to the implications of modern psychology
might suspect that such arguments disguised a deeper
masochistic impulse to cultivate suffering for its own sake, a
product of romanticism gone sour in New England air, of
the feminine sensibility *per se,* or of the introjection of
passions and resentments forbidden to find an outlet. And
the elements are there: the stern father whose children
could not break loose from his domination; the mother,
submissive, self-effacing, and dull; the subject a recluse with
nearly two thousand poems, her sister, a suspicious, sharp-
tongued old maid with nearly a dozen cats. The words
repression and *sublimation* come the more easily to mind
when one recalls that in the case of the first man Emily
picked love was inseparable from sin, that the second,
Judge Otis Lord, a family friend of long-standing, was the
most forbidding judge on the Salem bench, and that both
were nearly old enough to be her father. It fits, but only if
the critic does not appreciate the demands of the religious
life to which in 1862 a merciful God allowed Emily
Dickinson to commit herself. What the skeptic might call
rationalizing and the psychiatrist neurotic self-deception
the devout would understand as the apprehension of the
position death, suffering, and tantalizing uncertainty oc-
cupy in God's beneficent plan.

Such a response is, of course, supported by a long and
respectable religious – specifically Puritan – tradition: One
has only to remember Milton's forthright statement of the

intention behind his *Paradise Lost*. In her quiet way, Emily Dickinson, too, tried to justify God's ways: If, though elect, one still could not presume to count on the hereafter, "The Risks of Immortality are perhaps its' charm – A secure Delight suffers in enchantment –,"[98] or, to put it in poetry:

> In insecurity to lie
> Is Joy's insuring quality.[99]

"Remoteness," she wrote her friends the Norcross sisters, defending God's disinclination to provide us with incontrovertible evidence of His existence and our fate, "is the founder of sweetness,"[100] and then continued, in a quatrain hitherto unrecognized as such, to argue that His mystery is a function of His mercy. Not only does our uncertainty about who will achieve heaven deepen heaven's value[101] – just as the "letdown" felt by the soul after grace has touched it and passed on is used by the soul to measure the bounty of immortality[102] – but:

> Could we see all we hope,
> Or hear the whole we fear
> Told tranquil, like another tale,
> There would be madness near.[103] *

In addition to the argument that Dostoyevsky was to develop at such length and such power in *The Brothers Karamazov*, that mystery was the prerequisite of faith and was the gauntlet that it ran – or as Emily Dickinson expressed it – "Could Hope inspect her Basis/Her Craft were done –,"[104] she asserted that ambiguity tantalized rather than frustrated her intellect. Like Ishmael, and unlike Ahab or his modern and less self-confident de-

---

* This passage is printed here in quatrain form for the first time. Perhaps the fact that the letter, like all the letters Emily Dickinson wrote to the Norcrosses, exists only in transcript, has prevented readers of Emily Dickinson's prose from recognizing this poem.

scendant Joseph K., her response to the inscrutable is not rage, "outrage," or Angst, but curiosity. "The unknown is the largest need of the intellect," she wrote the Norcross sisters in 1876, and then added a backhanded compliment to the wisdom and magnanimity of her Creator, "though for it, no one thinks to thank God." [105] No one, that is, but Emily Dickinson, who was canny enough to prefer uncertainty to "a Fact of Iron," [106] the certainty of damnation:

> Sweet Skepticism of the Heart –
> That knows – and does not know –
> And tosses like a Fleet of Balm –
> Affronted by the snow –
> Invites and then retards the Truth
> Lest Certainty be sere
> Compared with the delicious throe
> Of transport thrilled with Fear – [107]

Puritan and not Papist, she finds that purgatory comprises rather than succeeds the mortal life, but like Dante and Eliot she appreciated "il foco che affina":

> Dare you see a Soul *at the White Heat?*
> Then crouch within the door –
> Red – is the Fire's common tint –
> But when the vivid Ore
> Has vanquished Flame's conditions,
> It quivers from the Forge
> Without a color, but the light
> Of unanointed Blaze.
> Least Village has it's Blacksmith
> Whose Anvil's even ring
> Stands symbol for the finer Forge
> That soundless tugs – within –
> Refining these impatient Ores
> With Hammer, and with Blaze
> Until the Designated Light
> Repudiate the Forge – [108]

Above all, the brevity of grace proved that both the immortal and mortal artist, both God and Emily Dickinson, shared the same view of aesthetics:

> Perception of an object costs
> Precise the Object's loss –
> Perception in itself a Gain
> Replying to it's Price – [109]

For this wealth that grace conferred, deprivation was, both agreed, the condition and the "just price." [110]

Such a use of metaphors of law, finance, and business was a practice of long and sanctioned standing in New England. In Covenant theology a contractual metaphor had incremented if not fully replaced the traditional erotic trope of marriage to define the tie that bound the creature to his creator, and though by Emily Dickinson's time the formal apparatus of the theocratic state had broken down in New England, the imagination that could simultaneously picture bridal beds and business deals was very much alive and intact. For all his disdain of the commercial life and his repudiation of even the vestiges of the Congregational Church, Emerson still saw the world as a balanced ledger; and in 1873, when he wrote out a contract – properly signed and dated – between himself and his maker,[111] Edward Dickinson assumed that if he was able to keep up his end of the agreement, the Universe, true to the principles of justice and accounting, would reciprocate. Mr. Dickinson did not make bargains (and he saw this as a bargain, not a gesture or an act of self-sacrifice) in bad faith: Not until twenty-three years had passed after his profession of church membership was he ready to write out and put his name to the deed "I hereby give myself to God," a pledge his daughter had made in 1862 and described with somewhat more fervor:

> I gave myself to Him – *
> And took Himself, for Pay,

163

The solemn contract of a Life
Was ratified, this way – [112]

. . .

myself to Him/Him all myself –

If Mr. Dickinson's verb calls up the erotic overtones
found in his daughter's frequent image of brides, be-
trothals, and marriages, his adverb, with its overtones of the
law office, ought, in addition to recalling Edward Dickinson's scrupulous propriety, to be a reminder that Emily
Dickinson drew as often on the vocabulary of politics, law,
and finance as on that of passion. And the sentence itself –
that laconic juxtaposition of tones, its intense yet regulated
and formalized vitality – is set to the Puritan mode. The
sentence reveals at once how much Emily Dickinson inherited from her father – even the militant "I say unto
you" with which he characteristically began family prayers [113] has its echo in her work – and how much both of
them owed to and drew from Congregational New England. Devout and orthodox, and no Arminian, Mr. Dickinson knew that his pledge had earned him not assurance of
salvation but solely the right to hope for it, terms that were
as satisfactory to him as they had been to the Amherst
Valley's first settlers and to his daughter, Emily, ten years
before when God through the benevolence of His grace
had made of her "the undivine abode/Of His Elect Content –." [114]

They were the terms of a marriage: to forsake all others:

Given in Marriage unto Thee
Oh thou Celestial Host –
Bride of the Father and the Son
Bride of the Holy Ghost.

Other Betrothal shall dissolve –
Wedlock of Will, decay –
Only the Keeper of this Ring *
Conquer Mortality – [115]

. . .

this Ring/the Seal

To dissolve the attachments of the will, a word that in Emily Dickinson's vocabulary signifies neither a pervasive and vaguely salutary instinctual drive nor, to turn from nineteenth century theories of instinct to nineteenth century justifications of free enterprise, a conscious and praiseworthy act of self-assertion. When she speaks of "will" here she draws upon the terminology of that faculty psychology on which the Puritans based their view of the nature of man, both fallen and redeemed,[116] the will not as Schopenhauer or Nietzsche understood it but as Milton described it to be after the Fall:

> For Understanding rul'd not, and the Will
> Heard not her lore, both in subjection now
> To sensual Appetite, who from beneath
> Usurping over sovran Reason claimed
> Superior sway:
>
> (*Paradise Lost*, IX, 1127 – 1131)

Only that marriage of which grace was the pledge could make it possible for the will to foreswear the "betrothal" it contracted while unregenerate, and even then, as Emily Dickinson implies by using the future tense in her second stanza, and, as other poems she wrote in 1863 and later state more directly, the old love did not die easy under this new marriage. Regeneration did indeed free the will – so the Puritans believed and so the elect discovered – but they found, and knew they would find, that election did not free the will from temptation. The bride of Christ might die to the world, might even dress in white to announce what she had done, and the wedlock of will might decay, but the deposed spouse sometimes refused to stay buried:

> If He were living – dare I ask –
> And how if He be dead –
> And so around the Words I went –
> Of meeting them – afraid –
>
> I hinted Changes – Lapse of Time –
> The Surfaces of Years –

I touched with Caution – lest they crack – *
And show me to my fears –

Reverted to adjoining Lives –
Adroitly turning out
Wherever I suspected Graves –
'Twas prudenter – I thought –

And He – I pushed – with sudden force –
In face of the Suspense –
"Was buried" – "Buried"! "He!"
My Life just holds the Trench – [117]

. . .

crack/slit –

The equation of this loss with death itself first made, as we have seen, in 1862, is continued as late as 1884.[118] By then this conventional romantic variant of a medieval cliché had long been incremented by the Christian paradox that he who loses his life shall save it. As early as 1863, when she wrote the Norcross sisters that "life is death we're lengthy at, death the hinge to life," [119] Emily Dickinson had worked out a complex but consistent usage of these terms in order to express the irony and the paradox that the price of living through Caritas is to die to Amor, and that regeneration combines an investiture of life with a renunciation of it. A quatrain, hopefully less enigmatic to us than it must have been to its recipient, Higginson, indicates that by 1864 she no longer felt that she had "died" in vain:

A Death blow is a Life blow to Some
Who till they died, did not alive become –
Who had they lived, had died but when
They died, Vitality begun.[120]

But though she could profess to "love the Cause that slew Me" [121] and perceived the difference between the "form of Life and Life," [122] between the imitation the ignorant will still stubbornly preferred and the genuine article she rationally knew she wanted, though she realized God's price was a just one, weighted to the gain, was "Even as the Grace –/Our lord – thought no/Extravagance/To pay – a Cross –"[123] that price, for all its fairness, at times seemed to her almost too steep to bear:

> To die – without the Dying
> And live – without the Life
> This is the hardest Miracle
> Propounded to Belief.[124]

No matter how reasonable were the demands God made in return for his "charity," no matter how freely human reason consented to them, the will, to the Puritan mind the weakest part of the psychic mechanism, resented the conditions of an "election" that in exchange for a hope of life deprived one of the sense of it:

> Denial – is the only fact
> Perceived by the Denied –
> Whose Will – a numb significance – *
> The Day the Heaven died –
>
> And all the Earth strove common round –
> Without Delight, or Beam * –
> What Comfort was it Wisdom – was –
> The spoiler of Our Home?[125]

. . .

numb significance/Blank intelligence
Beam/aim –

Thus it should not be assumed that by transferring her loyalty, her fidelity, from man to God that Emily Dickinson was merely taking an easy step up the social and celestial ladder, satisfying to her as this rise in status must have been. To take that step at all, she had to turn her back on the most celestial aspect of mortal life, mortal love, and forsake "The joyful little Deity/We are not scourged to serve –"[126] for a stern God and an unsure result. The recurrence in 1864 of poems affirming her constancy toward an absent lover,[127] as well as poems in which the lovers will

167

be rewarded in the afterlife for their renunciation of one another now,[128] shows the will's persistent struggle to "live" on its own terms. The terms of grace were no less than the rejection of the self that the self be – to use another term Emily Dickinson took from Puritan theology – "justified," what she described in her marvelously succinct definition of that "piercing virtue," renunciation, as:

> . . . the Choosing
> Against itself –
> Itself to justify
> Unto itself – [129]

Not that Emily Dickinson assumed that renunciation, or any other specific action on her part for that matter, would guarantee her membership in the "Justified Processions." [130] Even if she had not been aware of the Arminian heresy, her contempt for "works" and her unflagging belief in her own and her few close friends' superiority would have made her disdain a heaven open to anyone who kept his dues paid up. But history has provided a succulent heresy for every Puritan's taste, and those more sensitive and meditative souls who attended their inner workings instead of working in the world's vineyards, who cultivated their sensibility rather than their farms, flocks, trades, and neighbors, who would find callous, smug, and mercenary the Arminians' *quid pro quo,* might well sympathize with and be tempted by that arch-Antinomian, Anne Hutchinson, who had raised the rapture of the sensibility to a God-like power. Certainly Emily Dickinson's predilection for "enthusiasm" was strong – Perry Miller, in his essay "From Edwards to Emerson" alludes to one of her most famous poems when he wants to characterize the attitude of mind responsible for "the latest – and yet the oldest – form of New England infidelity," [131] and our examination of her early poetry has revealed how easily the slightest jag from nature could assure her that she had been selected for immortal life. Nor did the despair of 1861 – 1862 purge her of an exuberance both theologically and aesthetically suspect; during 1862 and 1863 the same tinny note of ecstasy is repeatedly and insistently struck, and all the tropes – crowns, robes, earls, carriages, and even one little gentian – are taken out of the toy box, dusted off, and set in their old places.[132] It is a brief return to childhood, though, the result of immediate release and rapture over the new hope held out to her rather than of presumption, arrogance, deliberate heresy, or naïveté. For in these same years, the last in which poems of this type appear, Emily Dickinson becomes aware of precisely what Anne Hutchinson lightly disregarded, the inevitability and imminence of the most awesome, tantalizing, terrifying and final moment of human life – the moment when God reveals His judgment.

From the beginning she had assumed that immortality was a "disclosure/To favorites – a few –" [133] and that the human race would be divided into the justified processions in heaven and "Being's Peasantry" [134] outside, and up through 1860 she was convinced she knew where she stood, more precisely, someday would eternally stand. During the following two years, whether in heresy or in despair, she was no less positive about what her position was. But by 1863 the emphasis has shifted from certainty to suspense; "Suspense – is Hostiler than Death –" [135] she wrote that year, fully aware of the irony that the elect are uncertain while the damned are secure and the despairing, in their own peculiar way, are content.

To the elect, that particular luxury was denied in favor of possible riches – and perils – to come. When Indian summer reminds her of the eternal "Summer of the Just," the thought is at once qualified by her recalling "this [summer] of Our's, diversified/With Prospect, and with Frost –." [136] Her reply to her own anxieties, that dread could be "a Spur – upon the Soul –," [137] a lively apprehension that served to increase our reverence, might justify God's ways, but it did not make the state of the elect any more secure, nor the soul in anticipating its journey toward the judgment any less apprehensive:

> Oh Future! thou secreted peace
> Or subterranean * wo –
> Is there no wandering route of grace
> That leads away from thee –
> No circuit sage of all the course *
> Descried by cunning Men
> To balk thee of thy sacred Prey – *
> Advancing to thy Den – [138]
>
>   .   .   .
>
> subterranean/unsuspected
> course/lines
> thy sacred Prey/the innocence

Even one of her most emphatic statements of commitment and devotion to God, the poem beginning "I live with Him – I see His face –," concludes with a more sobering affirmation of faith "Be Judgment – what it may –," [139] and in darker moments, she seemed to find the odds more heavily against her:

> No Other can reduce
> Our mortal Consequence
> Like the remembering it be nought
> A Period from hence
> But Contemplation for
> Cotemporaneous Nought
> Our Single Competition
> Jehovah's Estimate.[140]

The version above is a redaction, written in 1865, of an earlier version written in 1863. A comparison of the two reveals how divided Emily Dickinson's feelings were when she contemplated the possibilities that grace had opened for her. The stanzas below were rejected when Emily Dickinson returned to this poem in 1865:

> No Other can exalt Our
> Mortal Consequence

Like the remembering it exist –
A period from hence –

. . .

Invited from Itself
To the Creator's House –
To tarry an Eternity –
His – shortest Consciousness –

In several poems she tried to imagine this most decisive
and ultimate of occasions, the moment when the soul, risen
from the grave, stands at that "odd Fork in Being's Road
–," [141] the juncture of time with Eternity, the moment
when:

Circumference be full –
The long restricted * Grave
Assert her Vital Privilege * –
The Dust – connect * – and live –

Solemnity – prevail –
It's Individual Doom
Possess each separate Consciousness –
August – Absorbed – Numb * – [142]

. . .

restricted/subjected
her Vital Privilege/His Primogeniture
connect/adjust
Absorbed – Numb/Resistless – dumb

Here the soul has, to paraphrase another poem written two
years later, traversed the interval between experience and
experiment, the "most profound experiment/Appointed
unto Men –," [143] and by "experiment" she meant precisely what her Lexicon said, a method by which one – in
this case the most omniscient of savants – attempted to
"disclose the *qualities* in natural bodies." [144] Toward this
final test to determine whether "Eternity will be/Velocity
or Pause," [145] the soul, nominated by grace during the
term of its experience, and embarked at death on its voyage
from experience to experiment, at once fearfully and pas-
sionately aspires. And it goes this route alone; the paradox

171

that its identity remains at heel as a faithful companion is used by Emily Dickinson only to emphasize the soul's essential isolation. In this respect, as she made clear to Doctor Holland around 1866, life and death were not so different, and the wise could do worse than practice for the lonely journey to come. "The soul must go by Death alone, so, it must by life, if it is a soul," she wrote him, and then added wryly, lest he think she might be suggesting that all Amherst should or even could imitate her seclusion, "If a committee – no matter." [146]

Nor was this seclusion in white, this dying to the earthly life, this rejection of the pseudoheaven of secular love and acceptance of the "rack" of renunciation in itself any guarantee that one would be saved. In the poem below Emily Dickinson describes an ascending order of "triumphs" that the resolute soul may achieve both in life and beyond it, but each such victory, as the formal division of the poem into stanzas that are themselves separate grammatical units bears out, is a separate one, the precursor but not the cause of the one that follows:

> Triumph – may be of several kinds –
> There's Triumph in the Room
> When that Old Imperator – Death –
> By Faith – be overcome –
>
> There's Triumph of the finer Mind
> When Truth – affronted long –
> Advance unmoved – to Her Supreme –
> Her God – Her only Throng –
>
> A Triumph – when Temptation's Bribe
> Be slowly handed back –
> One eye upon the Heaven renounced –
> And One – upon the Rack –
>
> Severer Triumph – by Himself
> Experienced – who pass
> Acquitted – from that Naked Bar –
> Jehovah's Countenance – [147]

In this order of priority the triumph over death by faith is less important than the intellect's dedication to the truth on which faith is founded – and it is interesting that the soul is not apart from the mind but a refinement of it. The poem moves from the room and rituals of mourning to the isolated mind and its inner drama of anguish and its final suspense, from the Dickinson front parlor to Emily's room directly above, and from there to the antechambers of Paradise as the soul progresses from faith to grace, grace to sacrifice, and sacrifice to judgment, each trial preparing the way for the next, and each stage testing the soul anew. On this side of the veil God watches – that is His function or "department" in the scheme He has set up – but He does not prompt – and on the other side He waits to examine how His few select investments have disbursed the capital with which He endorsed or underwrote them:

> Growth of Man – like Growth of Nature –
> Gravitates within –
> Atmosphere, and Sun endorse * it –
> But it stir – alone –
>
> Each – it's difficult * Ideal
> Must achieve – Itself –
> Through the solitary prowess
> Of a Silent Life –
>
> Effort – is the sole condition –
> Patience of Itself –
> Patience of opposing forces –
> And intact * Belief –
>
> Looking on – is the Department
> Of it's Audience –
> But Transaction – is assisted
> By no Countenance – [148]
>
>   . . .

endorse/Confirm –
difficult/absolute
intact/direct – , distinct

"Transaction" – in one word the soul's progress from experience to experiment is united with the contract that made that progress possible. The poem describes the transaction, the bargain made between God and man and allocates to each the part each plays in man's salvation. The definition characteristically combines the two orthodoxies under which Emily Dickinson and most of the rest – certainly all of the better – people of Amherst lived, that of American Puritanism and that of American free-enterprise capitalism; God sets us up in business, but man conducts his business as he sees fit. Through grace the elect have been "gifted to discern/Beyond the Broker's insight –," [149] been given, one might say, the financial know-how to achieve the highest success (if Hooker is Emily Dickinson's spiritual ancestor, Horatio Alger is her literary contemporary, and her version of self-reliance is closer to Alger's than to Emerson's), and therefore the human will,[150] and not the machinations of Providence, should be held accountable if, refusing to economize, we fail to renounce gold for Gold or love for Love in this life, and end up bankrupt in the next.[151]

To Emily Dickinson the statement "God is love" was no commonplace. Indeed, before and during much of 1862 she violently rejected any such smug and casual contention, and even when she came to know better, when she employed the imagery of sanctified secular love to render the intense, ecstatic, evanescent union God made with those He chose to favor, she did not delude herself about the steep cost of momentary bliss and mortal hope. By love she did not mean the flutters of the heart but the laws of force by which the cosmos was moved and the soul was judged. For her, love, the "Initial of Creation, and/The Exponent of Earth –" [152] was indeed what made the world go round and what had started it moving, a power that was analagous to the forces of atoms rather than the sentiments of Valentines, the sheer incandescent energy of the sun, which, when Christ focused it through His passion as through a burning-glass, "annealed" [153] human love to a purity that made resurrection possible. This divine love is the blazing force that plays on the dust at resurrection to "reform[s] Vitality/Into Divinity," [154] a power so ultimate, so absolute, so infinite that it transcends the discriminations of language, a power incomparable, hence beyond simile:

> Love reckons by itself – alone –
> "As large as I" – relate the Sun
> To One who never felt it blaze –
> Itself is all the like it has – [155] *

Yet its difference from earthly love is one of magnitude, not of kind. Earthly love may be "but a filament . . ./Of that diviner thing," [156] but the poet insists on the connection. Emily Dickinson does not disparage human love – indeed one of her most satiric poems, the famous "What soft – Cherubic Creatures –" shows her contempt for those who do – but, while recognizing the relative pallor of its light, respects and validates it, and by assigning to human love a place and function in the divine scheme of regeneration, converts it from the weapon she had raised against God to the instrument by which He made her ready for His grace. "It may surprise you I speak of God" she wrote – "I know him but a little, but Cupid taught Jehovah to many an untutored Mind – Witchcraft is wiser than we –." [157]

---

* For a poem that celebrates but does define the limitations of human love, see Poem 1731. Poem 826 may shed some light on the "thought" inaccessible to language that is the subject of Poem 581, below:

> I found the words * to every thought
> I ever had – but One –
> And that – defies me –
> As a Hand did try to chalk the Sun
>
> To Races – nurtured in the Dark –
> How would your own – begin?
> Can Blaze be done * in Cochineal –
> Or Noon – in Mazarin?

words/phrase   done/shown

Thus Amor, "this lovely maze, which is not Life or Death – though it has the intangibleness of one, and the flush of the other –" [158] is no longer heretical but instead educative, a gift from God rather than a replacement for Him. It becomes the device by which the unregenerate, their consciousness still unextended by grace, can learn of Caritas if only by inference or "Comparatively –." [159] Her error had been to neglect the lesson for the device that was meant to teach it, to prefer the demonstration to the principle, to make ends of the means towards ends, an error of intelligence that God had intervened to correct, not out of petulance or jealousy as she had once thought but out of thoughtfulness, concern, and, in the fullest sense of the word, charity. When He laid down His "interdict," He granted at the same time "Our privilege": [160]

> You constituted Time –
> I deemed Eternity
> A Revelation of Yourself –
> 'Twas therefore Deity
>
> The Absolute – removed *
> The Relative away –
> That I unto Himself adjust
> My slow idolatry – [161]
>
> . . .
>
> removed/withdrew –

Through the relative, Amor, one is enabled to conceive of paradise and consequently to desire election to it; through the absolute, Caritas, paradise momentarily becomes apprehensible and one is given an opportunity to achieve it. The first is the precondition of the second: "Redemption Mental precedes Redemption Spiritual," [162] as she wrote Susan Dickinson in 1884, and the word "redemption" was one which she had, as early as the "Master" letters,[163] associated with human love. "To congratulate the Redeemed," she wrote to Higginson in 1879

on the occasion of his second marriage "is perhaps superfluous for Redemption leaves nothing for Earth to add": [164]

> We play at Paste –
> Till qualified, for Pearl –
> Then, drop the Paste
> And deem ourself a fool –
>
> The Shapes – though – were similar –
> And our new Hands
> Learned *Gem*-Tactics –
> Practicing *Sands* – [165]

The word *tactics,* implying as it does the artful deployment of intelligence for a desired end, reflects Emily Dickinson's belief that the Creator does not endow His creature
with immortality but "qualifies" him to achieve it, and that
the pursuit of salvation is a rational matter. What the
Creator does do is to provide, through the experience of
mortal love, a *modus operandi* which the creature would be
wise to follow. Thus in her mind the onus remained
precisely where the Puritans had placed it, upon man
"elected" not to a sinecure but to a candidacy from which
he would still have to conduct a rigorous, expensive, astute,
unflagging campaign for office, an office so immense that to
hope for it is not merely presumptuous but almost sac-
rilegious:

> Had I presumed to hope –
> The loss had been to Me
> A Value – for the Greatness' Sake –
> As Giants – gone * away –
>
> Had I presumed to gain
> A Favor so remote –
> The failure but confirm the Grace
> In further Infinite –
>
> 'Tis failure – not of Hope –
> But Confident * Despair –

Advancing on Celestial Lists –
With faint – Terrestrial power –

'Tis Honor – though I die –
For That no Man obtain
Till He be justified by Death –
This – is the Second Gain – [166]

. . .

gone/claimed
Confident/diligent – , resolute –

In the past she had been stupid enough to mistake plate
for solid silver [167] and mother of pearl for the pearl of
great price,[168] and, until forced to taste the difference, had
stubbornly persisted in husbanding chaff instead of God's
own wheat.* In 1862 God in His magnanimity had corrected
her vision and enhanced her taste, and for the rest of her
life she thanked Him for giving her the insight not to be
taken in again. Her insistence, first expressed in 1862, that
God's love was no momentary blazing of human blood but
an illumination by which the intellect's circumference was
made permanently and incomparably wider unless the will
chose to narrow or to extinguish it, that this love did not,
and was not intended to, protect, soothe, patronize, or
transfigure its human recipient, reveals an outlook thoroughly Puritan, an acute vision unsoftened and undistorted
by enthusiasm, transcendentalism, or Victorian sentiment.
For the rest of her life her business was to live, and to labor,

* Poem 1269, quoted below, is one of a number that become comprehensible when seen as a supercession of human by divine love:

> I worked for chaff and earning Wheat
> Was haughty and betrayed.
> What right had Fields to arbitrate
> In matters ratified?
>
> I tasted Wheat and hated Chaff
> And thanked the ample friend –
> Wisdom is more becoming viewed
> At distance than at hand.

See also Poem 1555.

by this light. If she had moments of doubt – as she must have when she wrote to Washington Gladden not long after Charles Wadsworth had died and when Judge Lord was seriously ill to ask this famous preacher whether immortality was indeed "true" [169] – she had none of disbelief, and she never returned to nature to seek evidence of immortality or to man to substitute for it. Nor did she feel obliged to castigate herself for those earlier failures to find pearls, jewels, or a viable love, or to disparage the earlier goals which, through a finer education, she had "outgrown." [170] She had learned her lesson, but she did not repent the education, nor continue to resent the teacher who had made her learn it. But after 1862 there was really no more to learn. After 1862 she, like her father, was pledged to God, her loyalties and her assumptions fixed. One can no longer speak of her development – there was no further place for her to go – but only of how her awakened faith informed and affected her conception of the principal aspects of experience that she chose to scrutinize: death, nature, and above all, the creative process itself.

At the earliest ending of winter,
In March, a scrawny cry from outside
Seemed like a sound in his mind.

He knew that he heard it,
A bird's cry, at daylight or before,
In the early March wind.

The sun was rising at six,
No longer a battered panache above snow . . .
It would have been outside.

It was not from the vast ventriloquism
Of sleep's faded papier-mâché . . .
The sun was coming from outside.

That scrawny cry – it was
A chorister whose c preceded the choir.
It was part of the colossal sun,

Surrounded by its choral rings,
Still far away. It was like
A new knowledge of reality.

Wallace Stevens, "Not Ideas About the
Thing but the Thing Itself"

Chapter 5

In 1859 Emily Dickinson, perhaps inspired by Emerson's statement in *Nature* that "the intellect searches out the absolute order of things as they stand in the mind of God, and without the colors of affection" and encouraged by his assurance a few pages later that "the laws of moral nature answer to those of matter as face to face in a glass," had tried to ferret out the evidence in the natural world that would validate the Christian hypothesis presented to her at school, at home, and at the Congregational meetings she chose to attend that immortal life was sure to come. To assume such analogies between natural and spiritual laws, indeed to assume that there were spiritual laws at all, came easily to a young woman, an aspirant poet aware of her need for instruction, whose favorite tutor, Ben Newton, had recommended Emerson, and whose most distinguished neighbor, the eminent geologist and president of Amherst, Edward Hitchcock, had testified that the observation of nature did indeed reveal evidence of the supernatural. It is a credit to Emily Dickinson's integrity that she refused to allow such respected authorities to distort her vision or compromise her experience. When "matter" refused to yield up such revelations, when the affections would not wash out but held fast, fast as Georgiana's birthmark, and when the glass, no matter how hard she peered, held but the Amherst landscape and the poet's questing, anxious face, she began, in opposition to the scientific temper of her time, to share Hawthorne and Melville's distrust not of the microscope but of the eye and the mind behind it. Even before 1862 she had abandoned such scientific investigation predicated on a faith in the intellect she could no longer share, and after that year she no longer needed evidence. By then, too, she had come to despise the audacity that would constrain God to any law – moral, natural, or otherwise – and had turned from searching for evidence and glorying in pride in her intellect as the micro- and telescope that would search evidence out to the more humble and vastly more important moral question first asked in America two centuries before: "How shall I be saved?"

The shift is a major one; it marks the third and final mode in which Emily Dickinson considered the subjects commonly held to be most important to her: death and immortality. Relying first on scientific method and transcendental optimism to determine the poet's *modus operandi,* then on the Romantic and the "graveyard" poets to define the field in which the poet operates, Emily Dickinson habitually turned contemporary conventions into metaphors through which an intense, indeed overwhelming private experience was, by being connected to a larger tradition, enhanced, projected, and controlled. This would seem to correspond to Tate's thesis that Emily Dickinson employed the vocabulary of a tradition without being limited to the vision for which that vocabulary was originally invented, but for her later work Tate's formulation turns out to be incomplete, and to the extent it is incomplete, inadequate. It is inadequate because for the greater part of her life and her work Emily Dickinson chose to commit herself to the tradition she at first had defied and then, as an artist, had made use of in the way Tate has described. What was convention in 1859 had become metaphor by 1862; what was metaphor in the beginning of 1862 had become dogma before that year was out.

When Emily Dickinson shifted the area of ambiguity from the fact of immortality to the possibility of achieving it, she reduced death from a fate to the instrument that prepared her for a fate still undisclosed, and thus made death at least potentially benevolent in character and beneficent in effect. By the time she could write that our fear of death, "The Porter of my Father's Lodge," [1] comes from conceiving of it as a "terminus" when it is actually a "Relay," [2] she had stopped thinking of death as a sentence from whose finality there was no longer an appeal.[3] Death was but God's "Alpine" requirement,[4] His "gentle Miracle," [5] "the Leisure of His Will," [6] or just the well-bred servant He dispatched to escort Emily Dickinson to her destination.[7] When she wrote to Susan Dickinson shortly after Hawthorne's death that "Ourself cannot cease – Hawthorne's interruption does not seem as it did –" [8] she was reaffirming what grace had taught her, that the self was more than that physical life to which death's power was confined.[9] "I thought since of the power of death," she wrote Mrs. Holland when a neighbor's daughter "young and in hope but a little while" died at the age of twenty-seven, "not upon affection, but its mortal signal," and then added one of the most succinct and telling descriptions of death she ever wrote, "It is to us the Nile." [10]

The image, recalling the terrible and exotic rapture by which Antony and Cleopatra were transfigured and undone, unites Christian mystery with human passion and brings together death's double and simultaneous function of destruction and regeneration. At the same time it shows that Emily Dickinson had a lively grasp of the immensity – and the consequences – of the way God chose to prove His love. Dedicated as she was, she sometimes had reservations about the technique by which the soul is wooed and won, and could resent the fact that death, though it gives way to eternal life, inevitably precedes it:

It came at last but prompter Death
Had occupied the House –
His pallid Furniture arranged
And his metallic Peace –

Oh faithful Frost * that kept the Date
Had Love as punctual been
Delight had aggrandized the Gate
And blocked the coming in.[11]

·   ·   ·

Frost/Sleet

Yet if at times she can resent death, she no longer fears or
despises it, for the possibility of salvation has dignified
death by raising it from a squalid terror to the hallowed
ground on which the great drama of "Felicity or Doom" [12]
must be played out. Though after 1862 she would agree
with Whitman that death was sacred, she would never
attempt to assimilate it to the human norm as Whitman
did by describing death as "sane." "Awe," and not easy
familiarity or comradeship is the emotion she feels and assumes she ought to feel. "Ample make this Bed –/Make
this Bed with Awe –" [13] she admonishes those who bury
the dead and demands from them the sole response adequate to this ultimate occasion. Of her own thirst for awe
she wrote obliquely, using her standard tropes for death,
winter, and wilderness, and distinguishing between herself
and the "satin races" who did not have the sense to share
her appetite and her austerity:

I think the Hemlock likes to stand
Upon a Marge of Snow –
It suits his own Austerity –
And satisfies an awe

That men, must slake in Wilderness –
And * in the Desert – cloy –
An instinct * for the Hoar,* the Bald –
Lapland's – nescessity –

184

The Hemlock's nature thrives – on cold –
The Gnash of Northern winds
Is sweetest nutriment – to him –
His best * Norwegian Wines –

To satin Races – he is nought –
But Children on the Don,
Beneath his Tabernacles, play,
And Dnieper Wrestlers, run.[14]

. . .

And/Or
instinct/hunger
Hoar/drear –
best/good

In the poems she wrote after 1862, there is none of the
stark terror of annihilation or the angry perplexity she had
formerly felt when confronted by the obdurate dead. Still,
though her gaze is calm, and her attitude toward death is at
times even cordial, and though she is fortified against death
by her new faith, she is still capable of seeing, from the
human perspective, a certain irony in God's employing such
an agency to lead her to His munificent rewards. When she
writes Susan Dickinson (who might have recalled these
words with a certain bitterness a year later when her two-
year-old niece died) in 1864 that "Life is Miracle, and Death,
as harmless as a Bee, except to those who run –" [15] the
tone has the exuberance and some of the fatuousness of the
recent convert. But when she wrote to Mrs. Holland a year
later, the actual event had made her less sanguine: "[Susan]
is still with the sister who put her child in an ice nest last
Monday forenoon. The redoubtable God! I notice where
Death has been introduced, he frequently calls, making it
desirable to forestall his advances." [16] And the occasion
itself seems to have inspired one of her grimmest pictures of
the dead and one of her bitterest poems of neglect:

They wont frown always – some sweet Day
When I forget to teaze –

They'll recollect how cold I looked
And how I just said "Please."

Then They will hasten to the Door
To call the little Girl
Who cannot thank Them for the Ice
That filled the lisping full.[17]

Less successful are the great majority of her poems about dead ladies – they seem so pleased and assured that they must surely be Emily Dickinson herself – lying snugly in their caskets, smug with the knowledge of their immortal worth and of our ignorance. The silence of these dead ladies is not meant to suggest disdain or mystery but is a prim hint that they have been hurt and slighted, a reticence that instructs the living that their mortal frailty is moral as well as physical.[18] These ladies intend to arouse feelings of "Gravity – and Expectation – and Fear –/A tremor just, that All's not sure," [19] and, alas, a tremor is all they provide as awe and irony give way to a saccharine optimism and death, "but the Drift of Eastern Gray,/Dissolving into Dawn away,/Before the West begin–," [20] becomes so benevolent as to be unrecognizable, and dying is reduced to a simple exercise in deportment. When soothed by her faith, Emily Dickinson's sensibility at times grows slack, and insight is replaced by simple presumption, and the profound by the merely pompous. The dead, we are told in all seriousness, know, where we but hope; receive, where we but pray; [21] and are not like us because they know their fate.[22] In an overrated poem that strains to make the banal profound, she merely belabors the obvious and reveals what is scarcely news: that the dead can't tell what they've found:

Those who have been in the Grave the longest –
Those who begin Today –
Equally perish from our Practise –
Death is the other * way –

Foot of the Bold did least attempt it –
It – is the White Exploit –
Once to achieve, annuls the power
Once to communicate – [23]

．　．　．

other/further

One of the few poems on the dead written after 1862 that
is not marred by either a mawkish or a cheerful insistence on
some self-evident fact about them – that they do not speak,
for example [24] – tries to define the way the dead extend the
consciousness of the living. As in all her most successful
poems about death, her emphasis is on the human observer
of the mystery rather than the mystery itself. Appropriately,
the poem is built around images of vision, of the dead as a
lens that leads the eye simultaneously forward to the
infinite in eternity and backward from the grave to the
finite life in time. And by this operation the lens performs a
second function: It readjusts the perspective from which
man views and appraises his life in time and his potential
life in eternity:

The Admirations – and Contempts – of time –
Show justest – through an Open Tomb –
The Dying – as it were a Hight
Reorganizes Estimate
And what We saw not
We distinguish clear –
And mostly – see not
What We saw before –

'Tis Compound Vision –
Light – enabling Light –
The Finite – furnished
With the Infinite –
Convex – and Concave Witness –
Back – toward Time –
And forward –
Toward the God of Him – [25]

187

Here at least the poet does not try to convince her audience that it will be startled to learn that dead men tell no tales, to amaze that audience with the revelation that the dead in some mysterious way are different, or to assure her readers that when their loved ones die they will feel their loss and regret their neglect.[26] Here the poem records an alert play of intelligence as the reader's eye, moving from the narrow tomb to infinite life, from the triumph of time to God's triumph and time's dissolution, follows, in images of perspective, focus, and insight that are organic outgrowths of the poem's statement, the poet's response to the occasion.

But this poem is not typical of those she wrote about the confrontation of the living with the dead. Except for "The last night that she lived" (Poem 1100) and the justly famous "Because I could not stop for death" (Poem 712), a poem which is in any case actually about the soul's progress after death toward what it "surmises" to be eternity and which deals with that "transaction" from experience to experiment that is always, perhaps because by definition it portrays a state of irresolution, one of her most congenial subjects, the remaining poems Emily Dickinson wrote on death reveal her at her most banal. In them she descends to simple asseverations of piety[27] or to quaint and rather tasteless "genre sketches" of village funerals and rural graveyards,[28] the stock in trade from which she started. And when she turns from the conventions at hand, she is apt to substitute her own, to work up some of the more simple-minded paradoxes that have, from overuse, degenerated from insights to habits, from genuine responses to mental reflexes before the dead. Thus the dead, though silent, "teach" us ("Paralysis – our Primer – dumb –/Unto Vitality!") ; [29] the grieving mourners stand in ironic contrast to the dead rejoicing in heaven; [30] the narrow grave contains both infinite life and infinite loss, momentarily arresting antitheses that have more of the neat balance of rhetoric than they do the dynamic tension of good poetry, that on reflection do not radiate or increment but collapse.

For example, the poem below, workmanlike to be sure, is a facile, too assured, almost flippant exploitation of paradox:

A Coffin – is a small Domain,
Yet able to contain
A Citizen * of Paradise
In it's diminished Plane.

A Grave – is a restricted * Breadth –
Yet ampler than the Sun –
And all the Seas He populates
And Lands He looks upon

To Him who on it's small * Repose
Bestows * a single Friend –
Circumference without Relief –
Or Estimate – or End – [31]

. . .

A Citizen/A Rudiment
a restricted/an inferior
small/low
Bestows/Conferred

Such posturing, whether it involves the substitution of sentiment for emotion or of rhetoric for intellect, is Emily Dickinson's characteristic vice and temptation. Attempts to "solve" the mystery of death invite the poet to indulge in platitudes or to inform us solemnly of what is true by definition, that death is changeless and democratic,[32] and apparently it is difficult for her critics to avoid a like solemnity when they discuss this theme, allegedly a significant one in her work.[33] Of course it is unfair to expect her pronouncements on death to be illuminating – she did not transmit her poetry through an Ouija board – but one may legitimately prefer those poems in which she consents to remain as baffled and awe-struck as the rest of us, poems in which she does not insist that she is on the inside track (that track inevitably turns out to be a well-worn groove) but where with full consciousness she reacts to the apprehensions, terrors, and uncertainties with which the dead inspire the living.[34] Her own poetic talent endowed her with an amazing ability to delineate the most delicate motions of her sensibility and to identify and define through metaphor the components of the most subtle emotion. Her mind was analytic, diagnostic, pictorial, and with equal efficiency she could define such abstractions as hope, despair, love, and faith, and describe the experiences for which these abstractions stand. But her mind was not a genuinely syncretic one – paradox, not synthesis, is her natural form of resolution – and when she tried to reach conclusions, or needed the assurance of them, she had to appropriate conventional formulations and pieties. Despite her wish for knowledge and her frequent pretensions to it, her statements of ignorance are more convincing, just as her campaigns are more interesting than her victories, and her progress toward heaven more so than her safe arrival, gowned and crowned, at the throne. Likewise, when she speaks of death, one is more moved by her sense of death's imminence than by her conclusions about it.[35] When she is evocative rather than didactic, as she is in the poem below, she is on her surest ground:

> Crisis is a Hair
> Toward which forces creep
> Past which forces retrograde
> If it come in sleep
>
> To suspend the Breath
> Is the most we can
> Ignorant is it Life or Death
> Nicely balancing.
>
> Let an instant push
> Or an Atom press
> Or a Circle hesitate
> In Circumference
>
> It – may jolt the Hand
> That adjusts the Hair

That secures Eternity
From presenting – Here – [36]

Her new belief in the possibility of her redemption was responsible for this sharp sense of how completely the physical life is contingent upon the divine will. Indeed in the poems she wrote after 1862 God's total power – His omnipotence, omniscience, and omnipresence – is fully recognized and accepted. No longer does Emily Dickinson attempt to test God out or to use her wit against His magnitude, and her disdain is replaced by ardor, her resentment by awe, her defiance, whether sullen or flagrantly rebellious, by oaths of fidelity and declarations of love. The ease with which God, for Whom the created universe is "but the Gambol/Of His Authority –," can dispose of human life, "inserting Here – a Sun – /There – leaving out a Man –" no longer angers her; as she considers the domestic economy of the cosmos she finds God to be a housekeeper after her own heart, and, to defend His omnipotence, she argues primly that "The thrifty Deity/Could scarce afford Eternity/To Spontaniety –." [37]

The tone is calm, but it is not complacent. Emily Dickinson did not disregard the new perspective she had been granted, an accurate sense of scale to measure man against the infinite, and she ridicules those whose sense of proportion is distorted, the gnats [38] and bees whose helter-skelter buzzing contrasts ironically with the sun's silent, immense, and vital "Yellow Plan." [39] And when these citizens can no longer ignore their minute – yet potentially stupendous – place in the cosmic design, they try to "insulate" themselves against such knowledge:

> The Lightning playeth – all the while –
> But when He singeth – then –
> Ourselves are conscious He exist –
> And we approach * Him – stern –
>
> With Insulators – and a Glove –
> Whose short – sepulchral Bass

191

Alarms us – tho' His Yellow feet
May pass – and counterpass –

Upon the Ropes – above our Head –
Continual – with the News –
Nor We so much as check our speech –
Nor stop to cross Ourselves – [40]

.   .   .

approach/accost

The failure is one of perception rather than reverence – to
force a distinction the Puritans, for whom reverence was the
rational reaction to the way things are, would not have
made. To tremble at the thunder, to arm oneself against
the supposed threat of lightning, is to misread the signs of
nature, but this misreading is inevitable until grace restores
in us the ability to apprehend the lightning's "news." Not
that the unregenerate can be held accountable for their
ignorance of news they are unequipped to hear or for their
alarm and caution in the face of the only attributes of God
they can see unaided.[41] Their reactions are indeed the
"natural" ones, for without grace, without the assurance
that salvation is possible, God does indeed appear as an
arbitrary and destructive force; and without the hope of
immortality there is, as Emily Dickinson demonstrated in
her caustic, defiant, bitter poems toward God in her early
years, no rational foundation for reverence. Grace itself
does not provide reverence, but reverence follows from it. It
is no influx of "blind faith" – for Emily Dickinson the
phrase would be a contradiction in terms – but a widening
and clarifying of vision, a true sense of the immensity of
God's power [42] and benevolence; and to this sense reverence was the logical response. Yet when one realized that
this omniscient [43] and omnipresent [44] God's aloofness in no
way implied indifference to the soul He would someday
judge, and that this new consciousness that comprised the
gift of grace was a lens that worked both ways, permitting
the regenerate to be apprehended as well as to apprehend, a

certain uneasiness was added to one's gratitude and one's devotions:

> Of Consciousness, her awful Mate
> The Soul cannot be rid –
> As easy the secreting her
> Behind the Eyes of God.

> The deepest hid is sighted first
> And scant to Him the Crowd –
> What triple Lenses burn upon
> The Escapade from God – [45]

This increased sense of God's omnipotence also affected her attitude toward nature. After 1862 she wrote no more poems resenting the natural world's indifference to human suffering, nor did she write about attempts and failures to find conclusive evidence of immortality in natural phenomena. God is in nature – as He must be if He is omniscient – but His presence is unaccessible to the unregenerate, and for the regenerate such "evidence" is no longer necessary. "I was thinking, today – as I noticed," she wrote Higginson in 1863, "that the 'Supernatural,' was only the Natural, disclosed – " [46] and added to her letter, perhaps to hint slyly that such disclosures weren't made to everyone, two lines, indented to indicate that they should not be considered as prose:

> Not "Revelation" – 'tis – that waits,
> But our unfurnished eyes –

The difference then, as she emphasizes by her use of dashes in the poem beginning " 'Heaven' has different Signs – to me – " [47] lies in the observer not the observed. The signs of heaven themselves turn out to be the familiar ones. Noon, with the sun at zenith, is the type of immortality; [48] sunset, regal, glorious, indifferent, a nightly drama of death and grandeur, is "Omnipotence' inspection/Of Our inferior face – ," [49] the birds' song at dawn, an "independant Extasy/Of Universe and Men – ," [50] seems to be an instinctive testament by nature to the resurgence after death of a force that is both spiritual, the essence of the body and, as in her earliest treatment of the image of the bird, aesthetic, the essence of the poem.[51] The "meaning" of dawn she defined in the following quatrain:

> Aurora is the effort
> Of the Celestial Face
> Unconsciousness of Perfectness
> To simulate, to Us.[52]

But the fact that Emily Dickinson found that the spirit of God manifested itself within the natural world should recall not Emerson but the Puritan tradition behind him, for Emily Dickinson never made Emerson's leap in logic from the premise that God operates in nature to the conclusion that God and nature were identical. Early in her career she had tested that hypothesis and had discarded it. And at no time did she share the transcendentalists' egalitarian belief that the ability to read the book of nature was an attribute of the species and not a grant by the divine. Nature, or one's intimations from it – if they were indeed from it – might reinforce the testimony the elect had already received, but nature did not, could not, testify by itself. To Emily Dickinson the tripartite equation of God, man, and nature at the heart of transcendental thought would have been inane, blasphemous, and naïve. She did not have to go out of her room, let alone to Concord, Europe, or down the open road to see how great a disparity there was between creature and creator, how wide the gulf between man and bug, snake, or hummingbird. She did not confuse the book of nature with its author, or, simply because she had been taught a few words, herself with the print. Responsive as she was to the natural world and to the intimations it sometimes seemed to provide of a world beyond it, she always felt that there was an essential discrepancy between the soul's linear progression from birth to death to judgment, where it might return to the eternal sphere from which it came, and the cyclical life of nature, exemplified daily by the sun and yearly by the seasons, a life secure, unalterable, and forever within the boundaries of time.[53] She might envy the creatures of this world for their innocence of good lost and evil got, for their indifference to the "little Mysteries/As harass us – like Life – and Death –/And Afterward – or Nay –," [54] or for their freedom from the anxieties and responsibilities of the regenerate,[55] but envy only emphasized the difference.

Another category of poems, and these are equally indicative of her sense of the separation of man from nature, are the many verbal portraits – in one of them she specifically invites comparison with a VanDyck landscape [56] – that she began writing during 1862 and continued until the end of her life. These are not poems about the "signs" of nature but are renditions of specific natural facts, exercises in which the poet deliberately tests and displays her capacity to catch and project the object in action. These vignettes – a summer shower, a storm, a snowscape, the moon, a cat's pounce at a bird, a balloon ascending, a railroad train, a spider at its web, a bluejay, a butterfly's flight, a humming-bird, a shower of rain [57] – are virtuoso pieces, demonstrations of her skill with her instrument,[58] language. In several of these pieces the separation of man from nature is the actual subject of the poem [59] in addition to being the premise from which the poet portrays her natural subject. In "A Bird came down the Walk" she tries and fails to establish rapport with nature (the bird will eat worms and politely step aside for beetles, but he takes off at the sight of Emily's friendly crumb) , and in "The Snake" she raises the possibility that a rapport can exist with some of "Nature's People":

> Several of Nature's People
> I know, and they know me –
> I feel for them a transport
> Of cordiality –

but in no poem, including that one, does any inhabitant of this world where birds eat worms, cats eat birds, and spiders' webs are flipped apart by well-trained housewives return this feeling. Her scrutiny of the natural world does not incline her to believe in transcendental harmonics:

> Our little Kinsmen – after Rain
> In plenty may be seen,
> A Pink and Pulpy multitude
> The tepid Ground upon.
>
> A needless life, it seemed to me
> Until a little Bird
> As to a Hospitality
> Advanced and breakfasted.
>
> As I of He, so God of Me
> I pondered, may have judged,
> And left the little Angle Worm
> With Modesties enlarged.[60]

The analogy, made tentatively and humorously, is one applied to nature rather than derived from it, an *exemplum* in the traditional manner of the Puritan – and indeed the medieval – sermon. This technique, and it is a technique and not a revelation, is one she frequently used in her later years, and it is a means by which moral conclusions may be illustrated rather than a god-given, apprehended analogy purposely established in the fallen world to allow natural man to progress from natural to spiritual fact. The spider's web, because it could represent equally a ruff for the nobility of the saved or a shroud for the damned, has the "Physiognomy" of immortality; [61] the violence of storms illustrates the desirability of the grave, where one is at peace and safe from nature; [62] the relationship of moon to tide is analogous to that of God to man; [63] the gentian is used to show us that "Fidelity is gain/Creation o'er – "; [64] the dew's evaporation and unknown fate, whether gathered into air or emptied into the sea, is a prototype of the possible fates, "Transport's instability/ And Doom's celerity"; [65] that await the soul; and the presence and passage of storm that, "like a Bugle," is associated with the day of judgment, emphasizes how the natural world continues on, heedless of "Doom's electric Moccasin" and the "flying tidings" the wind makes church-bells ring out.[66] But these, like her use of bees as pagans [67] or of crows as stuffbudgets,[68] are parables and not intimations or insights. The poet fabricates these relationships between natural and spiritual fact; she does not discover them.

Still for Emily Dickinson, no less than it was for the other major American writers of her time, the place the spiritual occupied in the natural world was a question of great importance. Each spring she shared with Emerson and Thoreau, and perhaps with everyone else who had survived another New England winter, a sense of the spirit's presence, but from that initial impulsive response she was never able to fashion a comprehensive and conclusive intellectual system. Spring, not only because it was the archetypal symbol of resurrection, but also because of the brevity as well as the intensity of its enchantment, sometimes recalled to her her experience of grace, and appeared to reaffirm that convenant and the possibility of entering the New Jerusalem.[69] Anderson, in discussing Poem 1333, quoted below, has an interpretation very different from the one implied here:

> A little Madness in the Spring
> Is wholesome even for the King,
> But God be with the Clown –
> Who ponders this tremendous scene –
> This whole Experiment of Green –
> As if it were his own!

If we take "own" to refer to one's own experiment, i.e., the test one will undergo at judgment (and we have seen that Emily Dickinson did indeed use the word in precisely this sense), and if we assume the phrase "God be with" in line three to mean that God, as opposed to madness, *is* with the clown, i.e., the poet, who has been enabled to try his own experiment, and who has the sense to think not merely of the cyclical drama of spring but of the unique drama in which his own soul will be engaged, then the poem can be seen as an affirmation of the poet's symbolic apprehension of spring rather than a rebuke of his presumption that he can literally *own* nature, as Anderson would interpret it.[70] Emily Dickinson compared spring itself, when she described how her own life was quickened in its presence, to the communion sacrament, an image she had used before to stand for grace:

> Friday I tasted life. It was a vast morsel. A circus passed the house – still I feel the red in my mind though the drums are out. . . .
> The lawn is full of south and the odors tangle, and I hear today the first the river in the tree.
> You mentioned spring's delaying – I blamed her for the opposite. I would eat evanescence slowly.[71]

Yet, no more than the presence can be found through chemical analysis of the wafer, could the source of this "life" communicated through nature be found by observing the facts of the natural world. When she tried to infer the general pattern of nature by observing a particular aspect of it, in this case "Four Trees – upon a solitary Acre –," [72] natural facts remained as taciturn about their mysteries as human corpses earlier had, and she was forced to conclude:

> What Deed is Their's * unto the General Nature –
> What Plan
> They severally – retard – or further – *
> Unknown – [73]
>
> . . .
> is Their's/they bear
> retard – or further –/promote – or hinder –

The "apprehensions" she received from nature were indeed "God's introductions –/To be hallowed – accordingly –" [74] but, she implies through the variant of the second of these two lines – "Extended inscrutably," – one could not ferret God out by tracking down His emanations to any source in the natural world. And in the best-known lines of this same poem she makes clear her belief that nothing in language, nothing in the phenomenalistic world upon which language is founded, can participate in man's intimation of immortality:

> Can the Dumb – define the Divine?
> The Definition of Melody – is –
> That Definition is none –

She goes on to insist that the line between spiritual fact ("Melody") and natural fact – and by extension the line between spirit and body, intuition and science – is a clear and absolute one:

> It – suggests to our Faith –
> They – suggest to our Sight –

And in a later poem states unequivocally that these intimations, these melodies that move her so deeply, will be understood only when death has allowed one to transcend nature:

> One joy of so much anguish
> Sweet nature has for me
> I shun it as I do Despair
> Or dear iniquity –
> Why Birds, a Summer morning
> Before the Quick of Day
> Should stab my ravished spirit
> With Dirks of Melody
> Is part of an inquiry
> That will receive reply
> When Flesh and Spirit sunder
> In Death's Immediately – [75]

199

Nature, then, is not the key to the mystery but the wall that blocks mankind from it; and under the term *nature* Emily Dickinson included the human eye. For from the first she was as wary as were Hawthorne and Melville of the evidence of perception, and aware as they that the mind is apt to create the meaning it thinks it sees. She did not go on to doubt the reality of appearances – her Amherst earth is hard as Doctor Johnson's famous stone – but she did believe that the Reality of realities, though it could be apprehended, did not appear until appearance ceased. The sun she saw from earth was apt, like the doubloon on the *Pequod's* mainmast, to flicker and swerve to the beat of the perceiving will:

> The Sun is gay or stark
> According to our Deed.
> If Merry, He is merrier –
> If eager for the Dead
>
> Or an expended Day
> He helped to make too bright
> His mighty pleasure suits Us not
> It magnifies our Freight [76]

Acquaintance with the "facts" of Emily Dickinson's inner life, the "dead" she is still eager for and the expended day when the sun for a moment shone on her in its full strength, as well as with her habitual use of the sun to denote God, extends the reference of this poem but does not change its primary statement that the mind creates the meaning it tries to draw from the external world. At deathbeds, funerals, and open coffins she had explored the ambiguities inherent in this assumption and portrayed her baffled state and her unsteady, often conflicting, feelings. But she is at times also capable of drawing another conclusion from this fact, one more important for an understanding of her vision of the poet: that the mind has an almost God-like power of creation. "I make His Crescent fill or lack – " [77] she writes of the moon, playfully putting the whole solar system under her control, but she knows that she has only framed a conceit, that the world goes on its unyielding way regardless of our shifting visions of it,[78] and in her last stanza she recalls how in reality both moon and man exist within a common system neither created, neither can understand, and neither may terminate:

> But since We hold a Mutual Disc –
> And front a Mutual Day –
> Which is the Despot, neither knows –
> Nor Whose – the Tyranny –

In the world of art, however, she believed man was the master, the poet standing toward his poem much as God did toward His created world. The modesty of the final clause of her famous aphorism "Nature is a Haunted House – but Art – a House that tries to be haunted" [79] should not prevent one from seeing how close a parallel she draws or conceal her implication that the poet shapes the dust of language and, if successful, breathes life into it. She did not make the specific connection between the creation of poetry and the word made flesh until late in her life,[80] but by 1862 she had already defined "life," as opposed to mere existence, as the active operation of consciousness, the operation that for her resulted in the creation of poetry. Higginson's article, which prompted Emily Dickinson to write him, his "Letter to a Young Contributor," [81] was probably responsible for her raising her instinctual conviction that she was alive only through the act of writing poetry into the aesthetic principle that the true poem is a creation the poet has infused with life. For in his article Higginson dismissed the colorless standard of style Professor Channing had taught him at Harvard and called for a language "so saturated with warm life and delicious association that every sentence shall palpitate and thrill with the mere fascination of the syllables." [82] In a subsequent article that appeared in the *Atlantic* of December 1862, an article

Emily Dickinson must have read because she ended one of her letters [83] to Higginson with a reference to it, he defined the poet's aspirations and the nature of his art still more forcefully, and the numerous descriptive poems of nature, poems of a type she first wrote during this year [84] and continued to write for the rest of her life, would appear to be her response to following the hints and challenges with which Higginson closed his essay:

> If, in the simple process of writing, one could physically impart to this page the fragrance of this spray of azalea beside me, what a wonder would it seem! – and yet one ought to be able, by the mere use of language, to supply to every reader the total of that white, honeyed, trailing sweetness, which summer insects haunt and the Spirit of the Universe loves. The defect is not in language but in men. There is no conceivable beauty of blossom so beautiful as words – none so graceful, none so perfumed. It is possible to dream of combinations of syllables so delicious that all the dawning and decay of summer cannot rival their perfection, nor winter's stainless white and azure match their purity and their charm. To write them, were it possible, would be to take rank with Nature; nor is there any other method, even by music, for human art to reach so high.[85]

By then she was used to reading Higginson closely. The careful attention she gave to Higginson's paragraph on style in his "Letter to a Young Contributor" is evident when one places that paragraph against her well-known statements in her second letter to Higginson (the first one she wrote him after his reply had given her some assurance a correspondence could develop) that for poets she has Keats and for prose Ruskin, two figures whom in fact she scarcely ever mentioned again.[86] But she had good reason to at this point; after calling for a vital style in the passage quoted above, Higginson gave a few hints about his own tastes:

> The statue is not more surely included in the block of marble than is all conceivable splendor of utterance in "Worcester's Unabridged." And as Ruskin says of painting that it is in the perfection and precision of the instantaneous line that the claim

to immortality is made, so it is easy to see that a phrase may out-weigh a library. Keats heads the catalogues of things real with "sun, moon, and passages of Shakespeare"; and Keats himself has left behind him winged wonders of expression which are not surpassed by Shakespeare, nor by any one else who ever dared touch the English tongue. There may be phrases which shall be palaces to dwell in, treasure-houses to explore; a single word may be a window from which one may perceive all the kingdoms of the earth and the glory of them. Oftentimes a word shall speak what accumulated volumes have labored in vain to utter: there may be years of crowded passion in a word, and half a life in a sentence.[87]

Scholarship has in part vindicated Austin Dickinson's skepticism [88] about his sister's utterances to Higginson. No one knows whether it was propriety, coquetry, or insecurity about the maturity of the poems she had sent and was still sending him that made her turn aside a question about how old she was (she was thirty-one) by replying "I made no verse – but one or two – until this winter – Sir – ," [89] but it is evident that she was lying, and by three hundred poems, give or take "one or two." And it is not impossible that it was in order to impress her mentor – surely his article was on her desk as she replied to his first criticisms and his friendly questions about her family life, her educa-tion, her reading, her attempts to publish – that she em-phasized that her lexicon, not the "Worcester's Un-abridged" to be sure, but Webster's *American Dictionary of the English Language*, 1847 edition,[90] was her "only com-panion." True, her sense of etymology and her delight in definition were acute before she ever wrote Higginson, but before Emily Dickinson is consigned to a lonely passage from *aardvark* to *zygote* she might be given credit for artifice and flattery, a few "stretchers," to use Huck Finn's word, that would help her to get the intelligent, informed criticism she felt she deeply and desperately needed.

Apparently she did not feel she could get it elsewhere, though she had two friends, Bowles and Holland, who were editors and who had already published one of the poems she sent Higginson in her first letter – a fact she carefully kept from Higginson then and later – but Holland's dislike of authoresses was well known,[91] and Bowles, however close he may have been to Emily Dickinson, did not inspire that kind of trust. Her reasons for selecting Higginson rather than Emerson, a preference that modern critics, invigorated by hindsight, have deplored, are justifiable once Higginson's sympathetic article, and, perhaps still more important, his stature in the eyes of her most cultivated friends, Susan Gilbert Dickinson and Samuel Bowles, are taken into account.[92] After all, Higginson, no matter how much he subsequently complained about the responses he received from eager "young contributors," asked to be selected. In his article, the tone is encouraging from the outset, assuring the young contributor that there is an audience for new voices, that the average editor is sympathetic – "not a gloomy despot, no Nemesis or Rhadamanthus, but a bland and virtuous man, exceedingly anxious to secure plenty of good subscribers and contributors, and very ready to perform any acts of kindness not inconsistent with this grand design." [93] In addition, Higginson's essay must have led her to conclude that his aesthetic criteria were essentially in sympathy with her own; he asked for economy, for concreteness of expression, and for a devotion to the art one practiced. His reflection that since Latin and Anglo-Saxon were "the two great wings on which our magnificent English soars and sings; we can spare neither" [94] corresponds amazingly well with the first analysis of her actual style made since the Johnson edition became available.[95] But the sentence of Higginson's that seems to have made the most profound impression on Emily Dickinson – despite her protestations to him that publication was as "foreign to my thought, as Firmament to Fin –" [96] – was one in which, in a paragraph discussing how few writers in any age achieve lasting literary fame, he described literature as "attar of roses, one distilled drop from a million blossoms," [97] a metaphor that soon inspired two of Emily Dickinson's most important poems on poetry, "Essential Oils – are wrung –" and "This was a Poet – ," [98] the latter written in the same year Higginson's article appeared.

Nevertheless, two of the principal critics who have written extensively about Emily Dickinson since the Johnson edition was published have both insisted that Emily Dickinson's aesthetic theory, to the extent they felt she ever had one, was fully worked out before she wrote to Higginson and that therefore Higginson's influence upon her work was negligible.[99] One can only insist that close attention to her poetry and to Higginson's essays does not bear their assertions out. For example, the word *circumference,* quite rightly considered to be a key term for the understanding of Emily Dickinson's aesthetic,[100] does not appear in any poem written before 1862, but is found in six poems written during that year,[101] and in July of 1862 she used the term in a letter to Higginson himself in a phrase we shall subsequently consider more closely – "My Business is Circumference – ." [102] The few poems she wrote about poetry before 1862 are an undistinguished lot: tributes to God the master artist [103] and "Mysterious Bard," [104] playful variations on Emerson's theories of poetic inspiration; [105] and the confused and inconclusive attempt below, where in the final stanza both thought and form peter out, to set forth a theory of her own:

> Alone, I cannot be –
> The Hosts – do visit me –
> Recordless Company –
> Who baffle Key –
>
> They have no Robes, nor Names –
> No Almanacs – Nor Climes –
> But general Homes
> Like Gnomes –
>
> Their Coming, may be known
> By Courtiers within –

Their going – is not –
For they're never gone – [106]

In 1861, perhaps because James Russell Lowell, author of
The Bigelow Papers, was then editor of the *Atlantic
Monthly,* Emily Dickinson had felt it necessary to declare
herself a regional poet and to compose a coy avowal of a
homespun New England provincialism she never possessed,
though she came to *think* New Englandly, more New
Englandly it would seem than anyone else around her. If
one has a view of New Englanders as *really* peculiar types,
one can argue that in that ecstatic and desperate succession
of years, 1860 to 1862, she *felt* New Englandly, but eye
never saw all those jewels, crowns, ermines, fancy cloth,
mountains, deserts, and exotic cities in Amherst, Massachusetts. The one poem in which Emily Dickinson seriously
and coherently discusses the poet and the value of what he
creates, the poem "Of Bronze – and Blaze – " on which
Anderson builds and rests his case, presents, in Anderson's
opinion, her belief that the poet can transcend the mortality of the poem by "centuries" if not forever, an assumption
that, if valid, would prove that at least one aspect of her
view of poetry had been formed before Higginson's essay.
To support his argument, Anderson pays particular attention to the following lines:

> My Splendors, are Menagerie –
> But their Competeless Show
> Will entertain the Centuries
> When I, am long ago,
> An Island in dishonored Grass –
> Whom none but Beetles – know.[107]

And yet the poem is susceptible to a very different interpretation if one assumes "their Competeless Show" to refer
to the northern lights that are described in the opening line
and that serve as the subject of the previous stanza, and not
to the poet's poems. Her own poems, the "Splendors" (a

term she uses ironically here when she compares her work to the aurora borealis), she describes as "Menagerie," a word Anderson admits having difficulty with [108] but that surely refers to the tawdry traveling circuses that annually passed through Amherst. Thus her comparison between the transient, grotesque, and flashy human attempts to create exotic entertainment and the grandiose energy of the "shows" of nature is a mocking and invidious one, though the poem *qua* poem slyly contradicts the poet's self-deprecation. By the end of 1862 she knew there was a chance of her ending up far beyond dishonored grass, and during that year, perhaps inspired by Higginson's challenge to the poet, she stopped abasing herself before natural creation and set herself to "distill" from nature that "life," that incorruptible essence, which, if not spoiled in the transfer from natural to artistic creation, she felt would enable the poem to be preserved.

It was not only her poems on poetry in 1862 and those letters to Higginson in which she began to define an aesthetic but also the very fact of her taking up Higginson's offer to be a "young contributor" (perhaps it was his adjective that made her reluctant to admit her age and her many years of work) that reveal the seriousness with which, beginning in 1862, she began to think of herself as an artist, that is as someone concerned with the nature of her medium, with acquiring a craftsman's knowledge of the techniques for working in it, and with her ultimate place among the best of those who practiced it. Though she replied to Higginson's admonition not to publish for the present that publishing was as foreign to her thought as "Firmament to Fin" (she didn't mention that one of the first poems she sent him had already appeared in print), [109] she went on to make clear that she was not unconscious of or unconcerned with the possibility of a final and enduring fame. "If fame belonged to me," she solemnly wrote the man she chose for preceptor, "I could not escape her – if she did not, the longest day would pass me on the chase

– ." [110] Fame, a subject she never raised in her work before 1862, is a major issue in every poem on poetry she wrote during that year and is discussed in many of the ones she wrote on poetry during the years thereafter.[111]

She wanted fame, for her work rather than herself, and she wrote to Higginson for the professional help she felt she needed to achieve it. From the outset she made clear to him why she had written: to get the objective appraisal of an intelligent and informed critic. The opening of her first letter to this eminent man she had never seen is distinguished by its lack of fanfare, coyness, or equivocation. Seizing directly on Higginson's central critical criterion, she asked him bluntly "Are you too deeply occupied to say if my Verse is alive?" [112] As the correspondence developed, Emily Dickinson took pains to prevent Higginson's natural sympathy and tact from interfering with the work she had asked him to do. Perhaps it was his request for a portrait that made her worry that rigorous judgment might melt into paternalistic solicitude, for in the same letter she made her charming refusal, itself a portrait better than any daguerreotype she could have had made and sent, and then drew upon their common equation of poetry with life to make clear as possible her reason for writing him in the first place:

Will you tell me my fault, frankly as to yourself, for I had rather wince, than die. Men do not call the surgeon, to commend – the Bone, but to set it, Sir, and fracture within, is more critical.[113]

By then she was no longer the sensitive amateur, the lonely misunderstood "Emilie" who sought a kindred spirit in commercial Amherst. From the young woman who had learned to use poetry to define, express, and control her deepest emotions, she had matured into an artist who cared more about the perfecting of her talent than any secret sense of power and superiority her talent might yield her. By 1862, for Emily Dickinson, poetry had become an end in itself and the created poem had become more important than the poet's release, relief, or aggrandizement.

It is hard to tell how seriously she took the advice she anxiously sought from Higginson, though clearly, over the years, the correspondence developed into one of friendship rather than professional instruction. Still, despite any irritation at Higginson's private estimation of his "cracked poetess" or impatience at his readiness to advise her to discipline her meter, her rhyme, and her thinking,[114] he is owed the recognition that a number of his published statements, as opposed to his private criticisms to and of her (to the extent they can be inferred from her replies and his own remarks to friends), apparently contributed to some of Emily Dickinson's major statements about her art. Into much of her own work she incorporated his image of the poem as a living creation rivaling the creations of nature. And there is further evidence of the esteem in which she held him: the poem, both a eulogy and a definition of poetry, she wrote to honor the poet with whom she felt a deep identification, Elizabeth Barrett Browning.

That Emily Dickinson made such an identification was no secret. Within a year of Elizabeth Barrett Browning's death three different friends had sent her a portrait of the poet, she told Higginson, asking if he wanted her to send him one of them.[115] One can understand why Emily Dickinson would have found sympathy with this poet who had for years led an equally lonely and circumscribed life and who had then found the ecstatic love that Emily Dickinson had to create by herself in fantasies to which Elizabeth Barrett's actual romance probably contributed and which it may have even inspired. When Emily Dickinson came to write her famous eulogy "This was a Poet," a "tribute" – and the poem shows how far beyond this genre she had progressed – to Elizabeth Barrett Browning, Higginson's image of literature as attar of roses and a sentence of his in an essay published in the *Atlantic* months before her first letter to him returned to her mind: "Literary amateurs go the tour of the globe to renew their stock of materials, when they do not yet know a bird or a bee or a blossom beside their homestead-door." [116] If we are to believe her statement to Higginson "I marked a line in One Verse – because I met it after I made it – and never consciously touch a paint, mixed by another person – " [117] (she then added, and here she does indeed "see New Englandly," "I do not let it go, because it is mine.") , she made no deliberate use of Higginson's words, but obviously they had impressed her so deeply that she had assimilated and transmuted them, a transformation that is a measure both of Higginson's influence and of Emily Dickinson's talent. A transmutation of another source, this time of a few lines by Elizabeth Browning, shows that Emily Dickinson could outvie her own model and makes it clear that she must have read "My Out-door Study," for the lines were quoted in a long article in that same number of the *Atlantic,* an article occasioned by Elizabeth Browning's death three months before.[118] From these lines:

> . . . poet true
> Who died for Beauty, as martyrs do
> For truth, the ends being scarcely two [119]

Emily Dickinson apparently fashioned her famous and far superior "I died for Beauty."

But "This was a Poet" has an importance beyond the evidence it provides of Emily Dickinson's fascination with Elizabeth Browning and of her respect for Higginson's essays. It is a definition of the archetypal poet as well as a eulogy for a particular one, and consequently it reveals a great deal about the aesthetic assumptions Emily Dickinson had worked out by this time:

> This was a Poet – It is That
> Distills amazing sense
> From ordinary Meanings –
> And Attar so immense
>
> From the familiar species
> That perished by the Door –

We wonder it was not Ourselves
Arrested it – before –

Of Pictures, the Discloser –
The Poet – it is He –
Entitles Us – by Contrast –
To ceaseless Poverty –

Of Portion – so unconscious –
The Robbing – could not harm –
Himself – to Him – a Fortune –
Exterior – to Time – [120]

Here the poet does not merely compete with nature, she "arrests" it, removing the natural object from the destructive flux of time, that is from the world to which, by virtue of its being a part of nature and not of humankind, it is in itself irrevocably confined. Not that she is merely reaffirming the commonplace that art survives nature – though to do so would be to reverse the statement she had made a year earlier in "Of Bronze – and Blaze" [121] – she goes on to say that only through the artist's skill and sensibility is nature allowed to survive itself; it is rescued from itself and transferred by means of poetry into an aesthetic, timeless "noon," precisely as the mortal soul, the "amazing sense" of the body is removed outside of time through the grace of divine power, while the body, the "ordinary meaning" is left to rot. God's motive power is love,[122] and the poet's is language; and the poet's unique and saving skill is his ability to sift the resources of language so as to yield words that will correspond to and hence transmit the amazing sense with which each natural object is haunted. The poet does not perceive "truth," in the sense of a deeper meaning beneath the surface of appearances, but perceives an essence, the word *soul* is not really too bold an analogy to make, which he rescues; and the creation of a poem is not an act of intellection so much as it is the saving of a life.

Emily Dickinson's description of what the poet does would

seem to coincide with Emerson's characterization of the poet as one able "to fasten words again to visible things," [123] or of the poet as "Namer or Language-maker, naming things sometimes after their appearance, sometimes after their essence, and giving to every one its own name and not another's, thereby rejoicing the intellect, which delights in detachment or boundary," [124] but the two part company once they advance from their common position that language must be adequate to its object. For the effect of Emily Dickinson's "disclosures" is not to rejoice or liberate the intellect of her audience but to reveal how limited their intellect is and to make them suffer by comparison. With Whitman's aesthetic she had even less in common, as is evident when we contrast her disclosure to the message Whitman announced in his preface to the 1855 edition of *Leaves of Grass*, "The messages of great poets to each man and woman are, Come to us on equal terms, Only then can you understand us, We are no better than you, What we enclose you enclose, What we enjoy you may enjoy."

This discrepancy is to be expected – it is consistent with the aristocratic bias that was a product both of her religious heritage and of her Amherst standing – but it should alert her readers to how little she reflected and participated in some of the major philosophical and political attitudes of her time. When Whitman was comforting the wounded in Washington field hospitals, Emily Dickinson was writing to her preceptor, Higginson, then commanding a Negro regiment in South Carolina, "War feels to me an oblique place – ." [125] And in her definition the poet is congratulated on his ability to be independent of the social and political conditions within which he resides; indeed, his good fortune lies precisely in his possession of riches at once so substantial he need not go to the world to increment them and so insubstantial, so incorporeal, that he cannot be despoiled by either time or humankind. To himself his gift is the immortality he gains through creating the poem and through his continued existence, in spirit, in it. To his reader, vulnerable, mortal, and imperceptive, his gift is an emotion compounded of envy and awe.[126]

It is a wry gift, a gift with a sting, and is no more than a by-product of that immortality it is the poem's function and the poet's reward to manufacture, a reward, as another poem inspired by Higginson's article indicates, that is not lightly won:

> Essential Oils are wrung –
> The Attar from the Rose
> Is not expressed by Suns – alone –
> It is the gift of Screws –
> The General Rose decay –
> While this – in Lady's Drawer
> Make Summer, when the Lady lie
> In Spiceless Sepulchre [127]

The poem is an elaborate web of juxtapositions and connections: the rack and the flower, the drawer and the tomb, the corpse turned to dust and the desiccated, fragrant petals in the sachet, the simultaneous tensions and fusions between inflicted pain and released pleasure that organize the first stanza and find their fullest concentration and power in "expressed," a word that is worked down to the root to pry out its ambiguities. The poem broadens when one applies to it a knowledge of the poet's characteristic images and habits of life. Holding very closely to her central image, the poet tells her readers what ladies who garden know by August, that Suns are not enough, that they wither the roses they have raised, that even at the height of blooming the garden's odor, or essence, is faint beside attar. The balance between divine inspiration and human craft is drawn, and the weight falls heavily toward our nearer side. With the creation of the rose, and of its perceiver, the sun's part is done; to preserve the essence, the rose-ness of the rose, takes human effort, human suffering, and human contrivance, but the result is an attar richer than any that emanates freely from nature.

213

Like her poem defining the poet, this poem moves from the poet's ability to preserve against time the essence of his subject to the poem as an act of self-preservation. Here the reference to the lady's drawer is sly but specific, a hint of what Lavinia Dickinson would find when she went through her sister's desk after the funeral; the distilled essence of a life, the impalpable sensed, caught, purified by the poet's consciousness, and by the pressure of the power of that consciousness condensed to form the poem. As she carefully bound her poems into the packets that comprised her "letter to the world," she must have assumed that someday the letter would be read. Certainly Howells in his review of the first edition of Volume I of Emily Dickinson's poems assumed they were written for publication. ". . . it was evident that she wished her poetry finally to meet the eyes of that world which she had herself always shrunk from." [128] In the closing stanza of her "letter" she explains to future readers the strategy she decided upon during her lifetime, to avoid the complications of notoriety, to trust to fame:

> This is my letter to the World
> That never wrote to Me –
> The simple News that Nature told –
> With tender Majesty
>
> Her Message is committed
> To Hands I cannot see –
> For love of Her – Sweet – countrymen –
> Judge tenderly – of Me [129]

The distinction Emily Dickinson made between fame and notoriety is consonant with and ultimately dependent upon the Puritan discrimination between the elect and the unregenerate, who heedlessly gather up their treasures in the wrong place and limit themselves to seeking recognition from their own kind. Temperament had made her too fastidious and grace had given her too great a moral intelligence to join in a scramble that against the backdrop of eternity seemed ludicrous [130] and with eternal renown a possibility seemed pathetic and even contemptible.[131] In addition, the very source of poetry made its exploitation a sacrilege. To trade on that combination of divine inspiration and the human imagination's god-like and god-given power was to indulge in the shoddiest and most degrading type of profiteering, as she made clear in her most forthright poem against publication.[132] Higginson, though he would not have defended her refusal to publish by referring to what was for him an outdated, even reactionary, theology, would have applauded her integrity, for in 1864 he was himself troubled by the effects of early fame upon the talent of one of his protégées, Harriet Prescott Spofford, whose literary career he had launched and one of whose stories he had, in fact, recommended to Emily Dickinson; [133] and he wrote to Harriet Spofford a severe warning against "that fatal cheapness of immediate reputation which stunts most of our young writers, making the rudiments of fame so easy to acquire, and fame itself so difficult – which dwarfs our female writers so especially." [134]

By 1872, however, Higginson was ready to expose Emily Dickinson to the perils of the public eye, and apparently by then others had tried to lead her to this dangerous temptation. Or so she told Louise Norcross, describing a "Miss P." to whom Higginson may have mentioned her, "Of Miss P—— I know but this, dear. She wrote me in October, requesting me to aid the world by my chirrup more. Perhaps she stated it as my duty, I don't distinctly remember, and always burn such letters, so I cannot obtain it now. I replied declining. She did not write to me again – she might have been offended, or perhaps is extricating humanity from some hopeless ditch. . . ." [135] She might at that time have been particularly dissuaded from adding to the sum of female poetry by the recent "chirrup" of her childhood friend, Emily Fowler Ford, whose volume *My Recreations* had been announced in the Amherst *Record* of

October 2, 1872 and had appeared later that month. One wonders if she read, and with what feelings, Emily Ford's introductory verse, "To the Public":

> I am no poet, and I know it.
> But if a wild bloom lingers
> Within my loving fingers,
> From the woods I joyful bring it.
> In my sweet friend's lap I fling it.
> Can you blame me if I show it? [136]

She also resisted the plea of a poet and friend she respected, Helen Hunt Jackson, "You are a great poet – and it is a wrong to the day you live in, that you will not sing aloud," [137] and only after further refusals did she finally give way to Helen Jackson's persistence and allow her "Success is counted sweetest" to be published anonymously in Thomas Niles' anthology *A Masque of Poets,* where it was mutilated by unauthorized editorial changes.[138]

Thus the prevailing taste, her experience with editorial revision, and her own disdain for the public eye supplied her with worldly as well as spiritual reasons for refusing to court a reputation in this life. And before judging her to be hopelessly ethereal or hopelessly mad, one ought to imagine Emily Dickinson being pried out of her Amherst room to be served up to the culturally fashionable on television or through the intimate "exclusive" taperecorded interview, and only then question the sanity of her decision, and only then decide just where neurosis lies. She had, after all, her precedents and predecessors, those anonymous painters and poets of the middle ages, artistic "martyrs" as she called them, who gave up their mortal lives that their essential ones not be obscured.[139] To illustrate – or, to remain consonant with her own metaphor, to illuminate – the relationship between poem, poet, and audience she thought to be the true one, she bent, with a firm and precise grace, twenty-seven words about the common figure of a kerosene lamp:

216

The Poets light but Lamps –
Themselves – go out –
The Wicks they stimulate –
If vital Light

Inhere as do the Suns –
Each Age a Lens
Disseminating their
Circumference – [140]

Anderson's valuable discovery that in Emily Dickinson's
lexicon "to animate" was one of the definitions of *stimulate* [141] makes clear that life as well as light is a major
subject of the poem. But in sophistication Emily Dickinson
has gone far beyond the commonplace of the poem as
lantern in the ignorant world and the poet as lamplighter.
At the same time her image differs markedly from the
striking figure of the poet that Whitman created in his
preface to the 1855 edition of *Leaves of Grass,* "High up
out of reach he stands turning a concentrated light . . . he
turns the pivot with his finger . . . he baffles the swiftest
runners as he stands and easily overtakes and envelops
them." For Whitman is not concerned with the discrepancy
between the poet's mortality (we can see why by reading
"Crossing Brooklyn Ferry") and the larger life of the poem,
nor does he bother with the way the poem will be affected by
the changing perspectives of the culture within which it
continues to live. For him, the poem functions independently of its audience, almost in defiance of it, and at the
same time is inseparable from its creator, is, as the image
implies, a mechanical extension of him. But Emily Dickinson conceived of her connections with her audience as
being at once more intricate and more tenuous. Her poem
presents a series of interdependent factors within a larger
condition: That the poem depends for its intensity on the
vital substance, the "light" – that elemental substance with
which God initiated the creation of His universe – that the
poet transmits from his hand to the poem. If that "vital

light" can animate the poem, the poem reciprocates by both preserving and magnifying the poet's light, making in effect a transfusion of life from poet to poem. But the poem by itself is no sun, as Whitman's spotlight is, that burns unmodified by history. Emily Dickinson, being at once more modern and more reactionary than the transcendentalists, does not share their disdain for the effects of time, and hence of history, nor does she relegate time and history to mere accidents that only disguise the eternal Now. She recognized that the poem was in part determined by the age that read it, that the circumference of its beam of light was modified by the bias of the retina through which it passed, and that therefore the *milieu* participated in the effect if not the creation of the poem. In Whitman's figure the poem is subordinate, being merely an extension of the poet from an eternal to a temporal plane, the microphone by which from the eternal Now he broadcasts to us. Emily Dickinson, on the other hand, limited the poet's role to that of setting the poem in motion, to generating it. She conceives of the poet as the begetter of the poem and hopes that she will bequeath to hers a strong and not a sickly constitution, but she does not assume that poet and poem become coexistent, that the reader holding the Johnson edition will have Emily Dickinson herself in hand. She wanted an audience, but she did not share Whitman's overwhelming need to feel that the poet must be so directly, so intimately present before it. Her strategy both in the conduct of her life and the disposition of her work was to avoid so highly personal a contact, and it was part of this strategy to leave the role of literary archeologist [142] to her sister, and hope that, when Lavinia untombed the poems from the drawer in which they had been laid away, their light, the resurrecting force of their language, would be strong enough to let them live.

But how can her assertion to Higginson, "My Business is Circumference – ," [143] be reconciled with her belief that the poem's circumference is as dependent on the sensibility of the age reading it as it is on "the amount of felt life" that went into its making? The term itself, one generally recognized to be central to her thought, is one she used less pervasively and less ambiguously than her most recent critic has assumed.[144] Its meaning is clear enough; it is the same one she found in her lexicon, where *circumference* was defined, with citations from Milton and Dryden, simply as "the space included in a circle." [145] The problem is not one of inconsistency of definition but one of variety of reference and context. But whether she refers to the mortal consciousness,[146] the immortal soul,[147] the totality of the poem,[148] or to God Himself ("the Stupendous Vision/Of His Diameters"),[149] the word is always used to describe and define an area of comprehension. And she knew perfectly well that in applying this word to One for whom:

> All Circumstances are the Frame
> In which His Face is set –
> All Latitudes exist for His
> Sufficient Continent – [150]

and Whose:

> . . . Eye, it is the East and West –
> The North and South when He
> Do concentrate His Countenance
> Like Glow Worms, flee away – [151]

she was risking a contradiction in terms. Aware that "There is no first, or last, in Forever – It is Centre, there, all the time –," [152] she probably drew, as Anderson has suggested, on Sir Thomas Browne's figure of the circle whose center is everywhere, whose circumference nowhere when she needed a definition and an image of the infinite.[153]

She could have taken her inspiration from Browne, but she did not need to; the figure of the circle with the mortal consciousness as the center, the extent of perception as the radius, and the area of comprehension the circumference was one so felicitous for illustrating and organizing some of the themes her poetry was concerned with from the beginning that its discovery could as easily and logically be attributed to the poetic imagination, whose business and gift it is to make precisely such discoveries. And her extension of the figure from mortal consciousness into the immortal sphere is merely the graphic equivalent of those transitions from the mortal to the immortal estate that comprise so much of her work. That by 1862 she was emphasizing the enhancement of her consciousness, from the "little circuit" of mortal life to the "new" [154] or "full" [155] circumference of the life to come, rather than her successful rise from rags to riches, indicates that her deepening identification of herself as a dedicated artist had made her change her mind about what mattered and redefine where status lay.

Definitions, Emily Dickinson knew, depend as much on what they exclude as on what they comprehend, and the space around and beyond her mortal circle played as active a part in her conception of this image as it would have had she painted figures on canvas and not with words. Beyond and giving shape to the limits of human judgment lay the larger consciousness or circumference one could not have until the line between dead and living, time and eternity, was crossed. When she felt closest to death, the despair that was death in all but body, she described herself as standing on that very line "out upon Circumference – ," [156] suspended between earth and heaven at the extreme range of the light of mortal consciousness. This is the fine but firm line she described elsewhere as that between "place" and "presence," [157] or "Twixt Firmament above/And Firmament below." [158] To look across it, to at least see where alive she could not go and once dead she hoped to – in her early years as a poet she looked to see if anything was beyond the line at all – Emily Dickinson scrutinized flowers, sunsets, and corpses. What she came to find was a barrier, as of one-way glass, through which the Almighty flashed intimations of the other side, intimations whose awesomeness and evanescence confirmed her ignorance as well as her hope:

> An impotence * a Sunset
> Confer upon the Eye –
> of Territory – Color –
> Circumference – Array – * [159]
>
> . . .
>
> impotence/ignorance
> Array/Decay

Through it, too, He flashed what she called "the News," the dazzling heliogram of His grace with its message that someday her own limited circumference might be congruent with His.

The most complex of her poems that uses the term "circumference" deserves a more detailed explication:

> When Bells stop ringing – Church – begins –
> The Positive – of Bells –
> When Cogs – stop – that's Circumference –
> The Ultimate – of Wheels.[160]

Here the figure is elaborated upon in a far more intricate manner, and combined with the idea of circumference is a view of Emily Dickinson's that we have encountered before, that the relationship between God's world and man's is one both of likenesses and of opposites. God's hardest blows, she learned early, could be construed and justified as lessons, and as a teacher He seemed to alternate between instruction by analogy and by negative example. Certain events accessible to mortal mind – sunsets, seasonal cycles, etc. – were analogues of the immortal estate; others – suffering, humiliation, restriction, the inevitability of death itself – gave man a lively anticipation and appreciation of the rewards of the life to come. The poem above depends in part upon such an interplay of opposition with similitude.

In it the relationship of mortal to immortal circumference is introduced by a particularly appropriate analogy, that of church bells, themselves concluding in a circular shape. Without the bells, Amherst will not go to its churches; without their ceasing, Amherst will not hear its ministers above the din. Whether we prefer reference to grammar ("Transitive") or photography ("Positive"), the implication is of a shift from one state to its opposite: Sound gives way to silence; the act of gathering to worship is replaced by worship itself. And the parallel structure of the two definitions that comprise the poem allows, indeed directs, the reader to set up the proportional equation bell is to church as cog is to circumference. The connection is evident: The cessation of the one is the condition for the initiation of the other. Yet the second half of the equation offers difficulties: Both cogs and wheels have a circumference, and the function of each is to move. Their relationship is one not of opposites but of analogies. But paradoxically, though the function of the cogwheel is to move, it achieves its ultimate extension when it moves no longer. The point is that what is nonsense in machinery makes supreme sense in mortal life, where man gains his ultimate when he ceases the function for which he is designed. Thus, just as the bell calls the worshipper to church but prevents him from partaking of church until its tolling ceases, so does the motion of mortal man, of his blood but more significantly of his consciousness, lead man toward that greater circumference which will be achieved only when both these human motions stop. That moment would be an infinite extension of perception for which, as she suggested when congratulating the sculptor Daniel Chester French on his newest and most renowned creation, the statue of John Harvard that is still in Harvard Yard, one's feeling of extended perception in the presence of great art is the most fitting analogy. Today it is ironic, even lugubrious that this same statue, painted blue year after year since Emily Dickinson's time by Yale undergraduates, should have been said, even out of politeness, to arouse that combination of terror and amazement with which Emily Dickinson reacted to the dead, the poetry she most loved,[161] and the prospect of immortal life.

The form that life would take, or, more precisely, the form one would take in it, was a subject about which both Emily Dickinson and her brother remained intensely curious, immoderately so in the opinion of their mother, who, as her eldest daughter once told Higginson, "does not care for thought – ." [162] "Austin and I were talking the other Night about the Extension of Consciousness, after Death and Mother told Vinnie, afterward, she thought it was 'very improper,' " [163] she wrote Mrs. Holland in 1880. For one to whom the equation of consciousness with life was literally true, to whom, as she wrote Maria Whitney after nearly twenty-five years of adult life in the Dickinson house on Main Street, "Consciousness is the only home of which we *now* know," (and then added, to show that the severity of the adjective did not mean she wanted to leave her real residence, her "fairer House than Prose –," [164] "That sunny adverb had been enough, were it not foreclosed," [165]) the question of the shape in which one survived the passage to eternity was not just an academic one. The reason is understandable: No tenant who had invested so much in her powers of perception would wish to be terminated with her lease.

What she wanted to know was whether the consciousness through which the substance of poetry was apprehended and the poem itself created would be dissolved with the body or preserved with the soul. The question, central equally to her aesthetics and her theology (a distinction she herself wouldn't have drawn) involves the relationship of soul to consciousness and the nature of each, and its answer has implications concerning the mode, source, and veracity of the poet's apprehension of what he perceives. The fact that she used the terms *soul, spirit,* and *consciousness* interchangeably to denote whatever of the mortal being persists after death may indicate that she observed no essential distinction between them.[166] Certainly when she wrote to Mrs. Holland in 1878 "How unspeakably sweet and solemn

– that whatever await us of Doom or Home, we are mentally permanent" [167] and described immortality, "the Disk to be – ," as "Costumeless Consciousness – ," [168] she was arguing for the persistence of something fundamental to the poetic faculty, and the famous analogy she drew for Higginson, "A Letter always feels to me like immortality because it is the mind alone without corporeal friend. Indebted in our talk to attitude and accent, there seems a spectral power in thought that walks alone – ," [169] shows she felt that the power with which the poet could inform human language was related to the power – love was one mode of it, beauty another [170] – with which God had informed human life. She would, she believed, survive as pure poet, and only as that; that power through which birds, beetles, snakes, citizens, the faces of the dead and the hearts of flowers had revealed their "amazing sense" to her narrow scrutiny would, if its vessel passed the test she had been elected to receive, return, unlimited by mortal lens, to the eternal infinite that had created it, to the "thought" of which the living poet was but "Corporeal illustration": [171]

> This Consciousness that is aware
> Of Neighbors and the Sun
> Will be the one aware of Death
> And that itself alone
>
> Is traversing the interval
> Experience between
> And most profound experiment
> Appointed unto Men –
>
> How adequate unto itself
> It's properties shall be
> Itself unto itself and none
> Shall make discovery.
>
> Adventure most unto itself
> The Soul condemned to be –
> Attended by a single Hound
> It's own identity.[172]

The opening stanza impressively affirms and validates the poet's perception by stating that it is his immortal part, the aspect of him that will confront his judgment and will be judged, and therefore is not fanciful but essential. In *The Poet* Emerson likewise related the artistic to the religious vision, but at the end of the first stanza, at the word *alone,* Emily Dickinson and the transcendentalists part company, the one to merge with a greater soul even before life is done, the other to wait, and to be tested. As the final stanza indicates, Emily Dickinson, not a lady to dismiss herself lightly, wanted no part of such indiscriminate merging but was resolutely insistent on holding her "self," her "Shaggy Ally" [173] – for she seems to have recalled her walks with her Newfoundland, Carlo, when she wanted a figure for the relationship of soul to identity – and her soul intact.[174]

Identity trails at the heels of the soul, but consciousness, "her awful Mate" [175] walks with her arm in arm. The adjective, stemming from *awe,* is meant to be not pejorative but paradoxical, uniting feelings normally conceived of as opposed, though no Puritan would have been startled by her contention that consciousness incorporates the pangs of conscience and cannot be separated from them.[176] To be conscious was to suffer, for the intuitive faculty through which "Mightiest Things/Assert themselves" [177] was also the route through which pain, remorse, grief, loneliness, and the overwhelming fear of damnation invaded the psyche, and Emily Dickinson, for all her ecstatic moments, would have sympathized with Eliot's famous statement that "only those who have personality and emotions know what it means to want to escape from these things." [178] But no matter how deeply she had suffered and despaired, or how keenly the memory of those times still tormented her – and she wrote about the torture and persistence of memory until the end of her life [179] – she was aware that:

No Drug for Consciousness – can be –
Alternative to die

Is Nature's only Pharmacy
For Being's Malady – [180]

Once granted, consciousness, that inner ear which picks up indiscriminately both the resonance of the soul and the sickness of the heart, was apparently inextinguishable and indivisible. Even the attempt to "abdicate" [181] consciousness through immersion into what would seem the opposite, the active life of "experience," was itself a mental activity:

Experience is the Angled Road
Preferred against the Mind
By – Paradox – the Mind itself –
Presuming it to lead

Quite Opposite – How Complicate
The Discipline of Man –
Compelling Him to Choose Himself
His Preappointed Pain – [182]

The consolation, for her to whom the fate of the soul after death was a "Drama" and not a foregone "Tragedy," [183] was that this faculty which brought to her so sharply and directly the pains and limitations of human life was also the faculty that made her "alive" beyond the normal circumscribed, mechanical existence. Moreover it was precisely through this faculty that she became aware of the force that had allowed her to be a candidate for the life to come, the force of which poetry that itself "breathed" was the outward and visible sign. Only those endowed with life could create life, she came to believe, and found in her talent hope if not assurance. That consolation was enough – she was well off and she knew it, as her many assertions about her wealth and the comparative poverty of most of Amherst testify – and the price to be paid was, though steep, a just one. "To have lived is a Bliss so powerful – we must die – to adjust it – " she wrote in 1877 to console a friend in his bereavement, "but when you have strength to remember that Dying dispels nothing which was firm be-

226

fore, you have avenged sorrow – ." [184] Time would tell, she knew, whether she had given her poems the strength to survive, and eternity would assay the firmness of her soul. In this life she had come to find God generous with His own, allowing her, as poet, to come as close as mankind could to playing the part of life's creator. As for the next life, she could only hope, but the bliss of this one justified any risk; and at least she was sure now that God was no usurer but had bargained in good faith and would deal fairly. Mr. Dickinson, by then somewhere far beyond his daughter's circumference – if he were in that "new house" which "though it was built in an hour . . . is better than this" [185] where Emily Dickinson had confidently assigned him – would have approved.

Conclusion

When I began this study of Emily Dickinson's work I had
no thesis beyond the assumption that human beings are
coherent, if not consistent, and that if they are artists their
coherence is reflected by the subjects they are habitually
concerned with and the ways in which they characteristically concern themselves with them. To the objection that
people change their minds – and any retrospective exhibi-
tion will bear out the fact that painters and sculptors as
well as poets change theirs – one can reply that while the
mind changes it does not alter, a word reserved for describing the brutal and unnatural effects of such intrusions as
lobotomies, or other operations less delicate than those of
the poetic sensibility. But until the Johnson editions of
Emily Dickinson's poems and letters appeared, it was not
possible to speak with much assurance – though a great
deal was said – about Emily Dickinson's sensibility, what it
was like, how it developed; no one was entirely sure either
of what Emily Dickinson actually wrote or of the order in
which she wrote it. So when, after a delay of just over one
hundred years, the Emily Dickinson retrospective show
opened, I thought I would see what I could see.

It was natural to expect that her work would show some development – the poems we have do extend over a period of twenty-eight years, and even a mind far less receptive than hers would, one assumes, have modified its views about something – but it was surprising to find that her work fell into such definite periods and, what is more, periods that seemed to have some connection with what we know of her life. Four such periods could be distinguished: a period of questioning in which she tried and failed to find conclusive evidence of that immortal estate she was told would compensate her for all that God and the mores of nineteenth century Amherst made human souls and un-married daughters of good family put up with here below; a period where, in resentment and defiance fierce to the point of heresy, she chose and indeed created (doing both quite without his permission) her own god, the Reverend Charles Wadsworth, who was promptly packed off to San Francisco by vigilant and higher powers; a period of de-spair, in every sense of this word she herself chose so care-fully; and, finally, a period in which all her wrongs were righted, in which the adversity that had seemed to be malignant was revealed to be instructive, and revealed in the way her heritage, her schoolmistresses, and her father had told her she could hope for if not expect, through God's own grace. The discovery of this pattern in her work was unexpected, but it made sense, more sense at least than had the wild vacillations found when reading her poetry at random or even in Johnson's order within any given year. And when, if her poems, her letters, and Johnson's dating were to be trusted, it turned out that her "despair," her conversion, and her decision to dedicate herself to becom-ing a major poet all occurred in 1862, the year in which, because of the sheer number of poems written in it, commentators have been forced to assume was a significant one, I was convinced that this pattern held.

If it does, and I hope I have shown it does, subsequent discussions of Emily Dickinson's work can at least proceed from a firm and common basis. At the same time, certain assumptions about Emily Dickinson will have to be changed and others be regarded with more confidence. For example, if her development is as I have described it, then the Biblical tropes and Puritan terms in her poetry are there because she believed in the concepts behind them and not because she found them useful tools for structuring and ordering experiences and beliefs for which they were not originally designed. Emily Dickinson's transcendentalism (or the watered-down version of it that lies behind her early poems about the intimations of nature) was a passing fancy, but Puritanism became a conviction and her commitment to it, as her white gown – a typically "slant" demonstration of truth – would have revealed to anyone with the wit to catch on, was absolute. And it is time to lay all the alleged lovers, of either sex, to the rest their upright conduct deserves. Wadsworth, I believe, did matter a great deal to Emily Dickinson's work, but that influence, profound while it lasted, was none of that worthy's doing. At the same time, Higginson should be given more credit; whatever literary historians may think of him, and whatever students of Emily Dickinson may think of his editing, his essays if not his letters did help Emily Dickinson to formulate many of her own aesthetic principles.

Her letters to him are a curious blend of coyness and hard-headed professionalism, but that is precisely her flavor. Toward Higginson the officer and gentleman she displayed the same calculated artlessness, the same dissembling pretense of helplessness and coquetry she used toward the world at large, telling him what she figured he wanted to hear and fitting herself to her sense of what he expected. But toward Higginson the critic she could be quite direct, even blunt, reminding him that she wanted advice and not sympathy and politely refusing the advice he sent when it would not work for her. For she was a pro, albeit a genteel one, and not a naïve and native warbler, who took her work seriously and did not leave its survival – or her own for that matter – to chance. Quite the contrary, she left it, this "estate real and personal," to Lavinia and through her to the world to which, during her lifetime, she had presented the faces required of her. In her early poems in particular she reveals how keenly she felt herself to be restricted, how both God and man required her to cut a properly submissive figure; later, with that fine economy which is by no means the least New England thing about her, she converted masks and manners from obligations to protections, means of keeping the world at its proper distance and of getting one's own work done.

This artfulness, this respect for artifice and calculation, shows Emily Dickinson at her most feminine. It is a mistake to locate the female side of this "poetess" in those sentimental excesses and "graveyard" tremors she was told young lady poets ought to feel and to write down, just as it is a mistake to say that ecstasy is feminine but irony is not. To be sure, impulsiveness is charming – until one pays the bills for impulse buying – but Emily Dickinson was no less of a woman because she checked her impulses out and gave whatever deal was offered a careful lookingover before consenting to it. To Amherst she never consented, though she outwardly gave in to its demands and quietly detested the "citizens" who forced her to do so. She did not consent even to God sight unseen – for some time she would not even receive him but with Yankee thrift and ingenuity she made herself a substitute out of material one would have thought to be intractable – until He came to call in person, and then only because He came with proof irrefutable that His offer held good.

Like all artists, she had a talent for turning adversity to account, but to this talent she added something of the housewife's skill and the lawyer's acumen. She came to share her father's beliefs, but she seems from the first to have shared his legalistic temperament. She was litigious by nature; again and again her poems are concerned with rights, rules, justice, arbitration, redress, evidence, spheres of authority, contracts, settlements, inheritances, and loopholes. When resentment and protest are qualified by respect for propriety and impulse qualified by shrewdness, one takes one's quarrels not to the whaling grounds but to the law courts. In addition she respected neatness, taste, and order, was a fastidious woman who loved to assign things to their proper categories and to fix the boundaries within which relationships, whether with society, nature, or God, are fittingly kept. She was tidy; she observed forms, both in her life and in her poetry, and though she was sometimes anarchic within these forms she would not break them. She disliked muddle, disliked nature untamed and unsurveyed, disliked people who overlooked distinctions, whether these people were transcendentalists or vulgar citizens, despised people too stupid to know their place. In the long run, transcendentalism could never have satisfied her: It was too messy, and too democratic, that is to say too presumptuous.

For perhaps, after all, the most important generalization to be made about Emily Dickinson is the one on which all her commentators agree – and then too readily dismiss – that she was a lady, a point she made clear to Higginson in that blunt and bold letter she first wrote him by enclosing her calling card in place of a signature. It was a point Higginson accepted and respected; when he wanted to clinch his argument that she should get out of the house and come to Boston, he assured her "all ladies do." She had a cultivated taste for fine wines, rare dress materials, expensive jewelry, rich perfumes and exotic ports-of-call. Her love of ceremony, her attention to the refinements of emotion, her sense of the proprieties to be observed with others, including God, and by others, her discriminating mind and eye, all these are the attributes of an aristocrat, secure in and sensitive to her class, a person who feels that everything has its proper place and that her proper place is in or near the top. Her decision to abjure the fuss and public display attendant on fame and to set the terms and conventions within which she would display herself at all was ladylike in its fastidiousness as well as practical in its effect.

When that fastidiousness was trained upon language, the

result was definition, when on men, the result was manners. And most of her poems are either poems of definition or poems of confrontation (if among the latter are included those in which she deliberately turns her back). In either case, they are poems in which a knowledge of propriety is of supreme importance. One can see, then, how Puritanism, with its legalistic bias, its concern for right behavior within conventions agreed upon and honored, with its innate and to her mind thoroughly justifiable sense of status, would have been congenial to her. Her very bringing-up, and by this I do not mean her religious education, had surreptitiously trained her for it. What lady, after all, would be at home to a God who lacked taste and discrimination? Moreover, and as a poet this aspect of Puritanism would have especially appealed to her, skeptical as the Puritans felt toward human intuition, they resolutely refused to accept a substitute for it, and they saw no opposition or contradiction between genuine intuition and intelligence, beween ecstasy and a hard, clear mind. Like her, they had little use for the one without the other. Her poetry reflects the uneasy harmony, or perhaps it is better to say the resolute counterpoint, within which the Puritan mind tried to hold discipline and passion. Her off-rhymes both reinforce the symmetry of her stanzas and emphasize the vitality and power of an impulse that tries to push both poem and artist aside, as if the poem, like the Puritan heart itself, were a controlled explosion.

To Higginson's criticism that she was "wayward" and disorganized – one can derive his statements through her reply – she answered ". . . when I try to organize – my little Force – explodes and leaves me bare and charred." Since she had written a number of highly organized poems well before mailing this letter, it is reasonable to assume that she is prevaricating in order to reject his suggestion tactfully. The metaphor is more significant; it indicates how intense and disrupting were the feelings out of which her poetry was made. She needed discipline, she knew, and she respected it. That she would turn to Puritanism, the one doctrine that did share her respect for control, order, intuition, and status, and be capable of such a reactionary choice is not surprising. She was conservative by temperament; she took no unnecessary risks; she spied the ground out first if she possibly could, and, judging from the earliest poems she decided were worth saving, when she first started to write she wrote about proper things in the proper way. When she wanted images, she took the standard ones, the solar and seasonal cycles, the winter of death, spring of resurrection, summer of eternal life, and then added more tropes from the Bible: pearls of great price, brides of Christ, martyrs' white robes, coronations, treasures in Heaven, and, by extension, fool's gold on earth. It is not her conventionalism that is surprising but how much she could draw out of the conventions she used. But she did use them, in poem after poem, to a greater extent and in a more consistent fashion than has been generally appreciated. In this respect the poems are more closely related than they have generally been assumed to be, and their settings, that is the times of day or night and the seasons in which the poems take place, of greater significance.

Yet, though she rejected the tone, the taste, and the assumptions of transcendentalism, though she was indifferent to the political questions and issues of her day, she had her own connections with the principal writers of her time. Like all of them, she kept asking "how much can I be sure of?," though, unlike some of them, her need for certainty deeply qualified her desire for assurance. Like them, she asked herself how much she could trust of what she thought she knew and looked to see how she had come to know it. She shares with the writers of the American Renaissance a fascination with the mechanics of perception and a distrust of the result. As she said, she did "see New Englandly," though not in the naïve way she played at seeing in that particular poem. Under the guidance of her first tutor, Ben Newton, she started off trying to see in the newest fashion,

Emerson's, but she ended up by seeing in the way New England had looked at things at its founding. She looked hard, with a clear eye for the ironic and the pretentious, and she wasted no words. She paid close attention to matters her contemporaries attended: what the eye saw, the way and the reason for the way it saw it, and the source of its light.

In this sense, rather than in terms of any specific intellectual movement, she was deeply influenced by the life of her own time; and, in addition, the scientific temper of that time, the great schemes of classification in the biological sciences that had so impressed Emerson when he visited the *Jardin des Plantes,* the increasing emphasis on measurement and observation as technology produced instruments more and more capable of exactness, the insistence on verification, were all congenial to Emily Dickinson's temperament. But she was even more influenced by the style of life she lived in that time, by her position – and her awareness of that position – as Edward Dickinson's daughter and as a woman in her father's masculine world of trade, business deals, litigations, finance capital, and political maneuvering. At one time or another her father was a lawyer, a Congressman, treasurer of Amherst College, a loyal churchgoer, a seller of grain, and a backer of the Amherst and Belchertown Railroad. His daughter Emily spent her whole life in her father's house. She needed to, and, times being what they were then, she would have had to. She was given a room of her own in that house, and she made it do.

Notes

CHAPTER 1

1. Ralph Waldo Emerson, "Nature," *Nature, Addresses, Lectures,* Vol. I of *The Complete Works of Ralph Waldo Emerson,* p. 60.

2. Herman Melville, *Moby Dick, or the Whale,* edited by Luther S. Mansfield and Howard P. Vincent, p. 193.

3. Her earliest editors, Mabel Loomis Todd and Thomas Wentworth Higginson, divided her poems into four categories: "Life," "Love," "Nature," and "Time and Eternity." In her edition of *The Complete Poems of Emily Dickinson,* Martha Dickinson Bianchi continues this method of arrangement. *Bolts of Melody,* edited by Mabel Loomis Todd and Millicent Todd Bingham, uses a different and more complex system. Their method of arrangement of the poems by theme is described in pp. 3 – 7 of this edition. Recent critical studies of Emily Dickinson that have been organized in terms of her themes are Thomas H. Johnson's *Emily Dickinson, An Interpretative Biography,* and Charles R. Anderson's *Emily Dickinson's Poetry: Stairway of Surprise.*

4. Richard Chase, *Emily Dickinson,* p. 8.

5. Genevieve Taggard, *The Life and Mind of Emily Dickinson,* pp. 107 – 9 and Appendix III contain references to these particular events. Further reminiscences of Emily Dickinson have been collected in the section "Supplement" in Vol. II of Jay Leyda's *The Years and Hours of Emily Dickinson.*

6. Anderson, p. 35.

7. *The Poems of Emily Dickinson,* edited by Thomas H. Johnson and Theodora Ward, Vol. I, Poems 1 – 8. Only Poem 4 was preserved by the poet. All future citations of poems refer to the numbering used in this edition.

8. *The Letters of Emily Dickinson,* edited by Thomas H. Johnson and Theodora Ward, Vol. I, Letter 105. See also Letter 77. All future citations of letters refer to the numbering used in this edition. Brief biographical sketches of the recipients of Emily Dickinson's letters and poems as well as of other figures of importance in her life in Amherst may be found in III, Appendix 1 of the *Letters* and in Leyda, I, xxvii – lxxxi.

9. Letter 121.

10. Letter 110. All italics appearing in quotations from Emily Dickinson's letters or poetry are hers unless otherwise noted.

11. Letter 56.

12. Letter 65. See also Leyda, I, 203, entry for June 30, Monday, 1851. Lavinia Dickinson to Austin Dickinson: "Emilie has fed you on air so long, that I think a little 'sound common sense' perhaps wouldn't come amiss *Plain english* [sic.] you *know* such as Father likes." (Italics hers.)

13. Johnson, *Letters,* I, Ch. IV. This chapter covers the period 1851 – 1854 when neither Susan Gilbert nor Austin Dickinson was in Amherst except for short visits.

14. Letter 172.   15. Letter 42.

16. Letter 63. See Letter 113 for Mr. Dickinson's opinions on literature delivered under similar circumstances.

17. Apparently Mr. Dickinson was not above opening her mail. See Letters 106 and 116.

18. Letter 77. The "king feeling" refers perhaps to the sense of secret power gained through her knowledge that she was a poet, or, at least, that she was endowed with the potential to be one.

19. Letter 80. See also Letter 54.

20. Letter 53.   21. Letter 142.

22. Leyda, pp. xx – xxi cites instances of scandal that took place in Amherst during Emily Dickinson's lifetime. See also Leyda's entries for June 26th and June 28th, 1853, p. 278 for evidence of crime, brutality, and violent accident in the community, and *ibid.,* I, p. 199 for evidence of drunkenness.

23. Letter 11.   24. Chase, pp. 42 – 43.

25. George Frisbie Whicher, *This Was A Poet,* p. 85.

26. Chase, p. 70.   27. Letter 110.

28. Whicher, p. 53. Professor Whicher cites Milton's use of Edward King in "Lycidas" in his discussion of Emily Dickinson's letter on Humphrey's death. I would extend the comparison to those of her later poems that mourn the loss of Newton or Humphrey.

29. See postscript to Letter 110 and editor's note, Johnson, *Letters,* I, 236, citing March 24, 1853 as the date of Newton's death. Emily Dickinson's letter to the Reverend Mr. Hale, Letter 153, was not written until January 13, 1854.

30. Letter 175. Letters 179 and 182 to the Hollands, and Letters 184 and 186 to John L. Graves also express similar feelings.

31. Certainly one striking characteristic of Emily Dickinson's poetry, when taken as a whole, is the presence throughout her work of hackneyed and conventional verse alongside of the most personal and original poetry.

32. Allen Tate, "Emily Dickinson," *Reactionary Essays on Poetry and Ideas.*

33. For more detailed accounts of Emily Dickinson's experiences at Mount Holyoke see Chase, pp. 50 – 59; Whicher, Ch. IV. See Letters 15 – 25 for Emily Dickinson's correspondence while at Mount Holyoke. Concerning Emily Dickinson's reluctance to join the church, her roommate at Mount Holyoke, Emily Norcross wrote: "Emily Dickinson appears no different. I hoped I might have good news to write with regard to her. She says she has no particular objection to becoming a Christian and she says she feels bad when she hears of one and another of her friends who are expressing a hope but still she feels no more interest." Entry for January 11, 1848 in Leyda, I, 135.

34. Whicher, p. 8.

35. Letter 35. See also Letters 30 and 36. That she did not follow the examples of her sister, her father, and her closest friends, including Abiah Root and Susan Gilbert, indicates that her refusal was the result of conviction.

36. For further evidence of Mr. Dickinson's extraordinary legalistic approach to religion see Chase, p. 57.

37. Poem 401.   38. Letter 30.

39. Letters 77 and 80.

40. Letters 96, 154, and 46 from which the following passage is taken. "I have just come from Church, very hot and faded, having witnessed a couple of Baptisms, three admissions to church, a Supper of the Lord, and some other minor transactions time fails me to record."

41. Letter 158. In Letters 193 and 194 ("Presume if I met with my 'deserts,' I should receive nothing. Was informed to that effect today by a 'dear pastor.' What a privilege it is to be so insignificant!") she shows a humorous resentment at the minister's opinion of his congregation's unworthiness. The "dear pastor" referred to is probably Edward Strong Dwight who was pastor of the First Church of Christ in Amherst from August of 1853 to September of 1860. Another resident of Amherst described Dwight as "a pretty nonentity . . . a very tedious – powerful imbecile of a Preacher." Leyda, I, 314. And still another, more restrained, but not uncritical wrote in her diary "He is stiff & set in his appearance. . . . He is very precise and uses a great many words." *Ibid.*, I, 334.

42. Letter 96.   43. Poem 465.   44. Letter 142.

45. Letter 85.

46. Letter 35. See Letter 36 for similar descriptions of the "change."

47. Letter 35.   48. Letter 35.   49. Chase, pp. 22 – 23.
50. Letter 173.   51. Letter 85.   52. Poem 125.

53. MacGregor Jenkins, *Emily Dickinson Friend and Neighbor.*

54. Henry W. Wells, *Introduction to Emily Dickinson.*

55. E.g., Genevieve Taggard.   56. Poem 146.

57. Poems 101 and 132.   58. Poem 151.

59. Poem 442. See also Poems 85 and 106 and Letter 233.

60. Poem 70.   61. Poem 214.   62. Poem 67.

63. Letter 69.   64. Chase, pp. 33, 43 – 50, 64, 99.

65. Apparently Emily Dickinson was not alone in having an effusive and voluminous correspondence. Letter 71, to Austin, mentions that Abby Wood had written "a letter of *16* pages to Eliza Coleman last week, and had just received one of *ten* in return."

66. Letter 85.   67. Letter 30.   68. Letter 73.

69. Letter 195 (". . . our man, Dick, lost a little girl through the scarlet fever. . . . Ah! dainty – dainty Death! Ah! democratic

Death! Grasping the proudest zinnia from my purple garden,
– then deep to his bosom calling the serf's child!") written in
1858, reveals the essential callousness of one who still confuses
sentimentality with feeling.

70. Letter 179.   71. Letter 184.

72. Letter 63. Letter 62, also to Austin, recounts a dream on
the same subject.

73. Letter 50.   74. Letter 182.   75. Letter 166.

76. Chase, p. 94.

77. Johnson's explanation. Johnson, *Emily Dickinson,* p. 57.

78. Letter 174.   79. Letter 178.   80. Letter 179.

81. Letter 182.   82. Letter 86.   83. Letter 191.

84. Letter 202.

85. The first reference we have to Emily Dickinson in the
character of "The Queen Recluse" is in a letter of Samuel
Bowles to Austin Dickinson written in 1863, probably in March.
Leyda, II, 76.

86. Chase, p. 104.

CHAPTER 2

1. The few poems extant of earlier date have been preserved
by other sources. See Poems 1 – 4.

2. Letter 190.   3. Letter 199.   4. Poems 143 and 148.

5. The clearest and most assured statement of the validity of
the poet's intuition of immortality is made in Poem 4, one of the
few poems extant written before 1858. See also Poems 48 and 97.
In Poem 191, in which again the bird is used as the symbol of
the poet's intuition, she argues that uncertainty is preferable,
and affects to *choose* not to ask her intuition to give her a definite answer.

6. Benjamin Newton had sent her a copy of the 1847 edition
of the *Poems* in 1850, cf. Johnson, *Emily Dickinson, An Interpretative Biography,* p. 72, and Whicher, *This Was A Poet,* p. 89. See
also Letter 750, written in 1882 not long after Emerson's death.
". . . the Ralph Waldo Emerson," she writes, " – whose name
my Father's Law Student taught me, has touched the secret
Spring."

7. Ralph Waldo Emerson, "The Poet," *Essays: Second Series,*
Vol. III of *The Complete Works of Ralph Waldo Emerson,* p. 7.

NOTES: CHAPTER 2

8. *Ibid.,* p. 5.

9. Poem 95. For poems with a similar theme see Poems 96, 132, 205.

10. Poem 155. 11. Poem 157. 12. Poem 214.

13. Poem 122.

14. Emerson, "Nature," *Complete Works,* I, 28.

15. Leyda, *The Years and Hours of Emily Dickinson,* I, p. liii, briefly describes the relations between the Hitchcock and Dickinson families. The Hitchcocks entertained the Dickinsons on several occasions, *ibid.,* I, pp. 161, 289, and Lavinia Dickinson and Jane Hitchcock, Edward Hitchcock's daughter, were intimate friends, *ibid.,* I, p. 163, and pp. 191–99. Leyda also states that "ED is known to have corresponded affectionately with all members of the family, but nothing of this is now among the Hitchcock papers at Amherst College," *ibid.,* I, liii.

16. Edward Hitchcock, *Religious Lectures on Peculiar Phenomena in the Four Seasons* . . . delivered to the students in Amherst College in 1845, 1847, 1848, and 1849. The titles of the four lectures were respectively "The Resurrections of Spring," "The Triumphal Arch of Summer," "The Euthanasia of Autumn," and "The Coronation of Winter."

17. Poem 22. For other poems in which nature is understood to be emblematic of immortality see Poems 7, 13, 65, 81, 100, 129, 140, 168.

18. Poem 137. Other poems that reflect some uncertainty as to nature's significance are Poems 28, 40, 60, 63, 66, 106, 111. Most of these poems are questioning, wishful in tone rather than disillusioned, but they do not have the definite conclusions about nature found in the poems cited in footnote 1 above. Note particularly the contrasts between Poems 13 and 63, and between Poems 129 and 66.

19. Poem 99. 20. Letter 225.

21. Letter 193. Contrast with Letter 220, written to Bowles in 1860.

22. Letter 207.

23. Letter 203. This was the first of Emily Dickinson's letters to Catherine Scott Turner Anthon, whose intimate friendship with Emily Dickinson was the subject of Rebecca Patterson's controversial book, *The Riddle of Emily Dickinson.*

24. Notably Poems 22, 35, 74, 89, 216.

25. Poem 216. Johnson, *The Poems of Emily Dickinson*, I, pp. 151–55 gives all texts and variants of this poem and a full account of the correspondence between Susan Gilbert and Emily Dickinson concerning the poem.

26. Poem 188. Poem 152 specifically describes her failure any longer to see any symbolic significance in the majestic colors of the setting sun.

27. Poems 40, 57, 79, and Letter 193.

28. The following poems, none of which were written before 1862, seem to me to be of this kind: 311, 328, 500, 507, 517, 605, 824, 986, 1172, 1177, 1279, 1298, 1340, 1356, 1359, 1379, 1387, 1388, 1448 (contrast with 173), 1561, 1575, 1635.

29. Poem 130. Presumably the "sacred emblems" refer to the emblems Emily Dickinson had once believed to exist in nature. For a very different analysis of the poem see Johnson, *Emily Dickinson*, pp. 187–88.

30. Poem 7.   31. Poem 69. See also Poems 88 and 168.

32. Poem 100.   33. Poem 149.   34. Poems 70 and 168.

35. ". . . it [Amherst College] owed its permanence to the scientific renaissance under President Hitchcock." Whicher, p. 48.

36. Poem 185. Enclosed in Letter 220.   37. Letter 220.

38. Letter 217, written to Lavinia Dickinson on receiving news of Lavinia Norcross'es death. Lavinia Dickinson had been at the Norcross home at that time.

39. Poem 201, enclosed in Letter 219. The poem is quoted in full below:

Two swimmers wrestled on the spar
Until the morning sun,
When one turned, smiling, to the land –
Oh God! the other One!
The stray ships – passing, spied a face
Upon the waters borne,
With eyes, in death, still begging, raised,
And hands – beseeching – thrown!

40. Poem 49.   41. Chase, pp. 102–3. Whicher, p. 108.

42. Johnson, *Emily Dickinson*, pp. 205–6. In Letter 11 Emily Dickinson describes her visit to Sophia Holland's sickbed.

43. Letter 86.   44. Poem 465.   45. Johnson *ibid.*, p. 214.

46. Whicher recognizes the possible ambiguity of the second line and anticipates my interpretation of it. Whicher, p. 108.

47. Chase, *Emily Dickinson,* p. 43. See Letter 183 for further evidence of Emily Dickinson's fondness for "graveyard" poetry.

48. Samuel L. Clemens, *The Adventures of Huckleberry Finn,* pp. 140–41.

49. Poem 104. For poems of a similar nature and quality see Poems 35, 39, 45, 78, 94, 96, 136, 169, 192, 205. Numerous poems on other themes could also be used as examples of Emily Dickinson's affinities with the cult of sentiment, as anyone who has read through the Johnson edition can testify. All letters written to female correspondents before 1861 also bear traces of this influence. Letters 10, 11, 86, and 195 are particularly fine examples of it.

50. "Every time a man died, or a woman died, or a child died, she would be on hand with her 'tribute' before he was cold. She called them tributes. The neighbors said it was the doctor first, then Emmeline, then the undertaker. . . ." Clemens, XIII, p. 143. For her own taste in "tributes" see Letter 183.

51. Chase, Chs. I and II and *passim.*

52. Poem 53. For similar poems see Poems 27, 60, 68, 74, 78, 104, 141, 144, 150.

53. Poem 147. For similar poems see Poems 43, 88, 114, 149.

54. Poem 144.   55. Poem 1100.   56. Cf. footnote 53, p. 38.

57. Poem 10. Compare with Poem 7 "Night is the morning's Canvas/Larceny – legacy –/Death, but our rapt attention/To Immortality" and also "My faith that Dark adores –/Which from its solemn abbeys/Such resurrection pours" to see how Emily Dickinson's attitude toward death is a function of her belief in immortality, and to see how vacillating that belief is.

58. Poem 52.   59. Poem 48.   60. Poem 88.

61. Poems 43, 149, 150.   62. Poem 71.   63. Poem 27.

64. Poem 71.

65. Poem 114. In one copy of the poem *go* is italicized. The poem itself, like Poem 144, is inconsistent in attitude, shifting from the assertiveness of the line quoted above to a flirtatious teasing and finally to the outright plea "Father! They wont tell me!/Wont you tell them to?"

66. Poem 160.

67. Poems 7, 9, 22, 24, 30, 40, 53, 62, 68, 70, 78, 98, 113, 117, 163, 164, 192, 193, 215.

68. Yvor Winters, "Emily Dickinson and the Limits of Judgment," *Maule's Curse*, pp. 149 – 68.

69. Poems 127, 141, 145, 177, 193.

70. Poems 53, 58, 68, 78, 98, 144, 171, 195.

71. Poems 75, 119, 127, 141, 145, 146, 177, 187.

72. Poem 177.   73. Poem 187.

74. Charles R. Anderson, *Emily Dickinson's Poetry: Stairway of Surprise*, pp. 229 – 30. I am indebted to Professor Anderson for his explanation of the etymology of "indolent." The irony he finds in Emily Dickinson's use of this word in this poem is not at all the irony I have in mind.

75. Poem 146. See also Poem 87. For a more mature treatment of the same attitude see Poem 874.

76. Poem 119.   77. Poem 141.

78. *Ibid.* See also Poem 145 and, for treatment of the same theme in a lighter vein, Poem 112.

79. Cf. footnote 71, p. 47.   80. Poem 7.

81. Whicher, pp. 105 and 324, and Johnson, *Emily Dickinson,* pp. 76 – 77 give the arguments for this conjecture. Evidence for it on the basis of the poetry of 1861 – 1862 will be discussed in subsequent chapters.

82. Lavinia Dickinson also feared and respected Amherst curiosity. According to Mabel Loomis Todd she had her royalty checks from the sales of her sister's poems cashed in Boston "so that the Amherst bank might not know how much she was getting for the poems." Millicent Todd Bingham, *Ancestor's Brocades: The Literary Debut of Emily Dickinson,* p. 362. Apparently she had no more respect for the professional reticence and honor of Amherst lawyers than she did for that of Amherst bankers, for in the famous lawsuit with the Todds Lavinia hired a lawyer from Northampton to avoid gossip. *Ibid.,* p. 339. That her precautions were justified is evident from the gossip that broke out when the lawsuit was initiated. *Ibid.,* pp. 351 – 52.

83. Poem 165.

84. ". . . she [Mrs. Samuel Mack] was seated next to a door which stood ajar, on the other side of which was Emily, and thus the conversation was carried on without either seeing the other's

face." From an article by Mrs. Henrietta Eliot (daughter of Mrs. Mack) in the *Sunday Oregonian,* March 19, 1899. Quoted in Leyda, II, 120. See also the quotation by Leyda from Clara Newman Turner's unpublished memoir "My Personal Acquaintance with Emily Dickinson," *ibid.,* II, 481, and the selections from the Journal of Mabel Loomis Todd (entry dated September 15, 1882), *ibid.,* II, 376 – 77. Mrs. Mack's visit is said to have taken place in 1866. Clara Newman Turner lived in Austin Dickinson's family from 1858 to 1869.

85. Poem 165.   86. Poem 677.

87. Poem 77. See also Poems listed in footnote 71.

88. Poem 384. See also Poem 613.   89. Poem 175.

90. Letter 65.   91. See Chapter I, *passim.*

92. Letter 268, to T. W. Higginson. "When I state myself, as the Representative of the Verse – it does not mean – me – but a supposed person." I take the term "supposed person" to be synonymous with *alter ego,* a projection of one aspect of the poet's personality.

93. Poem 178 ("I cautious, scanned my little life"), is perhaps the fullest expression of this strategy.

94. Poems 9, 65, 70, 77, 103, 112, 126, 133, 146, 151; Poem 163 "little Gipsey"; Poem 192 "little Heart"; Poems 196 and 215 for images that imply the voice of a child although the word is not explicitly used.

95. Poems 49, 117, 119, 121, 159, 166, 172, 179.

96. Poems 101, 132, 143.

97. Letter from Mabel Loomis Todd dated November 6, 1881, Leyda II, 357. The Todds moved to Amherst August 31, 1881.

98. Leyda II, 76. Cf. Higginson's description of his first meeting with Emily Dickinson in Letter 324a, dated August, 1870. For critical comment on Emily Dickinson's conscious cultivation of a myth and on the place of this myth in American tradition and culture see Chase, pp. 6 – 7.

99. Poem 105.   100. Cf. footnote 89.

101. At least we know that by 1862 she did not consider that these "Emilie" poems represented her best work. Of all the poems she sent to Higginson at that time only one, Poem 324, could be considered a poem of this kind. This poem was enclosed with her first letter to Higginson, and it would not be out of character

for her to be making a sly test of Higginson's critical acumen. By her eighth letter she had the temerity to select one of her starkest and finest poems, Poem 286, "That after horror – that 'twas *us*." The only poems written before 1861 that she chose for her first letter were Poems 67, "Success is counted sweetest," and 86. For a complete list of recipients and the poems sent to each see Johnson, *Poems*, III, Appendix 2.

102. For inferior poems using similar imagery see Poems 22 and 116.

103. "I was lately confirmed in these desires [to write a discourse on Compensation] by hearing a sermon at church. The preacher, a man esteemed for his orthodoxy, unfolded in the ordinary manner the doctrine of the Last Judgment. He assumed that judgment is not executed in this world; that the wicked are successful; that the good are miserable; and then urged from reason and from Scripture a compensation to be made to both parties in the next life." Ralph Waldo Emerson, "Compensation," *Essays: First Series*, Vol. II of *Complete Works*, p. 94.

104. Poems 8, 53, 58, 62, 68, 78, 79, 98, 117, 144, 150, 151, 171, and 192 are clearly based on this assumption. The critic who would see Emerson's theory behind Emily Dickinson's concept of compensation should keep these poems, and Emerson's essay, well in mind.

105. Poems 113, 126, 193, 207. For a slightly more skeptical examination of the same argument see Poem 121.

106. Poem 207.

107. Poem 193. The touch of irony in the first two lines anticipates the more directly critical Poem 167.

108. Contrast Poem 65 with the more qualified statements in Poem 63. See the discussion earlier in this chapter of Emily Dickinson's attempts to find in nature evidence of immortality.

109. Poem 73. Poem 65 shows a similar confidence.

110. Poem 63 (italics mine).

111. Both the stanza and the quoted phrases are from Poem 167.

112. Letter 207.

113. For the details of the publication of Poem 67 in *A Masque of Poets* and its ascription to Emerson see Johnson, *Poems*, I, pp. xxx–xxxiii, and Leyda, II, 302 – 3 for facsimile

of "Success" as it appeared in *A Masque of Poets* and for quotations from the New York *Times* and the *Literary World* reviews. The latter assumed the poem to be by Emerson.

114. Letter 268 accompanied this poem.

115. Whicher, pp. 304 – 5. Poem 135 shows very clearly her belief that "all that could be known at all was known by antithesis." I have tried to show that this assumption is implicit in other poems.

116. Poem 125.   117. Emerson, II, 98.

118. See Chapter I.   119. Poem 135.

120. Poems 10 and 139 are the only ones that imply at all that admission to heaven might be in the slightest degree selective.

121. Poem 98.

122. Jean Calvin, *Institutes of the Christian Religion,* I, 200.

123. *Ibid.,* I, 200.

124. Cf. footnote 103.   125. Letter 319.

126. One of Anderson's chapters is called "Immortality" and Letter 319 is quoted (p. 251) at the beginning of that chapter. Johnson entitled the section of *Emily Dickinson* in which he dealt with her major themes "Flood Subjects" and cited this same passage from Letter 319 (p. 233).

127. She had read Emerson as early as 1849. Letter 750. Poem 214 "I taste a liquor never brewed," written in 1860, was undoubtedly influenced by this essay. See Leyda, II, 20.

128. Emerson, "Self-Reliance," *Essays: First Series,* Vol. II of *Complete Works,* p. 49.

129. Emily Dickinson may have met Charles Wadsworth as early as 1855 (cf. Johnson, *Letters,* I, 289 indicating that earlier attempts to date their first meeting in 1854 are in error), and may have corresponded with him since that time (cf. Leyda, I, 352 and Whicher, p. 103). Emily Dickinson wrote no love poetry before 1860.

CHAPTER 3

1. Austin Warren, *Sewanee Review,* p. 576.

2. Even critics writing before the Johnson edition had observed that a number of poems reflected and described a severe emotional crisis. Chase, *Emily Dickinson,* p. 114 and Whicher,

This Was A Poet, p. 276 and Ch. VI *passim.* Three major studies that have appeared since the Johnson edition locate this crisis in 1861. Anderson, *Emily Dickinson's Poetry: Stairway of Surprise,* p. 293; Johnson, *Emily Dickinson, An Interpretative Biography,* pp. 81 – 82; and Theodora Ward, *The Capsule of the Mind.* Miss Ward's chapter "Ourself Behind Ourself" is written on this assumption. I cannot, as the subsequent discussion of Wadsworth and the "Master" letters in this chapter will make clear, share Johnson's certainty when on p. 80 of *Emily Dickinson* he states "she certainly never made demands on him that were other than proper for a minister of the gospel to meet."

3. Anderson, p. 293.   4. Whicher, p. 95.

5. Leyda, *The Years and Hours of Emily Dickinson,* II, 102.

6. Both quotations in this paragraph are from Letter 268.

7. Johnson, *The Letters of Emily Dickinson,* II, 472 – 76, includes the letters that Higginson wrote to his wife describing his first meeting with Emily Dickinson in Amherst, August 1870. Johnson also includes Higginson's diary entries, a postscript to a letter to his sisters that refers to "my singular poetic correspondent" and a pertinent quotation from Higginson's reminiscences of the interview twenty years later.

8. Letter 268.   9. Chase, p. 104.

10. Anderson, pp. 167 – 68.

11. See Bingham, *Ancestor's Brocades: The Literary Debut of Emily Dickinson,* pp. 16 –17, and Chapters XI and XIV *passim.*

12. *Ibid.,* Ch. XIV.

13. The so-called "Master" letters, Letters 187, 233, and 248.

14. Until recently, biographers thought that this meeting had taken place the previous year. Cf. Johnson, *Letters,* I, 289 for evidence that 1855 is the correct date. Also Letters 178 and 248.

15. Johnson, *Letters,* note to Letter 179.

16. Leyda, I, 352.

17. Letter 248a. Johnson places it immediately after the last of the "Master" letters, in 1862, but says that no date can be assigned. It seems logical to assume that it preceded the visit of 1860 and probably the earliest "Master" letter, Letter 187, which Johnson assigns to 1858. Letter 248a might, indeed, be the first letter she received from Wadsworth – certainly its tone does not indicate a close acquaintanceship – in which case it could have

been written as early as 1855. The only specific events that could
be classified as a trial or affliction in Emily Dickinson's life between 1855 and 1858 were her mother's illness early in 1856, and
Austin's typhoid fever in the fall of 1858. With reference to the
former see Letters 182 and 191, also Leyda, I, 324 and I, xxxix.
Leyda assumes the illness to have been a nervous breakdown. On
Austin's illness, see Letter 195.

18. Letter 248a.

19. Emily Dickinson's letter to James Clark, Letter 773, states
that on this visit Wadsworth was still in mourning for his mother,
who had died on October 1, 1859. In Letter 1040, to Charles
Clark, she says that Lavinia never saw Wadsworth. March and
April were the only months in 1860 when we know Lavinia to
have been away from Amherst (Letters 215 and 217).

20. Letter 773.

21. Letter 203. See also Johnson's note to Letter 222 "Kate
Scott . . . visited Sue on some four or five occasions during the
years 1859 – 1861."

22. Letter 222.

23. After her husband's death Catherine Scott Turner resumed
her maiden name. She did not tell ED of her marriage when she
visited Amherst in 1859, as the last sentence of the passage quoted
above makes clear. See Johnson's note to Letter 222 in *Letters,*
II, 366.

24. Texts of these drafts, and a facsimile of the second, appear
in Millicent Todd Bingham, *Emily Dickinson's Home,* pp. 420 –
29. In Johnson, *Letters,* they are numbered respectively 187, 233,
and 248.

25. Those portions of the drafts which Emily Dickinson crossed
out (a further hint that the drafts were the basis of actual correspondence) have been indicated by brackets.

26. Other critics have been more cautious about identifying
Wadsworth as the recipient of these letters, perhaps because of
Mrs. Bingham's reluctance to do so when she first published them.
The word "presbyteries," here taken literally to mean the church,
Mrs. Bingham feels to be used as a vague metaphor. In putting
forth her argument she neglects, however, to consider the import
of the phrase "holy Holiday" and the allusion to Revelations
7:13 – 14, "And one of the elders answered, saying unto me, What

are these which are arrayed in white robes? and whence came they?/And I said unto him, Sir, thou knowest. And he said to me These are they which came out of great tribulation, and have washed their robes, and made them white in the blood of the Lamb." The remaining verses of this chapter of Revelations are also pertinent here. Poem 325, written in 1861, shows Emily Dickinson to have been familiar with this passage. The failure of David Higgins, the only person so far to have dealt with these "Master" letters at any length, to recognize this passage as an allusion may have contributed to his thesis that the letters were addressed to Samuel Bowles. See David J. M. Higgins, "Portrait of Emily Dickinson: The Poet and Her Prose," pp. 133–34. Johnson, though his article "The Great Love in the Life of Emily Dickinson," *American Heritage,* pp. 52–55, is about the Reverend Charles Wadsworth does not, either in his notes to the "Master" letters or in *Emily Dickinson,* specifically identify Wadsworth as the recipient. Cf. Johnson, *Emily Dickinson,* p. 77. Other inconclusive references to these letters may be found in Ward, pp. 151–52, and Anderson, p. 167.

27. Whicher, p. 324. Johnson himself allows for the possibility that the second "Master" letter may have been written before 1862, for in his note to Letter 248 he writes that "accurate dating is impossible. The letter may have been written earlier, but the characteristics of the handwriting make the present assignment reasonable."

28. Leyda, II, 38.   29. Letter 241.

30. Charles Wadsworth, "A Sermon Preached in the Arch Street Presbyterian Church, Philadelphia on Thanksgiving Day, November 25, 1852," included in *Thanksgiving Sermons, 1852–1861.* I am indebted to John Stewart Wheatcroft, "Emily Dickinson and the Orthodox Tradition," for this information. The following quotation is taken from Wheatcroft's chapter on Charles Wadsworth:

"In cultural matters Wadsworth was an anti-intellectual. His values were rooted in the external, the collective, the organizational aspects of life, rather than in the interior and the individual. Politically, Wadsworth was a chauvinist who used not the doctrine of the Covenant but benighted conceptions of race and naive political commonplaces about democratic capitalism as his sanction. . . . And finally, Wadsworth showed himself insensitive to poetry, strikingly unaware of the nature and function of poetry, and antagonistic to the workings of the poetic imagination." pp. 313 – 16.

31. Poem 387.

32. In particular through *The Scarlet Letter.* Though Emily Dickinson does not specifically mention having read this novel there is a good deal of evidence that she and the rest of the family enjoyed Hawthorne's works and read them as they became available. By August of 1851 Lavinia was reading *The House of the Seven Gables,* published that spring, and Emily had read it by mid-November (Letter 62). Austin recommended *Mosses from an Old Manse* to Susan Gilbert, Leyda, I, 218. "Hawthorne's interruption does not seem as it did" Emily wrote Susan Gilbert a month after the author's death (Letter 292), and in 1879, discussing her estimates of the authors whom Higginson had treated in *Short Studies of American Authors,* which he had sent her as a gift, she says that "Hawthorne appalls, entices – " (Letter 622).

33. Letter 776.

34. Letter 222. See *supra,* pp. 77 – 78.

35. Poems 162, 208, 211, 249.

36. Poems 205, 246, 268, 275.

37. Poems 205, 236, 247, 270, 275.

38. Letters 233 and 248.

39. Poem 211.   40. Poem 213.

41. Poem 212. The image occurs in a similar context in Poems 162, 249, and 284.

42. Poem 246.   43. Poem 236.   44. Poem 273.

45. Letter 233.   46. Poem 270.   47. Poem 271.

48. Poem 199.

49. Poem 296 specifically distinguishes between God's grace and the lover's glory. See also Poems 343 and 349.

50. Poem 245. For another instance of Emily Dickinson's use of such imagery in speaking of Wadsworth see Letter 776. See also Chase, pp. 108 – 9, and p. 79.

51. Poem 232.

52. Poem 239. See also Poems 256 and 498.

53. Poem 262.

54. Poem 546.   55. Poem 299.

56. Poem 430. In her gentle refusal of a wedding invitation in 1884 she refers to India in congratulating the parents of the bride. "With proud congratulation that the shortest route to India has been supremely found." (Letter 900.)

57. Poem 485.   58. Poem 415.   59. Poem 398.

60. Poem 640.   61. Poem 495.

62. Poem 464. See also Poems 418, 636, and 644.

63. Poems 296 and 322.   64. Poems 322 and 387.

65. There are many poems in which Emily Dickinson emphasizes her fidelity. All poems using images of martyrdom and crucifixion also would come under this category. See Poems 275, 339, 366, 368, 438, 456, 464, 549, 573, 577, 611, 640, 648.

66. Poems 260, 295, 474.

67. Poems 225, 322, 394, 549, 553, 561, 573, 1072.

68. Judith Banzer, " 'Compound Manner': Emily Dickinson and the Metaphysical Poets," *American Literature,* pp. 415–33.

69. Poem 387.   70. Poem 400. Cf. Poem 263.

71. Poem 322. See also Poems 226, 260, 295, 325, 336, 344, and 625.

72. Poem 458. See also Poem 532.

73. Poem 474.   74. Poem 640.   75. Poem 495.

76. Poem 464. See also Poems 263, 418, 636, and 644.

77. Poem 294.   78. Poem 348.

79. Poem 1072. I cannot agree with Professor Anderson's interpretation of this poem (Anderson, pp. 182–83) as one referring to an earthly-heavenly marriage, and Anderson himself finds this purported marriage to be "curiously incomplete." For other evidence that Emily Dickinson thought of herself as "married" to Wadsworth see *supra,* p. 87.

80. Letter 242.   81. Poem 225.

82. Poem 264. *Compound* here certainly extends the nature of this pain beyond the physical. In Poem 244, written in 1861, the ache of the soul is contrasted to the ache of the bone in a grotesque juxtaposition of images that points out the poet's awareness of the discrepancy between the proper Miss Dickinson that Amherst saw in Sunday finery and the poet whom God had punished for apostasy:

It is simple to ache in the Bone, or the Rind –
But Gimblets – among the Nerve –
Mangle daintier – terribler –
Like a Panther in the Glove.

83. Poem 252.

84. Poem 1260. The penultimate stanza reads "If 'God is Love'
as he admits/We think that he must be/Because he is a 'jealous
God'/He tells us certainly."

85. Poem 690, sent in Letter 257. In *Poems* Johnson, on the
basis of handwriting, assigns this poem and the letter to 1861. In
Letters, however, assuming that the poem refers to the death of
Frazar Stearns, Amherst's first casualty in the Civil War, Johnson
moves the date up to March, 1862, the month Stearns was killed.
To me, this revised dating seems unwarranted.

86. Poem 281. 87. Poem 241.

88. Poem 272. See also Poems 244, 252, 269, 287, and 292.

89. Poem 412. 90. Poem 292. 91. Poem 278.

92. Poem 281. 93. Poem 286.

94. Poem 258. For a somewhat different interpretation see Anderson, pp. 215 – 17. Concerning the meaning of the phrases
"Heavenly hurt" and "Despair" he writes "It is then a mocking
light, like the heavenly hurt that comes from the sudden instinctive awareness of man's lot since the Fall, doomed to mortality
and irremediable suffering. This is indeed despair, though not
in the theological sense unless Redemption is denied also." Unlike Anderson, I assume that Emily Dickinson used the word with
a full appreciation of its theological significance.

95. Poem 290. I have in every case substituted variant readings
for the ones Johnson has chosen.

96. For an extensive and astute analysis of this poem see Anderson, pp. 47 – 54.

97. Poem 257. For other poems that depict evanescence as the
essential property of beauty see Poems 319 and 430.

98. Poems 219, 228, 243, 265, 266, 291.

99. Poem 273. 100. Poem 258. Cf. *supra,* p. 97.

101. Poem 273. 102. Poem 283.

103. Or so I interpret the last stanza of Poem 287. Anderson
is, I think, in error when he assumes that in this poem "her chief
concern is with the moment of death, however, not with the mo-

ment beyond." For Anderson's analysis of this poem, see Anderson, pp. 235 – 37.

104. Poem 422. For an inferior but related poem see Poem 372. R. P. Blackmur's extensive analysis and low evaluation of this poem may be found in "Emily Dickinson: Notes on Prejudice and Fact," *The Expense of Greatness*. Chase, p. 48, concludes that the poem's argument is "a little more meaningful than Mr. Blackmur senses, though the poem is scarcely better."

105. Blackmur, p. 126.

106. The full text of this poem was first published in *New England Quarterly*, XX (1947), 39 – 40.

107. Blackmur, pp. 127 – 28.

108. Poem 611. See also Poems 405, 425, and 577.

109. Poems 566, 616, 622, 648.

110. Poems 310, 314, 341, 358, 396, 411, 412, 414, 422, 443, 496, 510, and 539 all use death metaphorically.

111. Poem 379.   112. Poem 280.   113. Poem 314.

114. Poem 362.   115. Poem 315.

116. Whicher, p. 101. Anderson, p. 17, assumes that the poem describes "a hell-fire preacher."

117. Johnson, *Emily Dickinson*, p. 237.

118. Chase, p. 204.   119. Chase, pp. 204 – 5.

120. Cf. Jonathan Edwards' descriptions of grace in "Personal Narrative" and Whitman's description of the effects of music in section 26 of "Song of Myself."

121. Poem 410.   122. Poem 565.   123. Poem 556.

124. Poem 396.   125. Poem 650.   126. Poem 384.

127. Poem 341. For thorough explications of this poem see Anderson, pp. 211 – 12 and Francis Manley, "An Explication of Dickinson's 'After Great Pain'," *Modern Language Notes*, pp. 260 – 64.

128. It is significant that her first letter to Higginson, Letter 260, written in April of 1862, begins "Are you too deeply occupied to say if my Verse is alive? . . . Should you think it breathed – and had you the leisure to tell me, I should feel quick gratitude." Her inspiration for this metaphor may have come from Higginson's article, "Letter to a Young Contributor" which she had read in the April, 1862 *Atlantic Monthly*, and which had inspired her to write him. The article contains the following state-

ment: "Human language may be polite and powerless in itself, uplifted with difficulty into expression by the high thoughts it utters, or it may in itself become so saturated with warm life and delicious association that every sentence shall palpitate and thrill with the mere fascination of the syllables." Thomas Wentworth Higginson, "Letter to a Young Contributor," *Atlantic Monthly*, p. 403.

129. Poem 650.   130. Poem 305.

131. Poems 314, 315, 362, 410, 556, and 565, all previously considered, deal with this stage of the crisis.

132. Poem 510.   133. Poem 378.   134. Poem 510.

135. Poem 496.   136. Poem 470.   137. Poem 1071.

138. Poem 510.   139. Poem 419. See also Poem 599.

140. Poem 293.   141. Poems 443 and 618.

142. Poem 443.   143. Poem 618.

144. Poem 654. See also Poems 423 and 521.

145. Poem 187.   146. Poem 519.   147. Poem 612.

148. Poem 443.   149. Poem 382.   150. *Ibid.*

151. Poem 652.

152. The reference here is to Poems 384 ("the liberty of consciousness"), 652 ("prison"), and 411 ("either the inner or outer grave").

153. Poem 652.   154. Poems 430, 485, 584.

155. Poem 657.   156. Poem 652.   157. Poem 414.

158. *Ibid.*   159. Poem 348.   160. Poem 315.

161. Poem 620.   162. Poem 364.

163. Poem 620.   164. Poems 346, 364, 620.

165. Anderson, pp. 199 – 202.

166. Poem 588 ("I cried at Pity – not at Pain – ").

167. Poem 348.   168. Poem 632.

169. Poem 307. Poems 308 and 569 deal with the superiority of artistic to natural creation.

170. Poem 632.   171. Letter 268.   172. Poem 412.

173. Anderson, p. 207.   174. Poem 376.

175. Poem 437.   176. Poem 536.   177. Poem 376.

178. Poem 597.   179. Poem 621.   180. Poem 490.

181. Poems 419 and 576.   182. Poems 540 and 639.

183. Poem 350.   184. Poem 590.

185. Poem 646. See also Poem 623.

186. Johnson prefers the version "I think To Live – may be a Bliss/To those who dare to try –."

187. Poem 574. This illness, ". . . when I went in/To take my Chance with pain –/Uncertain if myself, or He,/Should prove the strongest One." is described as having occurred in early spring.

188. Poem 562.

CHAPTER 4

1. Johnson, *The Poems of Emily Dickinson*, Appendix 3 gives the figure 366. In arriving at my total I have departed from Johnson's practice of including a given poem under the year in which the *latest* draft was written.

2. Apparently Emily Dickinson's work was a topic for joking between himself and his friends as late as 1876, for the quotation is taken from a letter, cited in Leyda, *The Years and Hours of Emily Dickinson* II, 263, Higginson wrote to his sister describing without disapproval a mock-letter from Emily Dickinson that clever friends composed for amusement at a party. Presumably Higginson had shown them some originals!

3. See Johnson, *Emily Dickinson*, Chapter I.

4. Perry Miller, *The New England Mind: The Seventeenth Century*, pp. 25 – 26.

5. *Ibid.*, p. 9.　　　　　6. *Ibid.*, p. 8.

7. Specifically in his essay on Emily Dickinson in *Reactionary Essays on Poetry and Ideas*.

8. *Celebration of the Two Hundredth Anniversary of the Settlement of Hadley, Massachusetts* (Northampton: 1859), p. 79.

9. Letter 425. Dickens' *A Christmas Carol* first appeared in 1843, when Emily Dickinson was thirteen years old.

10. See Chapter III, *passim*, and, for example, Poem 640.

11. Poems 306, 356, 359, 424, 473, 503, 506, 513, 528, 535, 564, 579, 598, 603, 638, 679, 756, 1053.

12. Poems 393, 436, 439, 472. For a more detailed discussion of this theme and for subsequent poems that deal with it see pp. 158 – 63. Grace is mentioned in only two poems (293 and 296) written before 1862. In the first it is only a nostrum for others; in the second the word is discarded as inappropriate for des-

cribing what "one year ago" her beloved had brought her.
13. Letter 200 (italics hers) . 14. Letter 248.
15. Letter 275. 16. Poem 574. 17. Letter 277.
18. Letter 271. The phrase "shunning Men and Women" is presumably Higginson's since she places it in quotes.
19. Letter 261.
20. Letter 280. Higginson's article "The Procession of Flowers," appeared in *Atlantic Monthly,* X (December, 1862) , pp. 649 – 57. The procession refers to a peculiar phenomenon reported by a woman in Cuba concerning a crimson flower called Cupid's-Tears. Each day "she brought home handfuls of these blossoms to her chamber, and nightly they all disappeared. One morning she looked toward the wall of the apartment, and there, in a long crimson line, the delicate flowers went ascending one by one to the ceiling, and passed from sight." To the lady in question, to Emily Dickinson, and to Higginson the picture made a charming emblem of immortality. The actual cause of the procession, as the lady found, was that "each [blossom] was borne laboriously onward by a little colorless ant much smaller than itself."
21. Poem 393. 22. Poem 306. 23. Poem 513.
24. Poem 564. The manuscript has the phrase "the Heavens paused –" as an alternate for "Creation stopped –."
25. Poem 579. 26. Poem 598.
27. Poem 306. The manuscript has another reading " – to a Revering – Eye" for the second line of the stanza quoted above. This reading emphasizes the fact that the "favorites" referred to in the poem are believers rather than poets, and that the basis of election is therefore for Emily Dickinson religious rather than aesthetic. Thus the poem has to do with the soul and salvation, not with sensibility and inspiration, and is not derived from Emerson's theory of poetry or his concept of the poet.
28. Poem 593. 29. Miller, p. 25. Cf. pp. 138 – 39.
30. Poem 638. See also Poems 420, 839, and 1581.
31. Poem 1053. Johnson, using the 1865 version of this poem as his primary text, includes it with poems of that year, but the original version, included by Johnson as a variant, was written in 1862.
32. Poem 1039. 1733, an undated poem, is similar in theme.

33. For example, Revelations 22:17. "And the Spirit and the bride say, Come. And let him that heareth say, Come. And let him that is athirst come. And whosoever will, let him take the water of life freely." And Revelations 22:5, "And there shall be no night there; and they need no candle, neither light of the sun; for the Lord God giveth them light: and they shall reign for ever and ever."

34. For other poems that describe grace as "news" see Poems 827, 1319, and 1360. The significance of this association of grace with language will be treated in the discussion of Emily Dickinson's aesthetic theory in the following chapter.

35. Poems 122 and 128.   36. Poems 355, 614, and 1076.

37. Poem 640. See also Poem 387.

38. It appears in two poems in 1859, none in 1860, three in 1861, twenty-one in 1862, and five in both 1863 and 1864. After 1864 the word is used seldom: in two poems in 1872 and in one in each of the years 1865, 1866, 1871, 1874, 1875, 1877, 1883, and 1884. It does not appear in any of the poems for which no date has been assigned.

39. Poem 343.

40. Poem 508. I have adopted the variant readings "term" in the second stanza and "whimpering" in the third.

41. Anderson, *Emily Dickinson's Poetry: Stairway of Surprise,* p. 179. His statement that mortals do not achieve God's grace through their own choice is, of course, correct, but the choice in the poem involves the will of the elect after grace has been given, or, to paraphrase Emily Dickinson, after its second baptism.

42. Cf. Poem 313, where the "little Circuit" of ordinary life is contrasted to "This new Circumference."

43. E.g., "be thou faithful unto death, and I will give thee a crown of life." (Revelations 2:10); "the marriage of the Lamb is come, and his wife hath made herself ready. And to her it was granted that she should be arrayed in fine linen, clean and white." (Revelations 19:7 – 8).

44. Poems 232, 270, 283, 336, 366, 631.

45. Poems 58, 73, 79, 98, 144, 195.

46. Poem 356. See also Poem 493.   47. Poem 385.

48. Poem 803. See also Poems 373, 377, and 713.

49. Poem 1072.   50. Poem 473.

51. Poem 461.   52. Poems 1495, 1496, 1641.

53. Poem 1495. See also Poem 1297.   54. Poem 1641.

55. Revelations 3:5. In the first letter we have that makes specific reference to Emily Dickinson's decision to withdraw from society, Samuel Bowles' letter to Austin Dickinson in the spring of 1863, Bowles cites this passage, obviously recognizing that it is pertinent. "To the Queen Recluse," he wrote, "my especial sympathy – that she has 'overcome the world.' " The letter is quoted in Leyda, II, 76.

56. Psalm 51, v. 7.   57. Poem 922.   58. Poem 325.

59. Poem 365.   60. Poem 388.

61. For a different explanation see Anderson's comment (Anderson, p. 185) that:

To pin down the exact significance of "White" for Dickinson is impossible. . . . That she chose to dress in white exclusively for the last fifteen or twenty years of her life, probably beginning about the time she composed her poem on the "White Election," offers a fascinating field for conjecture. But she never gave an explanation for it (It may even have been an obscure whim, as with Mark Twain) .

However, Emily Dickinson's own explanation is given in Poem 388, cited above. An article in the *Springfield Republican* of July 25, 1878, and thus printed in Emily Dickinson's lifetime, also assigned various reasons for her decision to dress in white, wondering "whether it be a mourning for a friend, a religious notion like that of Hawthorne's Hilda [see *The Marble Faun*], or, perchance, the result of some decree of fate." The article, inspired by the possibility that Emily Dickinson was the author, or one of the authors, who had written under the pseudonym of Saxe Holm, is quoted in part in Leyda, II, 295 – 96. See also Leyda, II, pp. 239, 297 for other documents pertaining to the identity of Saxe Holm (Helen Hunt Jackson) .

62. Mrs. Todd's letter to her parents, dated November 6, 1881, is quoted in Leyda, II, 357. Cf. *supra,* Chapter II, p. 55.

63. Leyda, II, 472.

64. Higginson originally wrote this article, titled, "An Open Portfolio" for *The Century* to prepare readers for the forthcoming publication of the first volume of Emily Dickinson's work. It was found more convenient to print it in the *Christian Union,* where it appeared in the issue of September 25, 1890. The pref-

ace to Emily Dickinson's *Poems 1890* was taken from this article
(*Ancestor's Brocades,* p. 61).

65. Letter of Austin Dickinson to Thomas Wentworth Higginson dated October 10, 1890. The letter is quoted in full in Bingham, *Ancestor's Brocades,* p. 66.

66. Leyda, II, 295 – 96.   67. *Ibid.,* II, 297.

68. Poem 435. See also Poem 1692 (undated).

69. Poem 479. See also Poems 401 and 1611.

70. Anna Mary Wells, "Was Emily Dickinson Psychotic?"
American Imago, XIX (1962), pp. 309 – 21. The author reaches
no firm conclusion but the terms of her question reveal her
answer.

71. Letter 330a. Higginson goes on to describe the advantages
a trip to Boston hold over continued seclusion in Amherst:
I wonder if it would be possible to lure you [to] the meetings on the
3d Monday of every month at Mrs. [Sa]rgent's 13 Chestnut St. at 10 am
– when somebody reads a paper & others talk or listen. Next Monday
Mr. Emerson [rea]ds & then at 3-½ P.M. there is a meeting of the
Woman's [Cl]ub at 3 Tremont Place, where I read a paper on the
[Gre]ek goddesses . . . – or will the Musical Festival in June tempt you
down.

72. Poem 1054.

73. Poems 952, 1004, 1146, 1225, 1745, 1748.

74. For her contempt of ravers, moaners, and babblers see
Poems 1243, 1440, and 1748 respectively.

75. Jonathan Edwards, "Sinners in the Hands of an Angry
God," *The Works of President Edwards,* VIII, 169.

76. Poem 1380. See also Poems 1226 and 1645.

77. Poems 662, 1326, 1748.   78. Poem 1431.

79. Poem 789. See also Poems 780 and 1611.

80. Poem 395. See also Poems 773 and 855.

81. Poem 674. I have used the earlier version, incorporating the
variant reading for the last line ("The Mightiest – of Men –")
which was retained in the later copy she sent to Sue. Note the
variant reading "within" for "at Home," rejected in the final
version.

82. Tate, p. 15, "note the subtly interfused erotic motive, which
the idea of death has presented to every romantic poet, love being a symbol interchangeable with death." Tate's essay is presumably behind Anderson's interpretation of death in Poem 712

as a suitor rather than a coachman (Anderson, p. 242).

83. Susan and Austin Dickinson entertained Emerson in December of 1857. The occasion was Emerson's lecture in Amherst on "The Beautiful in Rural Life." According to the local paper, the Hampshire and Franklin *Express,* issue of December 16, 1857, "Ralph Waldo Emerson's lecture greatly disappointed all who listened. It was in the English language instead of the Emersonese in which he usually clothes his thought. . . ." But Susan Dickinson, his hostess, felt quite otherwise:

For years I had read him, in a measure understood him, revered him, cherished him as a hero in my girl's heart, till there grew into my feeling for him almost a supernatural element; so that when I found he was to eat and sleep beneath our roof, there was a suggestion of meeting a God face to face, or one of the Patriarchs of Hebrew setting, or, as Aunt Emily says, "As if he had come from where dreams are born". . . . I felt strangely elated to take his transcendental arm afterward and walk leisurely home.

Whether "Aunt Emily" refers to Emily Dickinson we cannot be certain, but Emily Dickinson must have known her sister-in-law's feelings and may well have been present at this occasion and may have recalled its effect on Susan when she wanted to find a metaphor adequate for her meeting with a thoroughly "supernatural element." All quotations taken from Leyda, I, 351.

84. Poem 679.   85. Poem 1055.

86. Poem 638. Cf. *supra,* pp. 143 – 44 for full text of this poem.

87. Poem 579. For poems not previously mentioned using the metaphor of a visit see 472, 796, and 1721, undated. All other poems using this metaphor are dated within 1862 – 1865. For poems using images of bread and wine outside of the context of the visit see Poems 383 and 791 as well as Poem 674 where she is eased of her "famine/At my Lexicon," surely a reference to a visitor far more imposing and rewarding than the book which, as she told Higginson, had until then been "my only companion" (Letter 261).

88. Poem 579.   89. Poem 815. See also Poem 1555.

90. Letter 318. See also Poem 1125.   91. Poem 1125.

92. Poem 1382. For other poems concerning the passing of grace see Poems 393, 436, 439, 472, 739, 752, 788, 840, 953, 985, 1018, 1046, 1118, 1240, 1376, and 1556. Poem 812 ("A Light exists in Spring") should also be included in this category.

93. Poem 393.

94. Poem 771. See also Poems 801, 1021, 1057, and 1240, and for a less resigned attitude toward "famine" Poems 872 and 1233.

95. Poem 1430. "Debases" and "surpasses" are alternative readings for "defaces."

96. Poem 393. See also Poem 1043.   97. Poem 1299.

98. Letter 353.   99. Poem 1434.

100. Letter 388.   101. Poems 807, 838, 1070.

102. Poems 771, 801, 1043, 1057.

103. Letter 388. For the Norcrosses' reasons for allowing only transcripts of Emily Dickinson's letters to them to be published, as well as for Mabel Loomis Todd and Lavinia Dickinson's estimations of Emily's "little cousins," see M. T. Bingham, *Ancestor's Brocades,* p. 238.

104. Poem 1283. See also Poems 779 and 915.

105. Letter 471.   106. Poem 1329. See also Poem 1462.

107. Poem 1413. See also Poems 1222, 1306, 1433, 1518, and 1642.

108. Poem 365. See also Poems 458, 744, 806, and 1113. The use of the color white and the term "designated" indicates that this poem is among those written in 1862 that reflect her experience of grace. The italics are hers.

109. Poem 1071. See also Poems 1036 and 1446.

110. Poems 1446, 1612, and 1725 and Letter 359.

111. This document is reproduced in Leyda, II, 200. For further evidence of Edward Dickinson's probity see Letter 311, "Father called to say our steelyard was fraudulent, exceeding by an ounce the rates of honest men. He had been selling oats. I cannot stop smiling, though it is hours since, that even our steelyard will not tell the truth."

112. Poem 580. See also Poem 1297.

113. Letter 432.   114. Poem 751.   115. Poem 817.

116. For a thorough treatment of Covenant theology and Puritan assumptions concerning the will, see Chapters IX and XIII in Perry Miller's *The New England Mind: The Seventeenth Century,* and for application of Edward's theory of the will to Emily Dickinson's work see John Wheatcroft's "Emily Dickinson's Poetry and Jonathan Edwards on the Will," *Bucknell Review,* pp. 102–27, and in particular his discussion of Poem 1216. Poems 677 and 1069 also use the term "will" in the sense described above.

117. Poem 734. See also Poems 784, 858, 876, 1123, and 1632.

118. In 1884, see Poem 1632, and for earlier examples see, in addition to much of the poetry mentioned in the previous chapter, Poems 907 and 951. Poem 1732, undated, the famous "My life closed twice before its close" seems to be associated with this image of the bereft poet in a state of living death. If it is, the three "closings" could refer respectively to the departure of Wadsworth, the "death" of despair, and the death to the world on the part of the regenerate spirit. The "third event" would be the fate after judgment.

119. Letter 281. See also Poem 931.

120. Poem 816. The version quoted above was enclosed in a letter (Letter 316) to Higginson. Other variants have a comma before *but* in the third line. See also Poems 332 and 483.

121. Poem 925. See also Poems 853, 1046, and 1304.

122. Poem 1101. See also Poems 1162 and 1294. In a related poem, Poem 454, she makes the same contrast in another way, "To take the name of Gold –/And Gold to own – in solid Bars –."

123. Poem 571. See also Poem 1040, where she states that "Below/Division is Adhesion's Forfeit – " and Poem 1612, discussed in Anderson, pp. 197 – 98.

124. Poem 1017. See also Poems 1013 and 1194.

125. Poem 965. See also Poems 762, 882, 1191, 1205, 1236, and 1548, as well as Poem 939, where she describes how her conscious faith in divine love is challenged by her memory of mortal love in dreams.

126. Poem 1771. See also Poems 1088, 1438, and Letter 361. The identification of secular love with idolatry persisted throughout her life, as several of her letters to Judge Otis P. Lord show quite clearly. In 1878 she wrote him "Oh, my too beloved, save me from the idolatry which would crush us both – " (Letter 560) , and still later, "While others go to Church, I go to mine, for are you not my Church, and have we not a Hymn that no one knows but us?" (Letter 790) . Poem 1771 was also sent to Lord. For the most complete account of Emily Dickinson's relationship with Judge Otis P. Lord see Millicent Todd Bingham, *Emily Dickinson: A Revelation.*

127. Poems 877, 968, 1013, 1022, 1260. In connection with 1260 see the undated poem 1719.

128. Poems 933, 968, 1001, 1231, 1260, 1383, 1476. Poem 1476

raises the possibility that this reunion may take place in "Woe –/ Or Terror – " as well as "Delight."

129. Poem 745. See also Poems 527, 792, 853, and 1153.

130. Poem 367.

131. Perry Miller, "From Edwards to Emerson," *New England Quarterly*, pp. 589 – 617. The allusion, made in Miller's final paragraph, is to Poem 214. Speaking of these new infidels, Miller says in conclusion "They were free to carry on the ancient New England propensity for reeling and staggering with new opinions. They could give themselves over, unrestrainedly, to becoming transparent eyeballs and debauchees of dew."

132. The little gentian appears in Poem 442. For the other tropes mentioned see Poems 373, 374, 385, 431, 460, 499, 542, 608, 665, 704, 717, 788, 946, and 964.

133. Poem 306. See also Poem 356.

134. Poem 385. See also Poems 367 and 432.

135. Poem 705.

136. Poem 930. See also Poems 1411, 1413, 1553, 1588, and 1662.

137. Poem 770. See also Poems 807, 838, 974, 1070, 1175, and 1678. For the opposite reaction see Poems 705, 879, 971, 1012, and 1331.

138. Poem 1631. A variant of the last two lines reads "To balk thee of the myriads/Departed to thy Den – ."

139. Poem 463.   140. Poem 982.   141. Poem 615.

142. Poem 515. See also Poems 524, 550, and 1000.

143. Poem 822. For a similar use of "experiment" see Poems 550 and 1770.

144. Anderson, p. 80 cites this definition. For other poems concerned with God's ability to determine and judge the moral stature of the individual soul see Poems 594, 683, 753, 894, 1216, 1453, 1598, and 1671. No poem written before 1862 has this as a central theme.

145. Poem 1295.   146. Letter 321.   147. Poem 455.

148. Poem 750. See also Poems 522, and for a similar image of "growth of nature" Poem 945. In Poem 750 "countenance," like "transaction," is used in more than one sense.

149. Poem 406. See also Poems 655, 843, 1117, 1189, and 1477.

150. Cf. footnote 116 on p. 165 as well as Poems 1014, 1090, and

1176. Her statement to Higginson "Whosoever will Own in Eden not withstanding Adam and Repeal" (Letter 319) is a clear statement of Covenant theology concerning this point. This passage is also printed as Poem 1069.

151. Poems 454, 1081, 1350, 1531.

152. Poem 917.   153. Poem 833.

154. Poem 809. See also Poems 491, 924, and 1597, as well as Letter 357.

155. Poem 826. See also Poem 1765.

156. Poem 673.   157. Letter 562.

158. Letter 559. See also Poem 1438.

159. Poem 534. See also Poems 800 and 1286.

160. Poem 1088.

161. Poem 765. See also Poems 313, 769, and 1601 as well as footnotes 126 and 128.

162. Letter 886.

163. Letter 233, "I forgot the Redemption [in the Redeemed. . . ."].

164. Letter 593.

165. Poem 320. See also Poem 1544 and Letter 593 as well as Poem 800 below:

> Two – were immortal twice –
> The privilege of few –
> * Eternity – obtained – in Time –
> Reversed Divinity –
>
> That our ignoble Eyes
> The quality conceive *
> Of Paradise superlative –
> Through their Comparative.
>
> · · ·
>
> Eternity – obtained – in Time –/Eternity – in Time obtained –
> conceive/perceive –

166. Poem 522. See also Poem 779.   167. Poem 747.

168. Poem 693. See also her statement in Letter 242 that "To take the Pearl – costs Breath – " as well as Letters 399 and 864. The primary source of this image is in all probability Revelations, the twenty-first chapter of which, describing the New Jerusalem, contains a number of images frequently used by Emily Dickinson.

NOTES: CHAPTER 4

169. Letter 752a and Johnson's note.

170. Poem 563. See also Poem 887.

CHAPTER 5

1. Poem 608.   2. Poem 1652 (undated).

3. For a poem in which death is so considered see Poem 412 and Chapter III *passim*.

4. Poem 914.   5. Poem 499.   6. Poem 820.

7. Poem 712. See also Poems 391 and 665. In Poem 1445, the image of the coach and escort is modified to emphasize that our destination after death is undecided until we have been judged. Hence the coach is "bisected" and death, because he may be her ultimate possessor, is raised from servant to "supple suitor" who leads her to a "troth unknown."

8. Letter 292.   9. Poem 976. See also Poem 1280.

10. Letter 318. See also Poem 1078 and her statement in Letter 360, where she says of her father during his illness, "I think his physical life don't want to live any longer."

11. Poem 1230. See also Poem 1236.   12. Poem 1760.

13. Poem 829. For other poems using the word "awe" see 525, 1370, 1397, 1620, 1678, and 1733.

14. Poem 525. See also Poems 1316 and 1558.

15. Letter 294. See also Poems 347, 692, 1307, and 1532.

16. Letter 311. This was the second of Martha Gilbert Smith's children to die in infancy.

17. Poem 874.

18. Poems 795, 804, 1135, 1272, 1318, 1527, 1752.

19. Poem 408. The capitalized "All" presumably refers to immortality. See also Poems 772 and 886.

20. Poem 721. For a very different evaluation of this poem and an extensive analysis of it see Anderson, *Emily Dickinson's Poetry: Stairway of Surprise,* p. 280.

21. Poems 499 and 547.

22. Poems 890, 900, 920, and 1221.

23. Poem 922. See also Poems 649 and 1204.

24. Poems 408, 417, 509.

25. Poem 906. See also Poem 856.

26. Poems 360, 363, 991, 1083, 1288, 1384.

27. Poem 698 for example.

28. Poems 389, 390, 813, 1147, 1396, 1473. The term "genre sketch" is taken from Anderson, p. 228, who applies it – without pejorative intent – to Poem 389. Johnson notes that when Emily Dickinson sent Mrs. Holland a copy of Poem 1396, she pasted on it a cutting, taken from a newspaper, of tombstones slanting against one another. See Johnson, *The Poems of Emily Dickinson*, III, 965.

29. Poem 689.

30. Poems 735 and 1344.

31. Poem 943.

32. Poems 583, 749, 897, 970, 1256.

33. For example, Johnson, in *Emily Dickinson*, p. 204, sums up the poems he has considered in his chapter "Death" as follows: "There seems to be one persistent thought that binds together this very large number of poems on death. It is the knowledge that death snaps the lines of communication with those we have known and loved, and creates the uncertainty in the minds of all mortals whether that communication can ever be reestablished." With respect to all too many of her poems, this is, alas, an accurate statement; indeed Poem 1288 is almost a redaction of Johnson's comment. I cite the passage to warn rather than to criticize; Emily Dickinson is a persuasive, indeed oddly seductive, figure, and it is easy for her admirers to accept her without reservation.

34. Contrast Poem 1100 with the poems cited in footnote 18.

35. Contrast Poems 708, 875, and 889 to Poems 390, 417, 499, 692, 735, 749, 813, 922, 943, 948, 949, 970, and 1065.

36. Poem 889. See also Poem 875. For a less successful poem that describes this "crisis" see Poem 948.

37. Both quotations in this paragraph are from Poem 724.

38. Poem 796.

39. Poem 591. For a more comic treatment of the same theme see Poem 885.

40. Poem 630.

41. For an example of how God appears to the unregenerate, to "ignorance," see Poem 1173.

42. Poems 820 and 871.

43. Poems 894 and 975.

44. Poems 750, 820, 871, 891, 975, 1238.

45. Poem 894. See also Poem 891.

46. Letter 280.

47. Poem 575. See also Poem 1115, where nature is characterized as "the Typic Mother."

48. Many poems use noon in this sense, among them Poems 327, 415, 420, 469, 498, 510, 512, 575, 579, 580, 581, 592, 593, 611, 620, 638, 654, 692, 714, 931, 960, and 1056.

49. Poem 552. "Analysis" is a variant reading for "inspection." See also Poems 560, 575, 595, 666, 667, 716, 757, 972, 1079, 1104, 1114, 1241, 1278, 1349, 1390, and 1642. In all these the sunset is assumed to be significant, though in the last two poems the nature of that significance remains in doubt.

50. Poem 783. "Deity" is a variant reading for "Universe."

51. Poems 783, 828, 1079, 1084, 1102, 1265, 1420, 1465, 1570, 1585, 1630, 1634.

52. Poem 1002. See also Poems 304, 783, 1053, and 1079.

53. Poems 592, 714, 811, 1068, 1330, 1422.

54. Poem 629. See also Poems 333 and 661.   55. Poem 1510.

56. Poem 606. For other landscapes, see Poems 354, 1140, and 1252.

57. Poems 794, 824, 311, 737, 507, 700, 585, 605, 1177, 517, 1463, and 1235 respectively. She also described orioles (1466), jays (1561, 1635), robins (1483), bobolinks (1279), butterflies (1387), arbutus (1332), mushrooms (1298), storms (1649, 1694), sunsets (1693), squirrels (1374), bees (1224, 1339), snakes (1740), frogs (1379), rats (1340, 1356), bats (1575), and caterpillars (1448).

58. Poem 700, in addition to being a demonstration of the poet's verbal virtuosity, has that virtuosity as its primary theme.

59. Poems 328 ("A bird came down the walk"), 986 ("The Snake"), 1379, 1388, and 1448.

60. Poem 885.   61. Poem 1138.

62. Poem 1172. Cf. Poem 1134.   63. Poem 429.

64. Poem 1424.   65. Poem 1437.   66. Poem 1593.

67. Poems 1522, 1536, 1628.   68. Poem 1514.

69. Poems 736, 844, 1333, 1404, 1425, 1519. In Poem 736 I assume the city on the hill to refer to the New Jerusalem. In connection with Poem 1519 see also Poem 1501.

70. Anderson apparently assumes the phrase "God be with" to mean "God help," and feels that the "King" as well as the

"Clown" stands for the poet, although "King" is a standard image for God in Emily Dickinson's poetry. For Anderson's interpretation see Anderson, pp. 79 – 81. Since this is the poem with which Anderson opens and on which he bases his discussion of Emily Dickinson's view of nature, this extended attempt to qualify his interpretation is perhaps justified.

71. Letter 318. See also Poems 812 and 1037, and for use of a similar image to describe the passage of summer, Poem 342.

72. Poem 742. See also Poem 1324.   73. Poem 742.

74. Poem 797. See also Poems 516 and 988.

75. Poem 1420.

76. Poem 878. See also Poems 300, 451, 526, and 632.

77. Poem 909.

78. Contrast Emerson's statement in "Nature" that "whilst the world is a spectacle, something in himself is stable" and hence the poet "unfixes the land and the sea, makes them revolve around the axis of his primary thought, and disposes them anew. . . . The sensual man conforms thoughts to things; the poet conforms things to his thoughts. The one esteems nature as rooted and fast; the other, as fluid, and impresses his being thereon." Thus what Emily Dickinson felt was a fatal defect in the imagination's grasp of reality, Emerson considered to be the definitive activity of the imagination. By his definition she is in the category of "sensual man." She would have agreed with the aim if not the appellation.

79. Letter 459a. See also Poems 1400 and 1583. For use of the metaphor of a house to stand for a poem, see Poems 488 and 657.

80. Poem 1587, and probably the undated Poem 1651. See also Poems 1212 and 1261 for more general statements about the "life" of the poet's words.

81. Thomas Wentworth Higginson, "Letter to a Young Contributor," *Atlantic Monthly*, pp. 401 – 11.

82. *Ibid.*, p. 403.   83. Letter 280.

84. The only poems before 1862 that appear to have been written as descriptive exercises are 140 and 173, both of which have a "moral" appended, and Poem 204. In 1861, Poems 219 and 228, revised in 1862 and 1864 respectively, could be considered in this category.

85. Higginson, "The Procession of the Flowers," p. 657.

86. Keats is referred to only once again; in connection with Helen Hunt Jackson's death Emily Dickinson wrote "Oh had that Keats a Severn!" (Letter 1018), and Ruskin is never mentioned again. The letter to Higginson is Letter 261.

87. Higginson, "Letter to a Young Contributor," p. 403.

88. Millicent Todd Bingham, *Ancestor's Brocades*. On p. 167 Mrs. Bingham, quoting from Mrs. Todd's journal entry dated October 18, 1891, states that, according to Austin, "Emily definitely posed in those letters." The letters meant are those to Higginson.

89. Letter 261.   90. Anderson, p. 31.

91. His novel, *Miss Gilbert's Career, an American Story*, a tale demonstrating the grief to which a female author comes when she learns that writing is no substitute for happiness and that her father places a higher value on his son's least achievement than on her highest success, was reviewed in *Atlantic Monthly*, VII (January, 1861), pp. 125 – 26. The synopsis above is drawn from that review. Both as a friend of the family and a subscriber to the *Atlantic* Emily Dickinson would have known of the novel. The point was one about which Holland had strong convictions, and sometimes he aired them in the Springfield *Republican*. See Leyda, *The Years and Hours of Emily Dickinson*, II, 81, 103, and 126. Holland's editorial "Leaves of Grass – Smut in Them" in the Springfield *Republican* of June 16, 1860 presumably was the cause of Emily Dickinson's reply to one of Higginson's questions: "You speak of Mr Whitman – I never read his Book – but was told that he was disgraceful – " (Letter 261), but one wonders why Higginson, who in 1867 wrote that it was "no discredit to Walt Whitman that he wrote 'Leaves of Grass,' only that he did not burn it afterwards" ["Literature as an Art," *Atlantic Monthly*, XX (December, 1867) p. 753], asked the question in the first place. Higginson's low estimation of Whitman remained as late as 1899. See Thomas Wentworth Higginson, "Whitman," *Contemporaries*.

92. Leyda, II, 46 quotes from a letter of Samuel Bowles to Susan Dickinson in which Bowles is evidently replying to Susan's request for a photograph of Higginson. Leyda assigns the letter to February of 1862, two months before Higginson's "Letter to a Young Contributor" appeared in the *Atlantic*.

93. Higginson, "Letter to a Young Contributor," p. 402.

94. *Ibid.*, pp. 405 – 6. 95. Anderson, p. 34.

96. Letter 265.

97. Higginson, "Letter to a Young Contributor," p. 410.

98. Poems 675 and 448 respectively.

99. See Anderson, p. 54. "Dickinson's esthetic theory was fully established before she opened her correspondence with Higginson in the spring of 1862," and Johnson, *Emily Dickinson,* p. 148, "It is of primary importance to bear in mind that when Emily Dickinson wrote her first letter to Higginson, asking him to pass judgment upon the poems she enclosed, her aesthetic theory was fully established."

100. Johnson uses the chapter he entitled "Circumference" for his discussion of Emily Dickinson's aesthetic theory, and Anderson uses the same word for one of the subdivisions of a larger section called "The Paradise of Art."

101. Poems 313, 354, 378, 515, 552, 633. 102. Letter 268.

103. Poem 155. 104. Poem 167.

105. Poem 214. 106. Poem 298.

107. Poem 290. Anderson's interpretation appears in Anderson, pp. 47 – 54.

108. *Ibid.*, p. 52.

109. Poem 216, "Safe in their alabaster chambers" was published in the Springfield *Republican* on March 1, 1862. In her second letter to Higginson (Letter 261) she recounted how "Two Editors of Journals came to my Father's House, this winter – and asked me for my Mind – and when I asked them 'Why,' they said I was penurious – and they, would use it for the World – ." She did not tell Higginson that she had given them, and "the World," what they had asked for.

110. Letter 265.

111. In 1862, see Poems 307, 406, 441, 448, and 544. In 1863 – 1865, see Poems 675, 709, 713, 880, 883, 982, and 1009. In 1866 – 1886 see Poems 1130, 1226, 1232, 1261, 1263, 1427, 1455, 1659, and 1763.

112. Letter 260. 113. Letter 268.

114. One can infer this advice from Letters 265 and 271.

115. Letter 271.

116. Thomas Wentworth Higginson, "My Out-door Study," *Atlantic Monthly,* VIII (September, 1861), pp. 302 – 9.

117. Letter 271.

118. "Elizabeth Barrett Browning," *Atlantic Monthly,* VIII (September, 1861), pp. 368 – 76. Perhaps her attention was initially called to this article by the Springfield *Republican's* announcement of August 24, 1861 that in the September *Atlantic* "T. W. Higginson gives us in 'My Out-door Study' one of his deliciously truthful pictures of rural scenes and diversions; and the number closes with an appreciative notice of the life and writings of Elizabeth Barrett Browning." Quoted in Leyda, II, 32.

119. *Ibid.,* p. 368. The quotation is taken from Elizabeth Barrett Browning's "A Vision of Poets." In the article the word *poets* was changed to the singular, presumably so that it would apply to Elizabeth Browning alone.

120. Poem 448. For a more conventional and far inferior "tribute" to Elizabeth Browning see Poem 312.

121. Poem 290. For the artist's superiority to nature see Poems 307 and 529 as well as her more lighthearted expressions of the same theme, Poems 308 and 1025. By contrast, in Poem 291, written in 1861, the poet feels inadequate to portray nature.

122. The relationship between the power of language and the power of love is stated directly in Poem 1651.

123. Emerson, "Nature," *Collected Works,* I, 30.

124. Emerson, "The Poet," *Collected Works,* III, 21.

125. Letter 280.

126. At best the poem can give its reader an experience very much like grace itself, or so Emily Dickinson described the effect upon her of first reading Elizabeth Browning's poetry in Poem 593, quoted in part below:

> The Days – to Mighty Metres stept –
> The Homeliest – adorned
> As if unto a Sacrament *
> 'Twere suddenly ordained – *
>
> I could not have defined the change –
> Conversion of the Mind
> Like Sanctifying in the Soul –
> Is witnessed – not explained –
>
> . . .
>
> Sacrament/Jubilee
> ordained/confirmed

Other poems written in 1862 and later that profess a more conventional view of the poet's function and contribution – that he sings out of gratitude to God, testifying to God's grace, glory, benevolence, and self-sacrifice – are so patently inferior to those discussed here and on subsequent pages that they seem to be products of dogma rather than of conviction. They do of course indicate that by 1862 she had committed herself to that dogma. See Poems 539, 544, 827, 828, 864, and 1348. For her opinion of the theory that the poet's duty is to help her fellow man, see her sarcastic statements about "Miss P." in Letter 380.

127. Poem 675 (version of packet copy H249). I am indebted to Anderson for the information that in Emily Dickinson's lexicon perfume is defined as "essential oils." Anderson, p. 65.

128. William Dean Howells, "Editor's Study," *Harper's Magazine,* LXXXII (January, 1891), p. 319. See also Poem 880, where she again uses the image of the rose in the drawer, this time insisting that the drawer must be opened for the rose not to become "superfluous," and Poem 261.

129. Poem 441. See also Letter 330.

130. Poems 888, 936, 960, 982, 1130, 1455.

131. Poems 406, 713, 1226, 1659, 1763.

132. Poem 709. See also Poem 488, an allegorical presentation of her refusal to publish. Here the poet, a carpenter, is solicited by a "builder" who informs the poet and her "plane" "Had we the Art of Boards/Sufficiently developed – He'd hire us/At Halves – ." The poet's reply is that she builds temples not houses.

133. Apparently he made this recommendation in the first letter he ever wrote to her. See her reply in Letter 261. For Higginson's role in Mrs. Spofford's career see Anna Mary Wells, *Dear Preceptor: The Life and Times of Thomas Wentworth Higginson,* p. 115.

134. *Ibid.,* p. 194. For Emily Dickinson's own thoughts on this subject, see Poems 1232 and 1427.

135. Letter 380.   136. Leyda, II, 191.   137. Letter 444a.

138. See Letters 476, 476a, 476c, 477, and 573a. Johnson, *Poems,* I, xxx – xxxiii gives a full account of the facts surrounding publication of "Success" (Poem 67).

139. Poem 544. See also Poem 711. For another treatment of the theme of the private poet see Poem 326.

140. Poem 883.

141. Anderson, p. 58. See also his discussion of Emily Dickinson and fame pp. 58 – 62.

142. Anna Mary Wells' statement that "Emily left no will; indeed she had passed through life with little more concern about property than was felt by the animals she preferred in many ways to people," is as untrue as it is insulting. On October 19th, 1875 Emily Dickinson bequeathed all her "estate, real and personal," to Lavinia, "to have and to hold the same to her and her heirs, and assigns forever," and she appointed Lavinia executrix. She was of course aware of what that "estate" consisted, and she must have smiled inwardly at the unintentional felicity of that legal commonplace. See Wells, *Dear Preceptor,* p. 274. Emily Dickinson's will is quoted in full in Leyda, II, 236 – 37.

143. Letter 268.

144. " 'Circumference' is a word that she returns to again and again. It is a pervasive image in her religious thinking and in her theory of art, though the meanings it carries are not always consistent." Anderson, p. 5. Actually, except for one *vers d'occasion* (Poem 1620 and the variant on it in Letter 898) she used the word only between 1862, the year in which, as we have seen, she began to work out her aesthetic theory, and 1866. I am assuming that the undated poem, 1663, in which it appears, was written sometime during those four years.

145. William Howard, "Emily Dickinson's Poetic Vocabulary," *Publications of the Modern Language Association,* LXXII (March, 1957), p. 238.

146. Poems 378, 802, 967, 1663.

147. Poems 313, 515, 552, 633, 798.

148. Poem 883.   149. Poem 802.   150. Poem 820.

151. Poem 871.   152. Letter 288.

153. Anderson, p. 55 and notes. Her statement to Mrs. Holland in Letter 950 that "The Bible dealt with the Centre, not with the Circumference – ," is also consistent with Browne's definition.

154. Poem 313. See also Poem 798.

155. Poem 515. See also Poem 936.

156. Poem 378. See also Poem 943 where death is described as "Circumference without Relief –/Or Estimate – or End – " as well

as the famous "I heard a Fly buzz – when I died – ," Poem 465, in which, even at the last instance of mortal consciousness, when the line is about to be crossed, the other side remains impenetrable.

157. Poem 1084. Like Poem 783, this poem uses the birds' song before dawn to signify the poet's apprehension of divinity invading the natural world. The bird, by singing, questions; the dawn, by its appearance, proves the hypothesis:

> At Half past Three, a single Bird
> Unto a silent Sky
> Propounded but a single term
> Of cautious melody.
>
> At Half past Four, Experiment
> Had subjugated test
> And lo, Her silver Principle
> Supplanted all the rest.
>
> At Half past Seven, Element
> Nor Implement, be seen –
> And Place was where the Presence was
> Circumference between.

158. Poem 1343.   159. Poem 552.

160. Poem 633. See also Johnson's brief explication in *Emily Dickinson*, p. 140.

161. See Emily Dickinson's famous definition of poetry as quoted by Higginson in Letter 342a: "If I read a book [and] it makes my whole body so cold no fire ever can warm me I know *that* is poetry. If I feel physically as if the top of my head were taken off, I know *that* is poetry. These are the only way I know it. Is there any other way." For her letter to Daniel Chester French, see Letter 898 and Poem 1620.

162. Letter 261.   163. Letter 650. See also Poem 1274.

164. Poem 657.

165. Letter 591. The Dickinsons moved back into the Main Street House in 1855.

166. For *soul* see Poems 524, 1142, and 1695. For *spirit* see 976, 1482, 1576, and 1630. For *consciousness* see 515, 622, 911, and 1454. Though these terms occur in many of Emily Dickinson's

other poems, I have limited myself to those specifically dealing with the manner in which one survives after death. Note also that in Poem 1421, quoted below, the essential, persisting quality is called mind:

> Such * are the inlets of the mind –
> His outlets – would you see *
> Ascend with me the eminence *
> Of immortality –
>
>   .   .   .
>
> Such/These
> see/know
> eminence/Table Land

167. Letter 555.
168. Both quotations are from Poem 1454.
169. Letter 330.
170. Poem 1474, quoted below:

> Estranged from Beauty – none can be –
> For Beauty is Infinity –
> And power to be finite ceased
> * Before Identity was leased.*
>
>   .   .   .
>
> Before Identity was leased/When Fate incorporated us –
> leased/creased

See also Poem 1630.

171. Poem 709.   172. Poem 822.   173. Letter 280.

174. In the last years of her life Emily Dickinson was especially troubled by the thought that neither she nor those she loved might be recognizable in the afterlife and that consequently after death she would never meet them again. The following statement to Susan is typical: "I sometimes remember we are to die, and hasten toward the Heart which how could I woo in a rendezvous where there is no Face?" Letter 856. See also Letters 859 and 872 as well as Poem 1576 which is enclosed with Letter 872.

175. Poem 894.

176. For poems in which Emily Dickinson equates consciousness with conscience, see Poems 594, 683, 753, 894, 1323, and 1598.

177. Poem 420.

178. Thomas Stearns Eliot, "Tradition and the Individual Talent," *Selected Essays 1917 – 1932,* pp. 10 – 11.

179. See Poems 670, 686, 1182, 1203, 1242, 1273, 1406, 1507, 1508, 1578, 1738, and 1753.

180. Poem 786. See also Poem 777.   181. Poem 642.

182. Poem 910.   183. Poem 1482.   184. Letter 523.

185. Letter 414. See also Letter 567.

Bibliography

TEXTS

Dickinson, Emily. *The Letters of Emily Dickinson,* 3 vols. Edited
by Thomas H. Johnson and Theodora Ward. Cambridge, Mas-
sachusetts: The Belknap Press of Harvard University, 1958.
—— *The Poems of Emily Dickinson,* 3 vols. Edited by Thomas H.
Johnson and Theodora Ward. Cambridge, Massachusetts: The
Belknap Press of Harvard University, 1955.

BOOKS

Anderson, Charles R. *Emily Dickinson's Poetry: Stairway of Sur-
prise.* New York: Holt, Rinehart and Winston, 1960.
Bianchi, Martha Dickinson, editor. *The Complete Poems of
Emily Dickinson.* Boston: Little Brown and Company, 1924.
Bingham, Millicent Todd. *Ancestor's Brocades: The Literary De-
but of Emily Dickinson.* New York: Harper and Brothers, 1945.
—— *Emily Dickinson: A Revelation.* New York: Harper and
Brothers, 1954.
—— *Emily Dickinson's Home.* New York: Harper and Brothers,
1955.
Blackmur, R. P. *The Expense of Greatness.* New York: Arrow
Editions, 1940.

Bradstreet, Anne. *The Works of Anne Bradstreet in Prose and Verse*. Edited by John Harvard Ellis. Gloucester, Massachusetts: P. Smith, 1962.

Calvin, Jean. *Institutes of the Christian Religion*. Edited by John T. McNeill, translated by Ford Lewis Battles, 2 vols. Philadelphia: Westminster Press, 1960.

Chase, Richard Volney. *Emily Dickinson*. ("The American Men of Letters Series"), New York: William Sloane Associates, Inc., 1951.

Clemens, Samuel Langhorne. *The Adventures of Huckleberry Finn*. Vol. XIII of *The Works of Mark Twain*, Definitive Edition. New York: Gabriel Wells, 1923.

Edwards, Jonathan. *The Works of President Edwards*, 4 vols. New York: S. Converse, 1829.

Eliot, Thomas Stearns. *Selected Essays 1917 – 1932*. New York: Harcourt Brace & Company, 1932.

Emerson, Ralph Waldo. *The Complete Works of Ralph Waldo Emerson*, 12 vols. Centenary Edition. Boston: Houghton Mifflin Company, 1903.

Hawthorne, Nathaniel. *The Scarlet Letter, a Romance*. New York: Modern Library, 1950.

Higginson, Thomas Wentworth. *Contemporaries*. Boston: Houghton Mifflin Company, 1899.

Hitchcock, Edward. *Religious Lectures on Peculiar Phenomena in the Four Seasons . . . Delivered to the Students in Amherst College in 1845, 1847, 1848, and 1849*. Amherst: J., S., & C. Adams, 1850.

Holland, Josiah Gilbert. *Miss Gilbert's Career, an American Story*. New York: Charles Scribner, 1860.

Jenkins, Macgregor. *Emily Dickinson Friend and Neighbor*. Boston: Little Brown and Company, 1930.

Johnson, Thomas H. *Emily Dickinson, an Interpretative Biography*. Cambridge, Massachusetts: The Belknap Press of Harvard University, 1955.

Leyda, Jay. *The Years and Hours of Emily Dickinson*, 2 vols. New Haven: Yale University Press, 1960.

Melville, Herman. *Moby Dick, or the Whale*. Edited by Luther S. Mansfield and Howard P. Vincent. New York: Hendricks House, 1952.

Miller, Perry. *The New England Mind: the Seventeenth Century*. Cambridge, Massachusetts: Harvard University Press, 1954.

——— and Thomas H. Johnson, editors. *The Puritans*. New York: American Book Company, 1938.

Moore, Marianne. *Collected Poems*. New York: Macmillan, 1957.

Patterson, Rebecca. *The Riddle of Emily Dickinson*. Boston: Houghton Mifflin Company, 1951.

Stevens, Wallace. *The Collected Poems of Wallace Stevens*. New York: Alfred A. Knopf, 1957.

Taggard, Genevieve. *The Life and Mind of Emily Dickinson*. New York: Alfred A. Knopf, 1930.

Tate, Allen. *Reactionary Essays on Poetry and Ideas*. New York: Charles Scribner's Sons, 1936.

Taylor, Edward. *Poems*. Edited by Donald E. Stanford. New Haven: Yale University Press, 1960.

Todd, Mabel Loomis and Millicent Todd Bingham, editors. *Bolts of Melody*. New York: Harper and Brothers, 1945.

Wadsworth, Charles. *Thanksgiving Sermons, 1852 – 1861*. Philadelphia: Moran & Sickles *et al.*, 1852 – 1861.

Ward, Theodora. *The Capsule of the Mind*. Cambridge, Massachusetts: The Belknap Press of Harvard University, 1961.

Wells, Anna Mary. *Dear Preceptor: The Life and Times of Thomas Wentworth Higginson*. Boston: Houghton Mifflin Company, 1963.

Wells, Henry W. *Introduction to Emily Dickinson*. Chicago: Packard and Company, 1947.

Whicher, George Frisbie. *This Was A Poet*. Ann Arbor: The University of Michigan Press, 1957.

Whitman, Walt. *Leaves of Grass by Walt Whitman reproduced from the First Edition (1855)*. New York: published for the Facsimile Text Society by Columbia University Press, 1939.

Winters, Yvor. *Maule's Curse*. Norfolk, Connecticut: New Directions, 1938.

ARTICLES AND PERIODICALS

Anonymous. "Elizabeth Barrett Browning," *Atlantic Monthly*, VIII (September, 1861), pp. 368 – 76.

Banzer, Judith. " 'Compound Manner': Emily Dickinson and the Metaphysical Poets," *American Literature*, XXXII (January, 1961), pp. 415 – 33.

Higginson, Thomas Wentworth. "Letter to a Young Contributor," *Atlantic Monthly*, IX (April, 1862), pp. 401 – 11.

—— "Literature as an Art," *Atlantic Monthly,* XX (December, 1867), pp. 745–54.

—— "My Out-door Study," *Atlantic Monthly,* VIII (September, 1861), pp. 302–9.

—— "The Procession of Flowers," *Atlantic Monthly,* X (December, 1862), pp. 649–57.

Howard, William. "Emily Dickinson's Poetic Vocabulary," *Publications of the Modern Language Association,* LXXII (March, 1957), pp. 225–48.

Howells, William Dean. "Editor's Study," *Harper's Magazine,* LXXXII (January, 1891), p. 319.

Johnson, Thomas H. "The Great Love in the Life of Emily Dickinson," *American Heritage,* VI (April, 1955), pp. 52–55.

Manley, Francis. "An Explication of Dickinson's 'After Great Pain'," *Modern Language Notes,* LXXIII (April, 1958), pp. 260–64.

Miller, Perry. "From Edwards to Emerson," *New England Quarterly,* XIII (1940), pp. 589–617.

Warren, Austin. "Emily Dickinson," *Sewanee Review,* LXV (Autumn, 1957), pp. 565–86.

Wells, Anna Mary. "Was Emily Dickinson Psychotic?" *American Imago,* XIX (1962), pp. 309–21.

Wheatcroft, John. "Emily Dickinson's Poetry and Jonathan Edwards on the Will," *Bucknell Review,* X (1961), pp. 102–27.

UNPUBLISHED MATERIAL

Higgins, David J. M. "Portrait of Emily Dickinson: the Poet and Her Prose," unpublished Ph.D. dissertation, Columbia University, 1961.

Wheatcroft, John Stewart. "Emily Dickinson and the Orthodox Tradition," unpublished Ph.D. dissertation, Rutgers University, 1961.

Index of first lines

"As Boy – should deal with lesser Boy –" *(from* Poem 597) , 130
"As a completed Man" *(from* Poem 443) , 121
Atlantic Monthly (periodical) , 271*n*91; Higginson and, 201-2, 206, 209, 210, 255*n*128, 258*n*20, 273*n*118
Authority, 123-24; impulse and, 6, 7, 8, 232; disguise and, 16-17, 53-54, 55, 232; death wish as reaction to, 48-49, 50-51, 53; of God, 56-59, 60, 61, 66, 83, 87; *see also* Order; Status; Tradition
"Auto da Fe – and Judgment –" *(from* Poem 620) , 126

"Ballots of Eternity, The" *(from* Poem 343) , 146
"Banquet of Abstemiousness, The" *(from* Poem 1430) , 159
Banzer, Judith, 253*n*68
"Baptized – this Day – a Bride –" *(from* Poem 473) , 149
"Beautiful in Rural Life, The" (Emerson) , 262*n*83
"Being's Peasantry –" *(from* Poem 385) , 148, 169
"Below/Division is Adhesion's forfeit" *(from* Poem 1040) , 264*n*123
Bianchi, Martha Dickinson, 237*n*3
Bible, The, 79, 151, 235, 250*n*26, 259*n*43, 260*nn*55-56, 266*n*168; language of, 143, 145, 148, 231; Emily Dickinson quoted on, 275*n*153
Bigelow Papers (Lowell) , 206
Bingham, Millicent Todd, 237*n*3, 261*n*65, 263*n*103, 271*n*88; "Master" letters and, 78, 250*nn*24, 26
Biography, 35, 70, 71, 74-75, 105; *see also* Criticism; *and see individual biographers*
Birds, 23, 26, 29; as emblems of the poet, 24-25, 52, 193-94, 241*n*5, 276*n*157
"Birds declaim their Tunes, The" *(from* Poem 364) , 126
Blackmur, R. P., cited, 100, 101, 255*n*104
Bolts of Melody (Dickinson), 237*n*3

Boston, Massachusetts, 154, 261*n*71
Bowles, Samuel, 71, 80, 250*n*26; letters to, 19, 29, 33, 81, 93, 142; on Emily Dickinson's isolation, 55-56, 241*n*85, 260*n*55; Higginson and, 203, 204, 271*n*92
Bradstreet, Anne, 141, 143, 145; quoted, 136,
"Brain is just the weight of God, The" *(from* Poem 632) , 127, 129
Brothers Karamazov, The (Dostoyevsky) , 161
Browne, Sir Thomas, 219, 275*n*153
Browning, Elizabeth Barrett, 143, 209, 210, 273*nn*118-20, 126
Bucknell Review (periodical) , 263*n*116
"But a filament . . . Of that diviner thing" *(from* Poem 673) , 175
"But – Madam – is there nothing else –" *(from* Poem 621) , 130
"But, most, like Chaos – Stopless – cool –" *(from* Poem 510) , 116, 118
". . . but the Drift of Eastern Gray" *(from* Poem 721) , 186, 267*n*20

California, Wadsworth call to, 21, 34, 35, 52, 69, 70, 71, 81, 82, 83, 88, 103, 230
Calvary Church, San Francisco, 82
Calvin, Jean, 248*n*122; quoted, 64
Calvinism, 82, 83; *see also* Puritanism
Cambridge, Massachusetts, 12
"Can the Dumb – define the Divine?" *(from* Poem 797) , 199
Capsule of the Mind, The (Ward) , 248*n*2
"Captivity is Consciousness –" *(from* Poem 384) , 111
Castle, The (Kafka) , 130, 162
Catholicism, 12, 162
Celebration of the Two Hundredth Anniversary of the Settlement of Hadley, Massachusetts, 257*n*8
Century, The (periodical) , 260*n*64
Channing, William Ellery, 201
Chase, Richard: on isolation, 4,

297

Poetry: commitment to, 5, 9, 15, 21, 23-24, 49, 66, 83, 113, 128, 201, 205, 206, 207, 208, 220, 223, 230, 238n18; convention and, 7, 24, 35-36, 37, 39, 46-47, 85, 86, 102, 105, 106, 115, 124, 182-83, 186-87, 188, 235, 239n31, 273n126; experience and, 9-10, 12-13, 17-18, 21, 33, 37, 39, 41, 47, 66, 73, 74, 84, 86, 95-96, 105, 113-14, 127, 179, 190, 218-19, 226; as liberating perception, 54, 76, 113-16, 127, 200-1, 211, 212, 222, 223, 224; on love, 69-70, 84-85; Wadsworth view of, 81; despair and, 111, 114, 134-35; aesthetics of, 199, 210-14, 216-19, 222-23, 224, 231, 233-34, 272nn99-100, 273n126, 274nn127-28, 276nn157, 161

"Poetry" (Emerson), 66

"Portrait of Emily Dickinson: The Poet and Her Prose" (Higgins), 250n26

"Power is only Pain –" (from Poem 252), 94

Prayer, 129-30, 142; Edward Dickinson's, 164

Predestination, doctrine of, 64, 177; Arminian heresy and, 147, 164, 168

"Procession of Flowers, The" (Higginson), 258n20, 270n85

Prose, 6, 15

Psalms, Book of, 151, 260n56

Psychology, 153, 160; Puritan, 165, 167

Publications of the Modern Language Association, 275n145

Punishment, 16, 17; the death of friends as, 18-19, 21; desire for, 83, 88-94; resignation to, 128-29, 131; grace and, 135, 141; see also Pain

Puritanism, 66, 162, 164, 225; self-reliance and, 53; grace and, 64, 84, 138-41, 145, 147, 148, 160-61, 192, 214, 255n120; predestination and, 64, 147, 164, 168, 177; status and, 157, 214-15, 234, 235; human will and, 165, 167, 178, 263n116; capitalism and, 174, 265n50; nature and, 194; sermon

techniques, 196; commitment to, 231, 234, 235, 273n126

Reactionary Essays on Poetry and Ideas (Tate), 239n32, 257n7

Reality: intuitive knowledge of, 3, 25, 26; prosaic versus poetic, 15, 117, 118, 127; natural "evidence" of, 26-29, 32-33, 133, 181-82; symbol and, 30, 117; appearances and, 43-44, 72-73, 74, 99, 118, 133, 154, 166, 200-1, 270n78

Reason: scientific method and, 27, 30, 32-33, 43, 45-46, 182; faith and, 46, 59-60, 65; emotion and, 47, 234; legalism and, 57, 128, 129; suffering and, 60-61, 62, 109-10, 220; grace and, 166-67, 177, 192

"Reform (s) Vitality/Into Divinity" (from Poem 809), 175

"Relay" (from Poem 1652), 183

Religion, 3, 9, 181, 215; formal, 7, 10-12, 15, 51, 54, 239nn33-35, 240nn40-41; imagery of, 10, 11, 31, 80, 86, 90-91, 93, 97, 104, 139, 145, 148, 149, 157-58, 163, 198, 253n65, 275n144; romantic approach to, 13-14, 15, 82; reason and, 46, 62, 64; of Wadsworth, 71, 77, 79, 80, 81, 82, 83, 89-90; punishment and, 83, 88-93; conversion to, 135, 138-79, 182-85, 190, 191, 227, 230; mystery and, 160-63, 192; see also God; Immortality; and see specific doctrines

Religious Lectures on Peculiar Phenomena in the Four Seasons (Hitchcock), 242n16

"Renunciation – is a piercing Virtue –" (from Poem 745), 168

Resurrection, see Immortality

Revelations, Book of, 79, 145, 148, 259n33; on white, 151, 250n26, 259n43, 260n55; on the New Jerusalem, 266n168

Reward: immortality as, 33, 38-39, 46, 50, 56, 57-59, 60-61, 83, 91, 120, 142, 221, 230; death as, 47-52, 93, 96; grace as, 146, 160

Rhyme, 24, 209, 234

302